THE OTHER COLD WAR

COLUMBIA STUDIES IN INTERNATIONAL AND GLOBAL HISTORY

COLUMBIA STUDIES IN INTERNATIONAL AND GLOBAL HISTORY

MATTHEW CONNELLY AND ADAM MCKEOWN, *editors*

The idea of "globalization" has become a commonplace, but we lack good histories that can explain the transnational and global processes that have shaped the contemporary world. Columbia Studies in International and Global History will. encourage serious scholarship on international and global history with an eye to explaining the origins of the contemporary era. Grounded in empirical research, the titles in the series will also transcend the usual area boundaries and will address questions of how history can help us understand contemporary problems, including poverty, inequality, power, political violence, and accountability beyond the nation-state.

Cemil Aydin, *The Politics of Anti-Westernism in Asia: Visions of World Order in Pan-Islamic and Pan-Asian Thought*

Adam M. McKeown, *Melancholy Order: Asian Migration and the Globalization of Borders*

Patrick Manning, *The African Diaspora: A History Through Culture*

James R. Fleming, *Fixing the Sky: The Checkered History of Weather and Climate Control*

Steven Bryan, *The World Economy in the Age of Empire: Adopting the Gold Standard in Japan and Argentina*

THE OTHER COLD WAR

HEONIK KWON

COLUMBIA UNIVERSITY PRESS   NEW YORK

Columbia University Press
Publishers Since 1893
New York Chichester, West Sussex

Library of Congress Cataloging-in-Publication Data
Kwon, Heonik, 1962–
The other Cold War / Heonik Kwon.
p. cm.— (Columbia studies in international and global history)
Includes bibliographical references and index.
ISBN 978-0-231-15304-1 (cloth: acid-free paper) —ISBN 978-0-231-52670-8 (e-book)
1. Cold war—Social aspect. 2. World politics—1945–1989. 3. History, Modern—1945–1989.
I. Title. II. Series.

D843.K95 2010
909.82'5—dc22 2010017652

Printed in the United States of America
c 10 9 8 7 6 5 4 3 2

References to Internet Web sites (URLs) were accurate at the time of writing.
Neither the author nor Columbia University Press is responsible
for Web sites that may have expired or changed since the book was prepared.

For David L. Schalk

CONTENTS

Contents

ACKNOWLEDGMENTS

This book grew out of my ethnographic experience in Vietnam and Korea, where I learned slowly over the years how, in these places, critical issues of world politics were familiar concerns in everyday communal life. It is thanks to my interlocutors in Korea and Vietnam that I came to see the cold war as human experience and its history as locally grounded and enduring *histories,* inseparable from unsettled memories of the dead and unresolved relations with neighbors.

I am also thankful to my former colleagues in the Department of Social Anthropology at Edinburgh University. Although none of them took cold war history as a specific subject of interest, they were nonetheless willing to share with me many fascinating stories of the cold war–era world that they had discovered in many different parts of the globe while doing field-work. My late colleague Charles Jedrej was special. I appreciate what he told me about his time in sub-Saharan Africa and our occasional concerted effort to place our separate experience within a broad, common spectrum of the global cold war.

This book has taken shape through close communication with the scholarship of international history and international politics. It is through reading and engaging with cold war international history that I was able to bring my ethnography into a larger picture of world history and, in turn, to bring that picture into a reflection on the ethnographic material. Marilyn Young and Arne Westad were a constant source of enlightenment and inspiration. So was David Schalk's intellectual history of France's Algerian War and America's Vietnam War. David showed faith in me, and I took great comfort in his encouragement while I grappled with postcolonial cold war histories and each time I came to doubt whether and how meaningfully comparative ethnography can relate to international history. This book is dedicated to our friendship.

I took comfort also in rediscovering the old literature of anthropology such as E. E. Evans-Pritchard and Meyer Fortes's *African Political Systems*, Max Gluckman's *Custom and Conflict in Africa*, and Edmund Leach's *Political Systems of Highland Burma*. In the mid–twentieth century, these eminent anthropologists believed that anthropology aimed to understand world politics just as the discipline of international relations did (although the world they were concerned with at that time was a particular world that they believed consisted of societies without states). This book, in spirit, inherits the important tradition of modern anthropology in which there was no clear, arbitrary boundary between local politics and world politics. I thank Keith Hart for encouraging me to keep this important tradition and showing the way to revitalize it.

Anne Routon and Peter Dimock of Columbia University Press have shown unfailing support for the book. Alison Rae offered valuable editorial advice in the early stage of writing. Mark Lawrence kindly shared his thoughts on the meaning of "the other cold war," which became the title of this book. Parts of the book were presented at seminars and lectures held in Edinburgh, St. Andrews, Oxford, Bologna, New York, Chicago, and Los Angeles and in various places in South Korea, including Jeju Island. I had engaging and memorable conversations at the 2008 Jeju April 3 memorial conference, at New York University's Center for the United States and the Cold War, and at the 2009 meeting of historians and literary critics at Yonsei University, held jointly with the University of Washington at St Louis. I thank especially Rhodri Jeffreys-Jones, Fabian Hilfrich, Christina Toren, James Weiner, Tony Crook, Emma Reisz, Rana Mitter, David M. Anderson, Antonio Fiori, Mario del Pero, Michael Nash, Marilyn Young, Emily Martin, Bruce Cumings, Julie Y. Chu, Viet Thanh Nguyen, Janet Hoskins, Cho Hung-Youn, Chung Byung-Ho, Victoria Sanford, Baskara T. Wardaya, Tessa Morris-Suzuki, Cho-Han Haejoang, Oh Myung-Seok, Kim Kwang-Ok, Shin Kyung-Sook, Gerald Early, Tani Barlow, and Hahm Hanhee. My early research in Vietnam received generous support from the Economic and Social Research Council. My research visits to Korea benefitted from the hospitality and generosity of the Academy of Korean Studies. The completion of this book was supported by a research development award from the British Academy. An earlier version of chapter 4 appeared in the volume *Sharing the Sacra: The Politics and Pragmatics of Inter-communal Relations Around Holy Places*, edited by Glenn Bowman (in press). Chapter 5 draws on an article published in the inaugural volume of *The Korea Yearbook: Politics, Economy, and Society*, edited by Rüdiger Frank, James E. Hoare, Patrick Köllner, and Susan Pares (2008), and in the *Asia-Pacific Journal*. Some of the book's main arguments appeared in my essay "Experiencing the Cold War," in *Experiencing War*, edited by Christine Sylvester (2010).

THE OTHER COLD WAR

INTRODUCTION

Storytelling reveals meaning without committing the error of defining it; it brings about consent and reconciliation with things as they really are.

—Hannah Arendt, *Men in Dark Times*

The story of the cold war, like that of any other war in human history, begins somewhere and ends somewhere. There is no consensus about the question of beginning. The origin of the cold war is an unsettled issue that continues to engender instructive debate among historians. Reflecting on the diverse ways to think about the origin of the cold war means rethinking the political history of the twentieth century and therefore considering the changing conditions of the contemporary world in new historical perspectives.[1] However, this openness to historical reasoning and imagining does not extend to the other end of the story. There is a strong consensus in contemporary literature that the end of the cold war is a fait accompli, a universal historical reality. The question of the end has no room for diversity and generates no such positive interpretive controversies like those about the origin.[2] The story of the cold war we tell ourselves today, therefore, has an open-ended beginning and a closed ending.

The term *cold war* refers to the prevailing condition of the world in the second half of the twentieth century, divided into two separate paths of political modernity and economic development. In a narrower sense, it means the contest of power and will between the two dominant states, the United States and the Soviet Union, that (according to George Orwell, who coined the term in 1945) set out to rule the world between them under an undeclared state of war, being unable to conquer one another.[3] In a wide definition, however, the global cold war also entails the unequal relations of power among the political communities that pursued or were driven to pursue a specific path of progress within the binary structure of the global order. The "contest-of-power" dimension of the cold war has been an explicit and central element in cold war historiography; in contrast, the "relation-of-domination" aspect has been a relatively marginal, implicit element. The debates about the origins of the cold war contribute to disclosing how complex the great bifurcation in the project of modernity has been for both nations and communities. The origin of the cold war is not merely a question of time but also, in significant measure, a moral question: Which side of the bipolarized human community was more responsible for bringing about the global order and engendering political and military crises? The moral question is intertwined with the chronological one, and their connectedness is more apparent in places where the bipolar conflict was waged in a violent form.

Imagining the political future of Korea, for example, is inseparable from locating the origin of the Korean War. For people who date the origin of the war to 1950, the culpability for the devastating civil war rests unquestionably with the northern Communist regime, which launched, with endorsement and support from Mao Zedong and Joseph Stalin, an all-out surprise offensive against the southern territory in June of that year.[4] For those who trace the war's origin to earlier years, the blame is apportioned equally to the belligerent, strongly anti-Communist southern regime, which instigated a series of border skirmishes and crushed domestic radical nationalist forces in a ruthless manner from 1947 to 1950. The latter measure provoked the outbreak of armed partisan activities in parts of the southern territory, which were effectively in a state of war from 1948 on.[5] For those who associate the origin of the Korean War with the end of the Pacific War in 1945, however, the main responsibility for the civil war lies instead with the United States and the Soviet Union, which partitioned and separately occupied the postcolonial nation after the surrender of Japan. (And we should add to these divergent views the official position taken by North Korea, which continues to paint its part in the war as an act of self-defense against the unprovoked aggression from South Korea, orchestrated by the United States, despite a wealth of evidence that points to the contrary.)[6] These diverse perspectives on the origin of one of the first violent manifestations of the bipolar global order are not merely matters of scholarly debate. They are also deeply ingrained in the society that endured what was at once a civil war and an international war, provoking heated public debate and developing conflicting political voices and forces. In this context, the origin of the cold war is largely the origin of the war-induced wounds felt in the society, thereby making the very concept of a "cold" war somewhat contradictory, so that claiming a particular version of the origin is simultaneously an act of asserting a particular vision of the nation's history and future.

In the wider terrain, too, the cold war's temporal identity continues to be revised as to the question of its origin. Conventional knowledge associates the origin of the cold war with the end of World War II and the breakdown of the wartime alliance between the Western powers and the Soviet state. However, several scholars have challenged this conventional view. For example, Melvyn Leffler retraces the origin to the period following the Russian Revolution of 1917, whereas William Appleman Williams famously argues that the seeds of the cold war were sown much earlier, during the nineteenth-century contest for global supremacy between the established European imperial powers and the newly rising American power.[7] Each of these revisions of the cold war's origin is simultaneously an attempt to reinterpret the meaning of the global conflict in modern history. Leffler's scheme foregrounds the importance of ideology (the antagonistic view to communism as a radically alien way of life incompatible with the market-based liberal world) in the construction of the cold war global order, whereas Williams shows how the perception of the alien ideological other mirrored for the United States at the turn of the twentieth century the nation's own ideological self-image defined in terms of so-called Manifest Destiny—the idea that America, as a sole benevolent and progressive power, confronts the backward and confused world infested with imperialist excess and colonial miseries.[8]

The identification of the origin of the cold war continues to be debated today and has even been revitalized recently. On the one hand, this continued interest is due to the accessibility of previously unavailable archival material held in the formerly Eastern bloc countries, which has enabled historians to introduce new facts to the early process of cold war construction and thereby to reassess how state actors on one side interpreted (or misinterpreted) the intentions and behaviors of the actors on the other side.[9] On the other hand, the origins of the cold war continue to be a vital question in relation to the explicit and implicit historical dimensions and meanings mentioned earlier. There is a notable tendency now in the international history of the cold war to bring the implicit, hierarchical dimension of the global bipolar order to the foreground of this ordering, thus challenging the traditional preeminence of the explicit, East/West reciprocal dimension. The increasingly common reference to "empire" in contemporary literature (with respect to the rise of American power or to the expansion of Soviet power) testifies to this tendency.[10] In this development, the history of the cold war is increasingly about a particular power structure of domination, invented and realized along the bipolarization of modernity, rather than singularly about the contest of power waged between opposing versions and visions of modernity.

Although the origin of the cold war remains unsettled to date and is therefore commonly expressed with the plural noun *origins* in contemporary debate, the same is not true with reference to the opposite end of cold war history. There is no plurality of time-space in our conception of the end of the cold war. In the media and across academic communities, it is widely assumed that the cold war era ended when the Berlin Wall fell in November 1989. In the subsequent decade, "after the fall" became the most popular means to express what was then perceived to be the new, hopeful spirit of the time and to contextualize contemporaneous events and developments on the basis of a radical rupture in time. The idiom has since become part of the language of social sciences, functioning as an essential spatiotemporal marker in discourses about new empirical realities and new conceptual tools. There have been prolific discussions about a new global order and about new social and cultural forms after the cold war, and they include propositions about novel analytical tools in accordance with the changed empirical world. These discourses have been advanced on the premise that the world "after the fall" is substantively different from the world before the fall and that the new world requires new instruments of description and analysis. Analytical discourses about new instruments of knowledge typically begin with a note about the fall of the Berlin Wall or other similar ways to express the end of the bipolar era, then they set out to chart the specific political, economic, and cultural issues with which the analyses are concerned (see chapter 1). This way, "after 1989" or "after the End" works in most contemporary analytical discourse as an indicator of the novelty of knowledge—a sign that the presented discourse is about aspects of the world here and now and not about the defunct order of things from the closed, nonexistent era.

The general consensus about the end of the cold war in chronological terms relates to a broad consent about the moral implications of the great End. The cold war ended because the Communist system ran out of steam to compete with the capitalist economy and liberal democracy. The Western industrial powers are not to be blamed for the demise of the Communist polities, apart from their having succeeded in building a system that is economically more efficient and organizationally superior. The year 1989 is the new "year zero," from which victorious liberal capitalism would herald a powerful move to transcend the ideological History that had entrapped humanity for a century.[11] These opinions of "triumphant liberalism" regarding the West's bloodless, peaceful victory against the East in the war of ideologies and in the competition between contrary versions of modernity were widely accepted during the first half of the 1990s.[12] Contrary voices and opposing interpretations existed at the time, though, and they have gained more decisiveness and coherence in subsequent years. Some pointed out the fragmenting, "disorder" aspect of the new world order; others highlighted a fundamental continuity, across the threshold of 1989, in the hegemonic propensity of American power.[13] The end of the cold war generated a multiplicity of ideas about the new order, and the contemporary transition was depicted "as a shift for the better, or for worse," depending on which perspective the contemporary history was seen from.[14] Nevertheless, the dissenting or pessimistic voices shared with the triumphant or optimistic voices the premise and certainty that the end of the cold war is a given reality. As Ian Clark notes, "Whether inaugurating something better or worse, the end of the Cold War was viewed by both sets of proponents as a significant turning point."[15] On the basis of this tacit consensus across different interpretative communities, the story of the cold war came to take on a singular, universal point of terminus.

The French political scientist Zaki Laïdi argues that in the cold war conflict, power and meaning were two sides of the same coin. Each of the two leading state actors offered a global meaning of the cold war within each geopolitical sphere it dominated. The cold war was as much a "battle for the appropriation of meaning" between two competing teleological systems of historical progress as a battle for power between two competing social systems. Laïdi believes that the appropriation of the meaning of progress was the fundamental origin of the cold war, "the first and only great polarization of modern History."[16] Christian Appy, historian of America's Vietnam War, also emphasizes the politics of knowledge in the constitution of the cold war order. According to Appy, the cold war was not only a struggle for power but also a struggle for the meaning of that power struggle—that is, a "struggle for the word" as well as a "struggle for the world."[17] Unlike Laïdi's consideration of the philosophy of history as the main battlefield for the appropriation and contest of meaning, Appy's notion of semantic struggle avoids any unitary explanation of the global struggle. Instead, Appy highlights the plurality in the "struggle for the world" and advocates the need to account for the variety of ways in which the struggle was perceived and understood by the different bodies of actors involved in it.

Why then is the "struggle for the *word*" engaged today in such a selective way as described earlier? What makes the end of the cold war an inappropriate subject for a semantic struggle? When we say the cold war is over, whose cold war and which dimension of the cold war do we refer to? Did the cold war end the same way everywhere, or was the "struggle for the world" the same everywhere?

The last two questions broadly define the aim of this book, which argues, among other things, that there has never been a conflict called *the* cold war. The bipolarized human community of the twentieth century experienced political bifurcation in radically different ways across societies— ways that cannot be forced into a single coherent conceptual whole. For nations in Europe and North America, the history of the cold war meant a "long peace" distinct from the previous era, in which these nations were embroiled in the mass destruction of human lives. But for many new postcolonial nations elsewhere the onset of the cold war meant entering an epoch of "unbridled reality" characterized by vicious civil wars and other exceptional forms of political violence.[18] Whereas the cold war in the first sense resulted in the culture of "ideological consensus" and "existential anxiety," the cold war in the second sense engendered a perpetual condition akin to what Georgio Agamben calls "the state of exception"—the suspension of the rule of law as a rule of the political order.[19] In certain parts of the world, the beginning of the cold war coincided with the end of imperial and colonial rule, whereas in other parts these two epochal political forms were disturbingly entangled and became practically inseparable. In some regions, cold war politics was viewed primarily as the business of the states and their alliances, largely unconnected to the routines of the civic order, whereas in other places people had to live the cold war as part of their everyday lives and in their most immediate, intimate domains.[20] The history of the global cold war consists of a multitude of these locally specific historical realities and variant human experiences, and this view conflicts with the dominant image of the cold war as a single, encompassing geopolitical order.

Other observers have cautioned against a uniform notion of the cold war, which runs up against many obstacles, including the variance between Europe and its former colonies as well as the equally important difference between the northern and southern parts of Europe, not to mention between the eastern and western parts. Walter LaFeber writes that the questions of *which* cold war and *whose* cold war are central to any debate about the cold war's origin and its aftermath.[21] In a similar light, Geir Lundestad and Odd Arne Westad have consistently emphasized the importance of political and revolutionary struggles for decolonization in the making of the cold war order.[22] For modern European history, Mark Mazower describes how the early cold war was experienced differently across European nations, demonstrating this point by highlighting the history of the Greek Civil War (1946–1949).[23] Bruce Cumings takes issue with the idea of a "long peace," pointing out that this primarily Europe-centered idiom of the cold war cannot extend to the experience of bipolar politics and conflicts in other parts of the world that resulted in prolific organized violence and millions of human casualties.[24] These insights from recent historical scholarship emphasize the locally contrasting experiences of the global cold war and the related need to shift the analytical perspective away from the centrality of the European and North American experience.[25] In fact, they unsettle the very semantics of the cold war (or the "imaginary war," as defined in contrast to the historically known and experienced real war) with which we are accustomed to grasping our immediate collective past. Cynthia Enloe notes that if the cold war was not a unitary phenomenon, the process of ending it was also not identical among different social groupings.[26] Although Enloe raises this point primarily with reference to the gender dimension of the bipolar politics, her statement can extend to other comparative contexts.

Taking on and extending these insights, this book confronts the idea of the cold war and the formidable semantic contradiction that is inherent in the idea. It does so in part by challenging the contemporary premise that the end of the cold war is a self-evident, given global reality. I argue that this premise draws on an abstract notion of the global, ungrounded in actual political realities and oblivious to the radical diversity in human communal experience of bipolar history. The projection of a definitive or "final" historical turning point, according to Hannah Arendt, rises from a falsely transcendental perspective of history. Following Arendt's participatory notion of the present time as interval and suspension between past and future,[27] I argue that the historical turning point glossed as the end of the cold war is actually an extended horizon of "what is not yet," a field of time-space that is open to creative political acting and moral imagining. I approach the end of the cold war both conceptually as an emerging horizon and proactive aspect of contemporary history, rather than as a given chronological reality, and empirically as a slowly decomposing process that involves a multitude of human actions arising from concrete, structured conditions within and across defined locales.

The phrase "decomposition of the cold war" broadly refers to this phenomenological approach to the temporality of the cold war, on the one hand, and to a rigorously comparative approach to its historical spatiality, on the other. Put in different terms, the decomposition of the cold war considers the end of the cold war as a participatory, ethnographic question rather than as a historical issue. It also proposes that cold war history is fundamentally an anthropological problem—both in the sense that an understanding of how the peripheral others experienced and recount the history of the cold war is central to putting into perspective the way in which the exemplary center conceptualizes the nature of this history and also in the sense that struggles between the image of the whole and the representation of the parts are critical to the understanding of the global cold war. If the cold war is an object of semantic struggles, the investigation of this object requires the same skill as that required for the investigation of cultural symbols. Eminent anthropologist Mary Douglas shows that placing the loud message of a symbol against the channels of tacit meanings concealed in the symbol is the first step to coming nearer to the social life of the symbol, which consists of a subtle interplay between explicit and implicit meanings.[28]

This book tells a new story of the cold war's power and meaning by attending to the diverse, implicit meanings of the war's power struggle. It aims both to extend the debate about the origins of the cold war to an understanding of the end of the cold war, freeing the latter from the falsity of uniformity, and to advance cold war history as a subject of comparative social and cultural research. These two objectives are closely interconnected. The comparative method is necessary for challenging the mistaken uniform notion of the cold war; the sociological perspective is necessary for bringing out the human dimension of the geopolitical order. The decomposition of the cold war thus involves a two-pronged shift of perspective regarding cold war history: from a geopolitical history to a social history, on the one hand, and from the exemplary central positioning of the cold war as imaginary or metaphoric war to a comparative positioning that privileges neither this peculiar history of war without warfare nor the peripheral "unbridled reality" of state terror and civil war, on the other. In the decomposition of the cold war, I do not consider these variant realities of bipolar political history in a "center versus periphery" scheme. Instead, I make the breakdown of this concentric conceptual spatial hierarchy the central element of this study's mode of inquiry. As illustrated, this change of perspective regarding the spatiality of the cold war makes it impossible for us to place our collective existence firmly and passively after the end of the cold war; instead, our collective being-in-the-world includes active engagement with ending the order of the cold war.

This book consists of three broadly divided parts. Part I examines how the idiom of "after 1989" and the related idea of a radical rupture in history cause some formidable conceptual confusions in fields of contemporary social research. Focusing on the literature on cultural globalization, postsocialist transition, and postcolonial criticism, the three chapters in part I view why bipolar history is commonly dislocated from research agendas in these fields and how this dislocation relates to the privileging of an abstract, geopolitical definition of the cold war. Chapter 1 examines how some contemporary discourses about global social forms relegate the bipolar global history as a whole to the past tense, thereby failing to engage with the enduring effects of bipolar conflicts on local social and cultural processes. This chapter also outlines a set of conceptual issues involved in approaching the cold war from an alternative, comparative sociological perspective and thus serves as an extended general introduction. These issues include the spatiality of the cold war as a geopolitical and social conflict, the contrast between imaginary and nonimaginary violence in the experience of the conflict, and the place of postcolonial struggles in the violent history of the cold war. Focusing on the latter issue, chapters 2 and 3 investigate why the historically interconnected processes of decolonization and political bipolarization are thematically separated in current social research communities such as postsocialist studies and postcolonial criticism and how this false separation is caused by a misguided, overly geopolitical conception of the global cold war. Part II illustrates these three issues with case studies based on Vietnam and Korea—two major sites of protracted, violent bipolar confrontation in Asia. Focusing on death-commemorative activities in a southern region of Vietnam and in a southern island of Korea, each of which continues to keep alive a bitter memory of civil war, the two chapters in part II describe how bipolar politics and ideologies are disintegrating in locally specific and culturally creative ways. These chapters thus explore the possibility of conceiving the end of the cold war as an emerging transnational reality that involves locally active social processes of conflict resolution. They also aim to demonstrate the importance of engaging theoretically with bipolar political and social history and discuss some relevant theories of social identity and moral and political action in this context. The conventional idea of the cold war invokes an image of the global that encompasses local social processes rather than an image that is revealed and made through the local, and the former abstract image of the global is intimately tied to the perceived end of the cold war as a universal event. In order to think of the global cold war in the context of local historical and social reality, therefore, it is necessary to rethink the conceptual relationship between local processes and the global dynamic. With this objective, part III further explores the conjuncture of postcolonial and bipolar histories based on the analytical discussion of part I and the empirical illustrations of part II. Chapter 6 reviews how some contemporary postcolonial theorists conceptualize the local/global spatiality and raises counterarguments to the way in which their conception of history and culture obviates the traces of bipolar history from the field of postcolonial culture by uncritically assimilating the dominant, Europe-centered scheme of the cold war as an imaginary war. Chapter 7 examines in a related light the idea of cold war culture, widely mentioned in the currently expanding field of cold war social and cultural history as a broad reference to the cultural politics of anticommunism. This chapter argues that the idea of cold war culture remains restricted within the paradigm of the imaginary war and biased in favor of a semiotic theory of culture, oblivious to the fact that the instrument of anti-Communist politics, in the wider postcolonial world, included naked violence and political terror as well as rhetorical or cultural symbolic instruments. "The decomposition of the cold war" refers to the diverse and locally specific ways in which the cold war is coming to an end. As such, it critically engages with the dominant geocentric, encompassing notion of the end of the cold war, which ignores the enduring social and cultural effects of the bipolarized political reality of the past century. The idea of decomposition also has an added, more literal meaning relating to the very concept of the cold war. The history of the cold war in non-Western territories was often an exceptionally violent one, involving mass destruction of human lives and political displacement of the victims' memories of this destruction. This book argues that how societies come to terms with the remains of the cold war's mass violence and death is vital for their political futures. In this sense, "the decomposition of the cold war" has a more literal meaning, which is to relocate the human casualties of the bipolar conflicts (and the actions concerning their decomposing bodies and troubled memories) from the invisible margins to a vital center in the history of the global cold war. The conclusion reiterates these objectives and their relevance.

PART 1

1

THE IDEA OF THE END

After the end of World War II, many communities in Greece were divided between the supporters of the Communist partisan forces and supporters of the government's anti-Communist drive.[1] In one village seized by the chaotic civil war, in the country's northeastern region, a partisan supporter was arrested in his home and subsequently sent to a prison camp on a remote island. The arrest was carried out by a group of men from outside the village, including one who was wearing a hood. The villagers later learned that the masked man was the arrested man's brother. Many people left the village after the civil war and now live in distant places. When these people later returned to their homeland for a visit, the remaining villagers organized a welcoming feast. The two brothers joined these gatherings if the visitors happened to be their close relatives or friends. However, the villagers never heard any greeting or conversation exchanged between these two men on that occasion or during many such occasions in subsequent decades.[2]

The civil war in Greece (1946–1949) was intimately connected to the civil war in Korea (1950–1953) in the international history of the cold war. They both were an "international civil war," in part driven by the Truman Doctrine of 1947 and in part grounded in each society's polarization into radical nationalist forces and anti-Communist nationalist forces.[3] The Truman Doctrine announced the active global leadership of the United States in the struggle against international communism, and the two civil wars marked the militarization and globalization of this struggle.[4] President Harry S. Truman in fact referred to Korea as "the Greece of the Far East" when a war broke out on the peninsula and said, "If we are tough enough now, if we stand up to [the Communists] like we did in Greece three years ago, they won't take over the whole Middle East."[5] In the southeastern region of the peninsula, there is a village once known as the region's Moskva (Moscow)—the wartime reference for a Communist stronghold.[6] Each year, people originally from this village return to their homeland in order to join the ceremony held on behalf of family and village ancestors. On these periodic occasions, the relatives from distant places are pleased to meet each other and exchange news—but not always.

When a man cautiously suggested to his lineage elders recently that the family might consider repairing a neglected ancestral tomb, this suggestion broke the harmony of the family meal held after the ancestral rite. One elder left the room in fury, and other elders remained silent throughout the ceremonial meal. The man who proposed the idea was the adopted son of the person buried in the neglected tomb, having been selected as the deceased man's descendent by the family elders for a ritual purpose, and the elder whom the man offended happened to be a close relative of the deceased. The ancestor had been a prominent anticolonial, Communist activist before he died at a young age without a male descendent; the offended elder's children were among the several dozen village youths who left the village together with the retreating Communist army in the chaos of the civil war. The elder believes that this catastrophe in village history and family continuity could have been avoided if the ancestor buried in the neglected tomb had not brought the seeds of "Red ideology" to the village in the first place.[7] Beautifying the man's neglected tomb was unacceptable to this elder, who believed that some of his close kin had lost, because of the ancestor, the social basis on which they could be remembered as family ancestors after their own deaths.

The morality of ancestor worship is as strong in Vietnamese cultural tradition as it is in Korean tradition. These two countries also share the common historical experience of being important sites and symbols in Asia for America's leadership in the global struggle against the threat of communism.[8] Since the end of the 1980s, when the Vietnamese political leadership initiated a general economic reform and regulated political liberalization in the country, there has been a strong revival of ancestral rituals in Vietnamese villages. The state hierarchy had previously discouraged these rituals because it regarded them as backward customs incompatible with the modern secular, revolutionary society.[9] In the communities of the southern and central regions (what was known as South Vietnam during the Vietnam War), a notable aspect of this social development has been the introduction to the ancestral ritual realm those identities and persons previously excluded from public memory. The memorabilia of the former "counterrevolutionary" South Vietnamese soldiers and other hitherto socially stigmatized historical identities became increasingly visible in the domestic and communal ritual space. Before the reform, the Vietnamese public ritual space was limited exclusively to the memory of the fallen revolutionary combatants from the Vietnam–American war. It is now increasingly becoming open to memories of the dead from the other side of the war and is therefore in conflict with the state-controlled public institution of commemoration, where one sees no records of deaths from what the Vietnamese call *ben kia* ("that side," meaning the American side).[10]

These communal developments and conflicts are common in societies where people experienced the cold war in forms other than the "long peace"—the idiom with which the historian John Lewis Gaddis characterizes the international environment in the second half of the twentieth century, partly in contrast to the war-torn era of the first half.[11] Gaddis believes that the bipolar structure of the world order, despite the many anomalies and negative effects it generated, contributed to containing an overt armed confrontation among industrial powers. As Walter LaFeber notes, however, this view of the cold war speaks a half-truth of bipolar history.[12] The view represents the dominant Western (and Soviet) experience of the cold war as an "imaginary war," referring to the politics of competitively preparing for war in the hope of avoiding an actual outbreak of war, but the identification of the second half of the twentieth century as an exceptionally long period of international peace would hardly be intelligible to most of the rest of the world.[13] The cold war era resulted in forty million human casualties of war in different parts of the world, as LaFeber mentions; how to reconcile this exceptionally violent historical reality with the predominant Western perception of an exceptionally long peace is a crucial question for grasping the meaning of the global cold war.[14] According to Bruce Cumings, it is necessary to weigh the dominant "balance of power" conception of the cold war, on which the idea of the "long peace" is based, against the reality of the "balance of terror" experienced in the wide world.[15]

The cold war was a global conflict. Yet this does not mean that the conflict was experienced on the same terms all over the world. One way to think about the cold war's encompassing but variable political realities is implicated in its name. The term *cold war* is both the general reference for the global bipolar conflict and the representation of this conflict from a particular regional point of view. Societies varyingly endured the political history of the cold war either as an imaginary war or as other than imaginary, either without or with large-scale violence and human suffering. Cold war politics permeated developed and underdeveloped societies, Western and non-Western states, and colonial powers and colonized nations: in this sense, it was a truly global reality. However, the historical experience and the collective memory of the cold war are radically divergent between the West and the postcolonial world. The cold war experienced as a long peace and the cold war experienced as a total war may not be considered within a single framework unless this framework is formulated in such a way that it can accommodate the experiential contraries and deal with the semantic contradiction embedded in the idea of the cold war.

The political history of the cold war has been the concern primarily of diplomatic history and international relations. In places where the cold war was waged as a civil war or in other forms of radical and violent bifurcation of social forces, however, its history may not be relegated merely to the specialty of these disciplines. In these places, bipolar politics permeated national society, traditional community, family relations, and individual identity. Diplomatic history alone, in such contexts, cannot do justice to the complex, multilevel reality of political confrontation unless it is creatively combined with social history. The bipolar conflict evolved not only according to the superpower state actors' intentions but also on the basis of existing, locally specific structural and normative conditions and orientations. The popularity of Communist partisans in post–World War II Greece was related to their moral strength as an active nationalist resistance force against the German and Italian occupations during the war; the same can be said about the Vietnamese and Korean Communists with respect to their resistance to the colonial occupations by France and Japan, respectively.[16] If the bipolar conflict involved a mass destruction of human lives, its wounds may still be vigorously alive in communal existence even though the superpower contest of power is declared over and done with. In these communities, these historical wounds were largely invisible in the public space under a self-consciously anti-Communist or revolutionary state, and they began to be acknowledged only after the cold war as a geo-political contest was over and when the structure of power within a political society began to change accordingly (see chapters 4 and 5). For this particu-lar history of the cold war, waged as the "balance of terror" rather than as the "balance of power," the narrative strategy that focuses primarily on the state and interstate actions is inadequate. We need to develop an alternative mode of narration, one that incorporates but does not exclusively privilege the state's perspective and agency.

The social dimension of the cold war has not been given much room in conventional cold war studies. Until recently, the focus of this academic field has been primarily on international politics, taking states (conceived of as actors or institutions) as its main units of analysis and aiming at explaining the behavior of these units within the sphere of activity called the "international system."[17] With a state-centric and systemic focus, the dominant approach was that of realism, stressing the importance of power balances and geopolitical considerations. However, the end of the cold war as a geopolitical order has affected the dominance of this realist paradigm in international relations and history. Not least because this paradigm failed to predict or explain the sudden collapse of the Soviet rule in 1989–1991, a number of younger-generation historians have since shifted their analytical orientation and now stress "the significance of ideas and beliefs, focusing on the importance of ideology and culture."[18] They are engaged in reconsidering cold war history in innovative ways, investigating the diverse sociocultural aspects of the global conflict and exploring ways to reconcile these aspects with the existing contours of diplomatic history. As a result, it is argued, "The story of the Cold War is likely to become more conten-tious as it becomes more interesting and complex, and it will continue to defy any single narrative."[19] In this new historiography of the cold war, the expansion of American power is not merely considered in the scheme of balance of power with the Soviet Union but also viewed according to vari-ous terms of ideological self-making and construction of social order. Thus, for instance, the idea of containment, which earlier referred to the geopo-litical reasoning about limiting Soviet power, now entails diverse aspects of societal ordering with regard to moral purity and dangers.[20]

The social and cultural dimension of the cold war is a neglected subject in other disciplines, too. In social and cultural anthropology, with which I am familiar, it is rare to find a specialist who addresses the social or cul-tural history of the cold war as a research question—even a specialist on a geographical area that is discussed among historians as a major site of the bipolar conflict. Mark Mazower, writing about modern Greece, writes bitterly of the almost complete absence of attention to the civil war history and the subsequent political history of anticommunism in the otherwise rich anthropological literature on Greek culture and society. He contends that the anthropology of Greece has instead contributed to establishing an image of rural Greece as "an unchanging, traditional, ahistorical world."[21] Geoffrey Robinson makes a similarly critical point about anthropological research on Indonesia. According to Robinson, the area specialists on Bali have neglected the impact of the cataclysmic anti-Communist state terror campaigns of 1965 on the deceptively peaceful, aesthetically rich, and seemingly apolitical Balinese cultural lives (see chapter 7). Against this representational tradition, Robinson says, it is necessary "to demystify Bali, to take the romance out, and to restore to their rightful place the conflict and the violence that have characterized the island's politics on and off throughout the twentieth century."[22]

Whereas historical scholarship currently shows a growing engagement with the social and cultural dimensions of the cold war, including Mazower's and Robinson's pioneering works, it is interesting to note an opposite tendency in other disciplines. In disciplines traditionally associated with cultural history and social analysis, there is now a strong inclination to disengage with cold war history altogether, to relegate it to the status of an old, unfortunate geopolitical episode that has little relevance for research agendas. The analytical break with cold war history is particularly marked in the academic discourse about globalization. The rest of this chapter reviews this trend and investigates how the analytical disengagement with the cold war relates to a problematic, incomplete understanding of the cold war in terms of balance of power.

The end of the bipolar era, according to the sociologist Anthony Giddens, "radically altered the nature of states' sovereignty," and in terms of economics it resulted in capitalism's "quantum leap to a completely different scale from the past."[23] Giddens observes that in the post–cold war world, capitalism has become a single option for the entire human race, facing no competing mode of economic development. This development has generated a profound sense of encompassment and inevitability, and in this triumphant march of capitalism after the "bloodless" victory over communism, money becomes sure of itself and more ruthless in pursuit of an absolute freedom of mobility.[24] Based on this observation, whose relevance is manifested in the recent global financial irregularities and meltdown, Giddens argues that there is an urgent need to reformulate key sociological categories such as state, society, family, and the individual according to the new global reality of a borderless economy and states without enemies (see chapter 5).

In a similar light, the anthropologist Arjun Appadurai also proposes "a new architecture for area studies" in the globalizing world after the cold war. He argues that scholars of area studies must redefine their object of inquiry, departing from what he calls the "trait geography"—the conception of localities and culture areas as discrete entities in possession of distinct traits of material and social life. This conception of the local, according to him, is an artifact "of a recent Western cartography of large civilizational landmasses associated with different relationships to Europe, and a Cold War–based geography of fear and competition in which the study of world languages and regions in the United States was legislatively configured for security purposes into a reified map of geographical regions."[25] The concept of the locale ought to be freed from the pigeonhole of cartographic tradition, Appadurai argues, and imagined anew as a locus of social actions and developments in constant interaction with global processes.

Appadurai explains how his current interest in cultural globalization, which he characterizes mainly as the deterritorialization of human lives and the circulation of cultural artifacts and ideas on a global scale, developed in critical reaction to the mode of knowledge practices dominant during the cold war era.[26] He states that the academic establishment of area studies in the United States, where he was involved as a specialist in South Asia, developed closely along with the policy directives of the cold war geopolitics. According to him, the U.S. state administration encouraged area studies (as did the Soviet bureaucracy) with the specific purpose of charting the politically polarized world with a detailed map of diverse cultural units and collective personalities. Appadurai is critical of this historical background of area studies and concerned about the future of area studies in what he calls "the world after 1989"—the environment in which the traditional specialty of area studies is no longer in demand from supporting institutions, at least in the form that developed at the height of the cold war conflict.

Philip Roeder observes in regard to the former Soviet and eastern European area studies: "The years prior to 1989 were the glory days for area specialists. The Cold War gave our special knowledge unique value: we knew the enemy and it was 'ours.' The quickening of changes in the mid-1980s temporarily inflated this value, but then came the crash."[27] Appadurai proposes a way out of this demise in area studies' political economy of knowledge production: "What does need to be recognized, if the area-studies tradition is to be revitalized, is that locality itself is a historical product and that the histories through which localities emerge are eventually subject to the dynamics of the global."[28] Appadurai reflects on the failure of traditional area studies to relate critically local histories and cultures that they investigated to the global political forces that propelled the investigation. The new area studies in the new age after the cold war must overcome this structural problem by means of a theoretical rebirth, which he paints largely as an analytical integration of local and global processes. Appadurai proposes as the main research focus of new area studies in the globalizing world a social process he calls "globalization from below." This process is defined in opposition to "globalization from above," which is, according to him, driven by free-floating financial capital and powerful states. Appadurai explains that his main concern is "the democratization of research about globalization[,] [which] could produce a global view of globalization."[29]

It is hard to disagree with Appadurai's general vision. Exploring the minute details of a local social form and doing so with an acute awareness of the wider historical process have in fact been a main objective of conducting anthropological research, which is partly a kind of area studies, too. In 1907–1909, Robert Hertz wrote his seminal works on death and the moral hierarchy of values. When he wrote these works, Hertz was also deeply engaged with the emerging political crisis in Europe that led to the outbreak of World War I, which not only killed Hertz's young life but also subsequently provoked a sea change in how the moderns would view mass death and value mass sacrifice to a national cause.[30] In the 1950s, Edmund Leach studied the political culture in highland Burma, in which he highlighted the coexistence of opposite political ideals and forms, equalitarian and hierarchical, among the Kachin who live along Burma's border with China. In doing so, Leach was conscious of the moral contradictions in British politics during and after World War II, which on the one hand made claims for the preservation of democratic values and national sovereignty against Nazism, but on the other worked against the demands for national independence and democratic governance rising from its own colonies.[31]

In 1954, Max Gluckman lectured the British public about the segmentary kinship and social system in tribal Africa. One of the central messages in his BBC lectures was about how although the segmentary kinship system divides the social world into two moieties, it is based on a complex network of crosscutting ties and loyalties. The division is laden with conflicts, whereas the network contributes to preventing the conflicts from running out of hand. Making this presentation about the idea of "peace in the feud" in the mid-1950s, Gluckman was conscious of what the idea would mean for the confrontational international environment and deepening political crisis of the time.[32]

However, there is a problem in Appadurai's vision of new area studies, particularly in how he conceptualizes local history in relation to global political processes. Whereas Appadurai is conscious of the impact of cold war politics on the development of area studies, such awareness is curiously absent from his characterization of the local. Appadurai states that his main analytical concerns are the long-distance migration of human labor and ideas, the weakening of national boundaries, and the growing "irregularity of ties between nations and ideologies."[33] They are some of the prominent social phenomena that he believes characterize "the world after 1989." He also notes that the legacy of colonialism continues to shape contemporary social processes. Between the enduring impact of colonialism on the modern world and the new horizon of transnational phenomena, however, there is no room in his rendering of local/global interactions for the particularly rigid, bipolarized regularity of ties between nations and ideologies. The history of the cold war is bracketed out from the depth of local history and removed from the expanse of globalization, even though in both spheres enduring elements of the colonial past are supposed be in interaction with the rising horizon of postnational futures.

Why this propensity to disown cold war history? What makes it necessary to obliterate the traces of the bipolar pasts from the local in a project whose stated aim is to give voice to the latter in the formation of the global? Does this approach mean that localities have nothing to say about the global cold war? The broad definition of the term *globalization* refers to the process in which nations and peoples are integrated into a larger community politically, economically, and culturally. Although the term is considered new and has emerged as a defining feature of the era after the cold war, it is understood that the underlying process of globalization is inseparable from "the evolution of the American Century."[34] Is it really possible to imagine the horizon of "globalization from below" without considering how nations and localities experienced the "American Century"?

We may say that this disengagement with cold war history is related to a disciplinary focus. John Borneman writes: "Given their concentration on peoples primarily located in the Third World, many anthropologists after World War II took up study of the decolonization processes in which their primary objects of research were involved. Because of this focus, anthropological contributions to understanding the making of the Cold War order have been minimal."[35]

But this explanation surely does not make sense, for the decolonization of political order and the bipolarization of politics were largely coeval, closely interconnected processes in the history of the twentieth century.[36] As Borneman also notes, "Decolonization, whatever its local aims or goals, could never proceed independent of Cold War order."[37] In my view, the analytical disengagement with cold war history points to a deeper problem than merely disciplinary focus. The historian Odd Arne Westad notes: "The Cold War is still generally assumed to have been a contest between two superpowers over military power and strategic control, mostly centered on Europe. [On] the contrary, the most important aspects of the Cold War were neither military nor strategic, nor Europe-centered, but connected to political and social development in the Third World."[38]

The way in which bipolar history is considered irrelevant in the formulation of area studies' research agendas results from a view of the cold war order as merely an abstract balance of power and from the related, mistaken assumption, as Westad puts it, that "the Cold War conceptually and analytically does not belong in the south."[39]

LaFeber insists that the cold war was not a unitary phenomenon but instead constituted diverse realities of varying intensity and temporality. He writes: "Before we conclude that the Cold War era has ended, it might be as well to decide which Cold War is under discussion. To telescope the past forty-five years into only a U.S.–Soviet confrontation might be convenient, but it is also ahistorical."[40] Cumings describes the cold war system as consisting of two projects: "the containment project" and "the hegemonic project." The containment side of the system was intended for the dominant state actors to secure their supremacy in their respective spheres of influence against challenges from enemies, whereas the hegemony side meant controlling the circulation of resources in order to secure supremacy against challenges from allies. For Cumings, the dominant definition of the cold war, focused as it is on the containment side of the bipolar system, has obscured the hegemonic project that in fact propelled the system.[41]

These scholars often warn us against viewing the cold war as a single monolithic phenomenon. Their writings suggest that understanding the history of the cold war requires a certain distance from the dominant perspective that sees the global conflict centered in the European and North American regions geographically and in the geopolitical balance of power conceptually. The conscious analytical decentering they advocate is at once a historical and anthropological question. It speaks of the fact that the West's understanding of the cold war is not necessarily extendible to how the non-Western world experienced it and that realizing this difference in experience and knowledge should be a central issue in assessing the history of the global cold war. The meaning of the cold war is thus open to critical comparison and reflection. This meaning is something that we need to continue to struggle for by questioning the dominant assumptions and attending to the diverse experiences, rather than something to be relegated to analytical closure by resorting to the convenient idiom of "after the fall" or "after 1989."

Appadurai mistakes the West-centered, geopolitical notion of the cold war for the global cold war and, because of this mistake, confuses the end of the geopolitical cold war with the end of the complexity of the cold war as a whole. He is concerned about the problematic division of labor between international studies and area studies, and he hopes to end this artificial division of knowledge production.[42] In attempting to achieve this goal, however, he reinvents the division at the same time. If the new area studies can obviate bipolar history from local history, this act can be justified only on the basis of the presumption that the end of the bipolar conflict as a geopolitical scheme is identical in meaning to the end of the conflict globally and across locales—that is to say, according to the same abstract language of the global bred by cold war–era knowledge practices. Appadurai proposes an integrative local/global analytical framework. By emptying the history before 1989 from this framework, however, he preempts the possibility of genuinely undoing the artificial division. He intends to create a new analytical tool that is free from the history of cold war power politics, yet he at the same time removes from the tool's instrumentality the capacity to engage critically with that history. Out of this disparity between reshaping the analytical tool and the purpose of doing so, cold war history may be removed from the horizon of local realities, and localities thereby appear to have nothing to say about the decomposition of the bipolar order. A properly revitalized area studies would have to strive to end the artificial division, both in the tools it employs and in the fields of inquiry in which it employs these tools. The field is a historically constituted one, and it must not be denied of its historicity with such a totalizing remark as "the world after 1989," which indicates that the conception of the global remains unanchored in the understanding of the local. Locality is a historical product, as Appadurai puts it, and we must stick to that.[43]

Furthermore, as briefly noted earlier, it is not viable to emphasize the enduring impact of colonial history on contemporary cultural and political developments, as Appadurai does, while at the same time removing bipolar history from this historical awareness. "The two processes, of decolonization and Cold War ordering, though spatially distinct are temporally and thematically inseparable," as Borneman notes.[44] Indeed, the First Indochina War (1946–1954) between France and Vietnamese resistance forces was for France rhetorically a moral struggle against communism, but in actuality it was an idiosyncratic, unethical attempt at colonial reconquest. After World War II, Algeria, Indonesia (by the Netherlands), and Malaysia (by Great Britain) also experienced mass violence that stemmed from the fusion between old colonial greed and the new language of anticommunism. For Korea, the end of colonial domination took place literally in the form of a cold war military occupation by the United States in the southern half and by the Soviet Union in the northern half. A similar situation prevailed in Iran, which after World War II was divided between the British rule in the southern territory and the Soviet occupation in the northern territory. In these contexts, postcolonial history and bipolar history are analytically not separable, as Borneman says, nor can the latter collapse thematically into the former.

Idioms such as "after 1989" give the false impression that the cold war was a single, globally identical phenomenon. The cold war did not have the same developmental patterns across territories, which becomes particularly apparent if we compare western Europe and its former colonies. For western Europe, according to Mary Kaldor, the cold war was an "imaginary war"—the anomalous condition of maintaining peace by mutually maintaining the threat of a total war.[45] Kaldor explains how the emergence of a new common external enemy contributed to post–World War II Western nations' being able to overcome their internal hostilities and past grievances and how the same situation in the Eastern bloc contributed to legitimizing the expansion of Soviet power and political integration within the bloc. In Europe's Asian and African colonies, on the contrary, the ideological division of the international environment after World War II often resulted in radical polarization of domestic political forces, which in turn led to devastating civil wars with prolific international intervention.

The experience of postcolonial Vietnam is again a powerful example in this respect. Vietnam's war with the United States, the Second Indochina War (1961–1975), was, according to Mark Bradley, the pursuit of a prevailing postcolonial vision in the era of a bipolarizing world.[46] At the end of 1945, France sent combat troops to the South China Sea using U.S. Merchant Marine vessels with the declared objective of protecting Vietnam from communism.[47] For French political and military leaders, the cold war was already in action in Indochina prior to their troop deployment, whereas for the Vietnamese nationalists it arrived on their horizon in the guise of French troops in American vessels. This example also indicates that the cold war had different temporalities even within the West. In the second half of the 1940s and in the early 1950s, western European states were experiencing the early age of cold war and the late stage of imperialism at the same time, and some of them pursued colonial reconquest on the basis of this split temporal consciousness. The United States was initially critical of these anachronistic attitudes held by its European allies and considered that their continuing colonial ambition hampered the mobilization of an effective international solidarity against the threat of communism.[48]

These conflictual views within the West are well illustrated in Jonathan Nashel's biographical approach to early cold war history. Nashel explores the life history of Edward Lansdale, the real-life figure used for the character Alden Pyle in Graham Greene's 1955 novel *The Quiet American*. Nashel examines Landsdale's "ethnographic encounters" with the Philippines and Vietnam in the late 1940s and in the 1950s.[49] Particularly interesting in his engrossing account, for the purpose of this discussion, is how in Greene's semifictional narrative of Lansdale's life, nostalgia about the "virtues of colonialism" (modeled on Thomas Fowler, the British journalist) confronts distrust of European empires (the attitude held by Pyle, the undercover American agent). Comparing this narrative to William Lederer and Eugene Burdick's 1958 counternarrative in *The Ugly American*, Nashel persuasively shows how in the decade after the end of World War II the declining European colonial power and the rising American power were imagined in complex schemes of structural continuity and moral discontinuity. If *The*

Quiet American foregrounds structural continuity (I acknowledge that this description somewhat oversimplifies the story), we may say that *The Ugly American* celebrates moral discontinuity, speaking of the confident view that America's civilizing mission to the non-Western world was substantively and morally different from Europe's.[50]

The sense of moral discontinuity was strong not merely among those who carried out the civilizing mission. The pursuit of national independence from colonial domination was often encouraged by the U.S. criticism of European colonialism.[51] There was also an important structural discontinuity between the colonial and bipolar age. According to Steven Lee, "the theory underpinning the United States' cold war empire differed significantly from the previous era of Great Power imperialism." Lee writes: "Whereas formal colonialism had sought the centralization of power for the benefit of the metropole, the United States concept of 'empire' was a decentralized one, based on the development of relatively independent local actors on the communist perimeter which were capable of holding back communist advances without direct American involvement or expenditure of resources."[52]

Although this idea of relatively decentralized informal imperial rule existed in the late colonial age (particularly within the British Commonwealth), the cold war formation was nevertheless unique, according to Westad, in that the informal rule was inherent from the very beginning.[53] Colonial rule and bipolar politics had questions of discontinuity both in moral-rhetorical and organizational terms, and careful consideration of these questions is crucial for furthering our understanding of each formation (see chapter 6).

Related to this issue, it should be added that the cold war invented different material and symbolic forms across territories. In western Europe, the wall that divided the city of Berlin was the prominent material symbol of the cold war.[54] In North America, however, the symbol of the cold war took on different forms. Alan Nadel suggests that for Americans, the central symbol was the atomic bomb, and Kenneth Rose similarly describes how the underground nuclear fallout shelters became a national obsession across the United States during the Berlin and Cuban crises at the beginning of the 1960s.[55] The U.S. administration built dug-out shelters for the White House staff and members of Congress, and it encouraged banks to do likewise to protect their most valuable objects from nuclear destruction—the dollar notes and the credit slips. Communities and families took to self-help on this matter, too, resulting in a boom in the commerce of formulaic domestic nuclear shelters.[56] Margaret Mead took great interest in the question of human survival from thermonuclear disaster during this period and made a series of public appeals for the need to prepare a collective survival shelter for a group of young, healthy, and reproductive couples. The eminent anthropologist's Bible-inspired idea of species survival was widely disseminated by the media and affected the public culture of fear and survival. The idea of nuclear fallout shelters and the technology of "blast-resistant structure" also came to western Europe in the following decade, but it did not affect the public imagination as forcefully as it did on the other side of the Atlantic Ocean.[57]

The regional variance in the material culture of the cold war relates to a certain disunity in the political cultures and moral worldviews in the West. There was, for instance, a substantial disparity between the European and American public in assimilating the ideology of anticommunism. In response to the survey question in 1961, "Suppose you had to make the decision between fighting an all-out nuclear war or living under communist rule—how would you decide?" 21 percent of the British opted for the war option, but 81 percent of the American respondents chose death over life under Communist rule.[58]

The Berlin Wall thus is only one of many different instruments and symbols of containment that existed in the world; likewise, the fallout shelters were a particular, place-specific symbol of deterrence and survival.[59] The politics of ideological containment in non-Western regions may have taken less materially tangible and more socially diffused forms than the wall or the shelter. This is one of the important lessons that we learn from the expanding literature on the social history of the cold war. Recent works show how even for the Berliners, it was in their ideas of kinship and in their everyday activity such as consumption that the two Germanies' bipolar contests were waged most vigorously.[60] In societies that experienced the cold war as a violent civil war, as discussed later (see chapters 4 and 5), the political repression and violence of ideological containment were waged most radically in the domains of family and kinship relations. The politics of anticommunism in these societies invented a unique technique of social control, "punishing thoughts and beliefs rather than acts" and developing punitive measures against politically subversive individuals that criminalized the entire moral collectives to which these individuals belonged.[61]

Last, something has to be said about the "irregularity of ties between nations and ideologies" and the related prolific cross-border traffic of human labor and ideas, which Appadurai highlights as key features of the world "after 1989." His remark gives the misleading impression that the world before 1989 should be characterized with the regularity and stability of cross-national ties and movements. The transnational circulation of objects and ideas was hardly unfamiliar in the apparently highly regulated world of the cold war era. Consider the forceful idea of Red scares and the related mechanism of social control that swept nations and communities across the world from the geopolitical power center to the distant peripheries. The idea was adapted to specific local conditions, sometimes becoming more radical and destructive in the process of dissemination and developing into a massive force of anti-Communist state terrorism across regions from the 1950s to the 1980s. If kidnapping individual ideological suspects was a notable form of anti-Communist terror in places such as Chile and Argentina, the so-called collective-responsibility system mentioned earlier, which punished an individual's thoughts by criminalizing his or her entire web of blood ties, was one of the most notable instruments of societal control in places under anti-Communist military rules, such as Indonesia and South Korea.[62] The penal practices against alleged ideological crimes often had no rule-of-law boundary and distorted the traditional conceptions of social subjectivity and moral liability. The globalization of these pathological formations and their local variations are an important subject matter in the investigation of cold war political culture.

The cold war era also saw prolific circulation of material objects and human labor across territories. In Soviet Russia, several ethnic and national groups were relocated from one end of the Eurasian continent to the other for no other reason than the state authority's suspicion of their loyalty. In wider international terrain, even as East German, Russian, and Hungarian engineers came to Vietnam in order to help reconstruct the country's shattered postwar economy, Vietnamese laborers migrated widely to what are now Slovakia, Croatia, and other places within the Eastern bloc to earn the badly needed hard currencies. In the Western bloc, the massive influx of refugees from the conflict zones provided a significant labor force for the recovering economies of western Europe in the mid–twentieth century and for the affluent American economy afterwards. Later, the emerging South Korean industrial capitalism shipped technology and labor to the Middle East after having consolidated its know-how partly in the theater of the Vietnam War as a key U.S. military ally, and at the same time the then strong North Korean arms industry supplied cheap weapons to this same region and later to other war zones in northern and central Africa. Even as North Korea forced upon libraries in Malta, Zimbabwe, Sudan, Uganda, Iran, and elsewhere large quantities of free books—its bible of the "self-reliance" revolutionary philosophy—the resistance forces in Zimbabwe and Mozambique, on their own initiative, imported from Cuba and Vietnam the philosophical ideas of a people's war and logistics for jungle warfare.[63] The Cuban military and its Vietnamese counterpart maintained close ties in one bloc, regularly exchanging personnel and experiences of resistance war; the Israeli army and its South Korean counterpart likewise instituted a similar exchange program of their own kind in another bloc. Arms, money, labor, and ideas of population control and political resistance thus migrated widely, not only from the geopolitical center to the periphery but also between the peripheral actors.

One of my favorite stories from this transnational history of the cold war is from Sudan. Charles Jedrej, my late colleague in Edinburgh and an Africanist, told me how North Korean advisors failed to deliver their Asian political art to Africa. The advisors tried to teach the Sudanese how to perform the "mass game"—the renowned public art that performs revolutionary slogans using thousands of hand-held multicolored pickets that are raised in a series of absolutely synchronous movements—but eventually had to give up.[64] The advisors concluded that the Africans, compared to the East Asians, lacked the strict bodily and spiritual discipline required for the performance of totalitarian art. The Africans, for their part, assimilated the Asian cold war influence on the margins of their aesthetic life. Followers of a regional Sudanese popular religion incorporated the memory of migrant workers from the People's Republic of China into their traditional spiritual category of "strangers," which previously had consisted mainly of other tribes and white colonists. A militant Ugandan cult group, during that country's civil war, promoted the spirit of Chung Po to a key position in its hierarchy of spirit helpers. Chung Po symbolized the supplier of arms from North Korea.[65] Most of these episodes of cold war mobility remain unstudied, but that does not mean that they are an insignificant part of local histories or an irrelevant aspect of international history. The age of ideological extremes witnessed some great transnational migrations of animate and inanimate objects on both sides of the frontier, and it will be important to chart these movements so that we can situate the contemporaneous mobility in a proper historical context.

In view of the previous discussion, we can conclude that the cold war was a globally staged but locally diverse regime of ideas and practices. Calling this regime "a global conflict" does not mean that it was experienced as a single monolithic phenomenon across places. George Mosse has written about the myth of national experience of war with reference to the world wars. In Mosse's accounts, modern warfare has to invent the idea of the nation as a community of common fate and identical experience, and this is achieved partly through the institution of war commemoration, whose primary function is to incorporate the locally and communally divergent experiences into the unifying scenario of a common struggle against external enemies.[66] Elaborating on this idea, other historians bring forward the divergent experiences of World War I in various European cities and residential communities, thus disclosing aspects of the war hitherto concealed under the narrative of overarching national histories.[67] If the idea of a national experience of war is a myth, so is the idea of a global experience of the cold war. If there is such a thing, it is likely to be a product and instrument of the politics of war.

As Christian Appy puts it, our historical understanding of the bipolar struggle for the world should be at the same time a "struggle for the word"—a competition over the very explanation and meaning of the global struggle.[68] The "struggle for the word," as discussed earlier, also applies to the idea of the end of the cold war. The cold war is surely over, if we mean by it the contest of will and power between two powerful, mutually hostile state actors and the blocs of other relatively weaker states under their respective influences.[69] Within this geopolitical scheme, it is correct to think that the cold war ended with the series of dramatic events in Europe during the period from 1989 to 1991. It is possible within this scheme to think that one side won an irrevocable, bloodless victory over the other side, ending the long drawn-out military standoffs and political confrontations of the bipolar era.[70] The empirical historical fact does have to be acknowledged that the economic and political structures of the Eastern bloc states began to disintegrate in the late 1980s, generating a domino effect, which soon led to the implosion of Soviet political unity at the end of 1991.

Turning our attention from geopolitical to social and cultural dimensions, however, it is not clear if we can as easily claim that the cold war is over. The eminent British historian E. P. Thompson once noted that the cold war was a formative experience for modern man. If this was the case, it is difficult to imagine how such a powerful historical experience would be traceless in the emerging new world order, whichever form we imagine this order to take. It is unthinkable that the human experience of bipolar politics is as easily removable from the lived world as the rubble of the Berlin Wall was. According to Stephen Whitfield, the cold war was much more than "a geopolitical contest between the two major states which filled the power vacuum after World War II." Addressing mainly American readers, he writes: "[Because] the perceived threat from international communism receded by the beginning of the 1990s, we run the risk of remembering the nation's crusade against Communism as an isolated historical happening, one that affected only diplomatic and military policies of the Cold War. On the contrary, that struggle deeply scarred the nation's social order as well."[71] The central message of Whitfield's pioneering book *The Culture of the Cold War* is that the cold war constituted aspects of social order as well as aspects of geopolitical order and that these two dimensions have different developmental cycles.

Whitfield suggests that the end of the cold war as a social order is a slow process of *decomposition*: the cold war did not end simply, nor is it a simple process to end it, as Cynthia Enloe observes in her work focusing on the gender aspects of militarism and postwar life.[72] Whitfield's suggestion implies that our disengagement from the bipolar era is a suspended, liminal period of twilight. Just as the decomposition of a dead body is considered across cultures a critical and perilous time when the physical death of a person coexists with the symbolic vitality of the person's animus, the "decomposition" of the cold war is the unsettling situation in which the lived reality is not really free from the immediate past and has not reintegrated the past into the time present as a past history—that is, it has a kind of spectral existence.[73]

Slavoj Žižek argues against the idea of "postideological society." According to Žižek, the postulation that history has moved beyond the grid of ideology is itself a deeply ideological statement. What he calls "the spectre of ideology" addresses the unresolved relations of domination and issues of social justice that, according to him, are cryptically concealed in the rhetorical practice about the end of an ideology-driven historical era.[74] Part of Žižek's argument applies to the issue that concerns us here. Like the end of ideology, the idioms such as "the end of the cold war" or "the world after 1989" are not to be taken for granted. Sheldon Pollock and others ask the questions: "What defines our *times*? What times are *ours*? It is too easy to name our moment as post–Cold War or transnational. . . . Do we live in a post–Cold War world *tout court,* or in the long shadow of that disastrous postwar experience of superpower collusion and competition that deformed the development of the rest of the world?"[75] Peter Kuznick and James Gilbert note: "How we understand this troubling though fascinating period in human history [referring mainly to the 1930s and 1940s in the United States, which they define as the time when a cold war society took root] will go a long way toward determining the kind of future we collectively shape in the twenty-first century and beyond."[76] If the language of a radical, universal discontinuity is partly an ideological statement rather than merely a referential device, as Žižek claims, the chronological punctuation of the history of the cold war should also be a subject for critical reflection and analytical scrutiny. The language may hinder a critical understanding of the contemporary transition inasmuch as it can be a convenient idiom for contemporaneous reality.

If we seek a genuine end to the cold war, I would argue that doing so requires us to come to terms with the diverse ways in which the global conflict was waged and is now coming to a closure. The failure to place the cold war history within the spectrum of social research makes understanding historical transition to a new era critically incomplete. Equally important, societies that experienced the cold war both as a politically bifurcating and radicalizing social order and as a geopolitical order, may also have created the art and technology of keeping the dismembered social body alive. If that is the case, we should be able to understand how the cold war is coming to an end, slowly and varyingly, in concrete places and at the same time to assess the locally specific, emerging strategies of conflict resolution.

The process of decomposition is a period of liminality; it also occurs—according to Marilyn Strathern, who tellingly describes it within a Melanesian context—when people take apart an image "to see/make visible what insides it contains; . . . this is a process that gives the elicitors of those insides, the decomposers, power as witnesses to their own efforts of elucidation; [and] the elicitor/witness is in a crucial sense the 'creator' of the image."[77]

In this understanding of decomposition, witnessing the process is a valuable and creative experience, for it is through this witnessing that we can see how the whole was in fact constituted by many individual parts and further that we will eventually be able to create a new image of the whole—that is, with the many constitutive parts no longer hidden behind what was before a deceptively monolithic, organic whole. The elicitation of the parts can change the image of the whole and may also ironically contribute to keeping the memory of the cold war as a whole—just as Strathern describes the meaning of active human engagement with the process of decomposition in Melanesian mortuary art, which is to remember the dead creatively.[78]

Is the cold war over? The answer to this question depends on what dimension of the conflict the question refers to. Like any conception of radical rupture in time, the notion that the world we inhabit has resolutely departed from the structure of the old world has elements of mystification as well as revelation. Saying this, I do not mean to question the premise that we are moving beyond the era of a bipolarized world, which would be empirically absurd. The point is rather that the great End may not be presumed, but rather understood. This is particularly the case with the discipline of anthropology, the traditionally rooted grace of which is, among other things, to represent the human experience and voices from the horizons beyond the West. "After 1989" is much more than a chronological marker; it also represents a particular view of history that privileges the experience of Europe and the geopolitical explanation of the human world. Anthropological research can contribute to eliciting the partiality of this view and enriching our understanding of the contemporary transition by bringing into the light the diverse decomposing processes of the cold war in concrete contexts of social life. It is true that the cold war's East/West divide does not fit the anthropologist's traditional comparative divide between the West and the rest. Yet it is also true that these two great divides crosscut each other in modern history and that an understanding of their crossings is pivotal to an understanding of each divisive trajectory. I believe that it is in modern anthropological knowledge practices that we will find an instrument to scrutinize the unifying category of the West in the East/West bipolar divide, for it is in the cumulative body of these practices that anthropologists have sharpened their awareness of the mystified, holistic West in the divide between the West and the rest or between the developed North and the underdeveloped South. It is through a revitalization of the critical comparative perspective and the expansion of its horizon from a two-dimensional to a three-dimensional formation, incorporating both sides of the great divide of the human community in the past century, that anthropological knowledge, in turn, may develop a more historically grounded understanding of the merits and limits of this knowledge.

In order to move toward this hopeful direction, it is necessary to free our understanding of cold war history from the centrality of Europe's imaginary war; that is, we need to think of the history as a genuinely global history. It is equally necessary to free our historical awareness from the illusion that the cold war was merely a business of the rich and powerful nations and that its history does not belong to the developing nations in the South. The first step toward an understanding of cold war history as a genuinely global, locally grounded history will be to ask ourselves, when someone tells us that the cold war is globally over, Whose cold war and which aspects of the cold war is that person talking about? And we must ask these same questions when someone tells us about his or her new research vision for the new world that is based on an unexamined, totalizing notion of a global historical break between the cold war and this new world.

2

TWO COLOR LINES
OF THE TWENTIETH CENTURY

The problem of the twentieth century, W. E. B. Du Bois famously wrote in 1903, "is the problem of the color-line,—the relation of the darker to the lighter races of men in Asia and Africa, in America and the islands of the sea." Du Bois conceptualized the color line as a problem for whites as well as for blacks and saw the resolution of this problem, in the spirit of Frederick Douglass, not merely as the extension of liberty to the black population, but as the protection of the white population's liberty as well. He reflected on the history of the American Civil War (1861–1865) in this light and objected to Booker T. Washington's idea of self-enlightenment as a precondition for equal rights, which Du Bois believed was a scheme to relegate "the burden of the Negro problem to the Negro's shoulders."[1] The British anthropologist Max Gluckman described in 1955 what he called the "color-bar" of South Africa in a similar perspective: "I've called this analysis 'the bonds in the color-bar' not because the Africans and Indians of South Africa are chained by discriminatory custom; but because discriminatory custom against the Africans and other colored groups chains the dominant White group."[2]

Both Du Bois's "color-line" and Gluckman's "color-bar" were primarily about skin color and the related ideology of racial difference and hierarchy; however, the problem of the twentieth century, as it unfolded, turned out to be as much about the color of human belief and thought as about the physical color of the human body. Being a white person or person of color was a major determining factor for an individual's life career for a significant part of the past century, but so was the relatively novel color classification of being "Red" or "not Red" in many corners of the world, including the United States and South Africa.[3] The apartheid regime in South Africa justified its race-based political order in part by an ideology of anticommunism and went against the moral and political demands for racial justice and civil rights using the polemics of Red menace that labeled these demands as Communist-inspired agitations.[4] The United States maintained a distance from the rising white-supremacy claims made by South Africa's National Party during the second half of the 1940s, considering these claims to be in line with the politics of the Nazi regime against which it had just fought a major war. When a war broke out in the Korean Peninsula in 1950, however, this view changed, and the Harry S. Truman administration, concerned primarily with the preservation of stability in the non-Communist world, decided to support Pretoria and subsequently became what Thomas Borstelmann calls "apartheid's reluctant uncle." According to Borstelmann, "Within two months [after the Chinese communist troops entered the Korean War] American loans and arms sales to the Union had been arranged, and American weapons were soon being used to guarantee the domestic stability of the apartheid regime. The igniting of the Cold War into actual large-scale fighting welded the common interests of South Africa and the United States into a solid alliance."[5] It is worth remembering that South Africa's National Party did not lift the ban on the African National Congress and release Nelson Mandela until the early 1990s.

Questions of racial justice were critical in the domestic arena of the United States, too, and were also closely intertwined with the political imperatives of combating communism. According to Mary Dudziak, U.S. administrations from the late 1940s to late 1960s were preoccupied with "the Negro problem," believing that the unresolved domestic problems of racial segregation and inequality were America's "Achilles heel" that seriously undermined America's leadership of the world in the global struggle against communism.[6] The question of racial inequality in general and of the segregationist force in America's South in particular, Odd Arne Westad points out, became a "cold war liability" for the John F. Kennedy and Lyndon B. Johnson administrations.[7]

Ann Stoler approaches the color line of the colonial era in an innovative way. The colonial rule, according to Stoler, suffered from the inherent and irreconcilable self-contradiction between the rhetorical inclusion of the colonial subjects in the metropolitan sovereignty, on the one hand, and the political imperative to exclude them from the rights of citizenship in the polity, on the other. Stoler calls this structural contradiction "the tensions of empire"—"the tension between a form of domination predicated on both incorporation and distancing at one and the same time"— and she illustrates these contradictions and tensions with the legal debates and moral confusions about the status of racially mixed children (parented by a European man and an indigenous woman) in the Dutch Indies and French Indochina. The legal and political status of "mixed-bloods" was a highly contentious issue for colonial administrations because it threatened to destabilize the biopolitical foundation of the colonial rule, which, based on a rigid hierarchical ordering of racial and cultural roots, linked "domestic arrangements to the public order, family to the state, sex to subversion, and national essence to racial type."[8]

Issues of "mixed blood" were equally critical in the history of the ensuing cold war era. The two countries Stoler focuses on, Indonesia and Vietnam, proclaimed political independence in 1945, and both of them experienced violent bipolarization of political forces in their postcolonial eras. Against this background, Benedict Anderson writes: "Vietnam and Indonesia came together for me in a new way" through a series of events in the mid-1960s.[9] The two societies were seldom considered in comparative terms by specialists on Southeast Asia before the events of the 1960s, according to Anderson, whereas after these events their political histories appeared to be connected to each other and to the wider horizon of international politics. A large territory of Indonesia was devastated by the anti-Communist terror campaigns waged amidst a political crisis in 1965–1966, resulting in an estimated one million human casualties. Observers note how the legacy of extreme political violence from this era continues to haunt Balinese and Javanese lives today (see chapter 7).[10] Genealogical history in southern and central regions of Vietnam is crowded with a history of radical political disunity relating to the bifurcated mobilization to fight the Vietnam–American war, whose force of destruction reached its apex in the second half of the 1960s.[11] In both theaters of destruction, state violence against individuals who were believed to harbor subversive political ideas took on and was justified by the idioms of biological or racial differences, and it often targeted the collective social units where these individuals belonged. If a person had consanguine ties with someone considered ideologically impure, that person could be classified as a subversive individual in the light of kinship ties and punished as such. Families with a politically impure ancestral heritage may also have a politically contrary genealogical history, though, especially with the background of a civil war. If not, they might try to escape from the status of a politically damned family by actively joining the very political campaigns that made them suffer in the first place. The histories of these families are also stories of "mixed blood," and a close examination of them can also illuminate "the tensions of empire"—the novel imperial order of the cold war era.

The bipolarization of social forces reached a critical point in Southeast Asia in the postcolonial era; nevertheless, it had deeper roots in the region's colonial histories. Melvyn Leffler observes that the Russian Revolution of 1917 was not a particularly impelling event for most Americans until the 1940s: "Most Americans were more concerned with Bolshevism at home [domestic communism and other forms of radicalism] than with Bolshevism abroad."[12] In the colonial world, however, the Russian Revolution had a formative impact on intellectual discourses and political imaginations beginning as early as the 1920s. Hue-Tam Ho Tai describes how Vietnamese intellectuals, impressed by events in Russia, began to imagine different roads to freedom and independence during this period, and other historians of Vietnam write similarly that the Vietnamese struggle for freedom, contrary to its portrayal in the official history in contemporary Vietnam, took on bifurcated visions of the country's postcolonial future—some revolutionaries believing in liberal ideals, but others following the Russian example.[13] In Indonesia, the charismatic leadership of Sukarno, the unchallenged hero of the anticolonial independence war, managed to hold in check the conflicts between left-wing and right-wing nationalist forces until the crisis of 1965, when some army groups, supported by the U.S. administration, launched the "holy war of cleansing communism from the national body politic."[14] In these contexts, foreign interventions and geopolitical tensions distorted and radicalized the existing ideological color line, the formation of which was nevertheless rooted in the pursuit of a world without the injustice and the contradictions of the colonial color line.

The racial and ideological color lines coexisted for much of the twentieth century across territories, colluding in various ways and sometimes becoming practically indistinguishable. The Vietnam War magnified their connectedness on the U.S. home front, where civil society was bitterly divided on questions of racial inequality amidst the mounting crisis and debacle in the distant, overseas theater of containment of communism. Jeff Woods shows how the radical segregationist polemicists in the American South, like the apartheid regime in South Africa, went against the advocacy of racial integration by propagating that this advocacy was an act of collusion with Communist ideology or even a concerted Communist-directed agitation.[15] If Dudziak focuses on the impact of the domestic racial issue on American foreign-policy making, Woods examines how the international politics of anticommunism affected the horizon of racial conflicts in mid-twentieth-century America. Against this historical background, Douglas Field rightly concludes that the containment of racial conflicts and the containment of communism are two sides of the same coin in modern American history, despite the fact that they are often treated as separate subjects in existing literature.[16]

If questions of racial segregation were imagined in the idioms of the cold war, the questions of ideological difference could be translated into biological or racial terms. The tragic civilian killings during the Vietnam War were caused, to a large proportion, by the transformation of the two color lines into the mystified image of a generic ideological enemy.[17] War-generation Vietnamese, in particular those in the southern and central regions, are familiar with the expression *hat giang do*. This idiom, literally meaning "red seed and red plant," referred to people believed to be "Communists born and bred." Widely used in the former South Vietnam during the political campaigns to uproot communism from communal lives, the idiom implied that uprooting communism from society required eliminating not only the "plants" of individual suspects but also the "seeds" of their social, genealogical origins. Civil war–generation Koreans are familiar with similar idioms, such as "red blood line."[18] For people whose genealogical backgrounds include ancestors once classified as Communist subversives, sympathizers of communism, or defectors to the Communist North, "red blood line" has been a terrifying idea associated with the memory of summary killings and mass murder, surviving family members' experience of social stigma, and the restriction of their civil rights. The expression came from the actual physical appearance of the public-security record system, which highlighted the profiles of such families and individuals with red-colored lines and circles. In another such case, the massive anti-Communist violence unleashed in Bali and elsewhere in Indonesia in 1965 was based in part on "the logic of associative guilt and the need for collective retribution," which aimed to destroy the ideological enemies within the society "down to the roots."[19] In these historical contexts, it was possible for individuals to be labeled "Red" just because they belonged to a specific social group and to experience accordingly something akin to extreme racial discrimination in society even if they had the same color of skin as everyone else. If racial colors were ideological constructs, not biological conditions,[20] political ideologies, in turn, took on biological and racial imagery in the history of the twentieth century.

Although the racial and ideological color lines overlapped in many ways during the past century, it is important to note that the two forms of division nevertheless had different dimensions. Bipolar politics not only took particularly violent forms in the decolonizing world but also affected societies across the old colonial color line. The ideological color line was distinctive in that its formation encompassed the traditional boundaries of racial and cultural hierarchies.

After World War II, the United States staged vigorous campaigns in Europe to "win the battle for the hearts and minds of Western Europeans."[21] In Austria after May 1945, for instance, the U.S. occupation authority ran an elaborate, if not always successful, public-relations program aiming to educate the local population about the dangers of harboring sympathy for Communist ideals and about the superiority of American liberal ideals, as manifested in the thriving material and popular cultures of the countries where these ideals were held.[22] The campaigns stressed America's material-cultural superiority in terms of "People's Capitalism" and defined the latter against "the wretched socialism of the Soviet, concealing behind its barbed wire and its low living standards, slave labor, and cruel restrictions on personal freedom."[23] In parts of postwar southern Europe, the possibility that the Communist Party might take over political power was real, and this prospect triggered the announcement of the Truman Doctrine in 1947, which some observers consider the official beginning of the global cold war.[24] In 1951, a French politician named Cavaillet campaigned in favor of an amnesty law that would pardon former Nazi collaborators of the Vichy regime. This initiative was necessary, as Jacques Derrida recalls, "to repair the national unity meant to re-arm with all available forces in a combat which would continue, this time in a time of peace, or of a war called cold."[25] A similar "geopolitics of forgiveness" was practiced in other postwar European states and emerging postcolonial nation-states.[26] For the latter, the amnesty concerned collaborators with the colonial regimes, and these acts of forgiveness, often conducted against the population's expectations and wishes, weakened the state's moral legitimacy and distorted subsequent political developments. The new bipolar color line encompassed societies previously divided by the traditional colonial color line, in part replacing the latter in significance and in part further complicating it. If the cold war was a global conflict, it merits this characterization probably in the sense that it formed a common human experience of division across the racially and culturally divided world.

The previous discussion is intended to highlight the similarities and differences between the terms and scales of colonial politics and those of bipolar politics. As such, it serves as a broad introduction to this chapter and the following chapter. It is one of the main arguments in this book that a careful consideration of the juncture between these two epochal political forms is crucial for comparative cold war social and cultural history. The previous chapter touched briefly on this issue while reviewing a proposal for new area studies in the globalizing world "after 1989." In the next two chapters, I explore the thematic relationship between colonial history and bipolar history from other angles and with reference to two specific genres of social research that are particularly relevant for my discussion: postsocialist research and postcolonial studies. I investigate why research in these currently thriving genres commonly tends to ignore the conjectural histories of decolonization and bipolarization in pursuing their specialized interest in this or that trajectory. For the rest of this chapter, however, I focus on postsocialist studies, which appeared as a distinct field of social research at the same time that the cold war ended as a geopolitical order.

Among scholars who specialize in former socialist societies in Russia and eastern Europe, there are currently some concerns about the viability of the referential term *postsocialism*, which defines the object of their inquiry. These concerns are caused mainly by the intensifying incorporation of the former Eastern bloc political entities into the economic and political structure of the formerly Western bloc. These scholars also point to the growing diversification in the ways in which these entities, having previously constituted a coherent transnational unity under the banner of socialism, are now making a break with their past in favor of an alternative mode of economic relations and political organization.

Caroline Humphrey defends the referential validity of postsocialism against the suggestion that the concept is more a heuristic device than a signifier of an existing reality. Humphrey writes: "While 'post-socialism' is certainly a construct of the academy, it is not ours alone, and it does correspond to certain historical conditions 'out there.' "[27] There was an "actually existing socialism" in the vast Eurasian territory, according to her, and the elements of social-structural homogeneity among the social and political units in this territory extend to a certain commonality among them in experiencing the transition away from their socialist pasts. Humphrey suggests that the empirical research of the transition from socialism requires a conceptual umbrella to cover the radical variety in transitional forms across regions with a relatively homogenous historical heritage.

This conceptual struggle and the reality principle of a transitory social process are not unrelated to the discussion in the previous chapter about the idea of the end of the cold war. I argued that the cold war has different dimensions and development cycles as a geopolitical order and as a social order; likewise, the ideology of socialism has varying relevance as a transnational institutional framework and as locally specific historical experience. Humphrey elsewhere describes how in communities of the former Eastern bloc the imported ideas and imposed forces of the liberal market are negotiated with the preexisting economic practices and norms that she calls the "everyday economy." The latter in this context refers to the experience of the relative economic security within institutional, bureaucratic socialism and of the informal economy, which prospered in socialist societies in parallel with the institutional forms. Humphrey emphasizes the informal barter network and practices in Soviet Russia and Mongolia, whose importance, in her account, continues and even rises in the current situation of increasing deregulation of economic life.[28]

This concern with the referential viability of postsocialism or postcommunism is widely shared among other specialists in Russian and eastern European studies and is closely intertwined with two questions of comparison. One question is about the radical divergence of sociopolitical forms found in the transition countries in the former Eastern bloc. Philip Roeder argues, "The 1989 revolution that swept the communist world replaced the apparent homogeneity of a single Soviet-inspired model of command politics, command economics, and command societies with a dazzling diversity of liberal and illiberal states."[29] Defining "postcommunism" as "different forms of extrication from communism," the historian Charles

King expresses doubts about the comparability of these dazzlingly diverse societies. Emphasizing "highly variable success in the move away from one-party rule and planned economies" ranging from "prosperous social democracies to sultanistic or even dynastic regimes," he argues that "[p]ost-communism, ten years into the transition, now seems bizarre as a moniker for governments, societies, and economies as vastly different as those of Poland and Tajikistan." King argues that "there is little utility in continuing to treat all twenty-seven (or more) transition countries as a natural set."[30] However, the question of comparison also involves imagining alternative trajectories and horizons of comparison beyond the perspective anchored in the defunct socialist system as well as beyond the perspective focused on the similarities and differences between the transition societies and established Western liberal market democracies. Thus, it is argued that a theory of politics developed in Western democracies may apply to a handful of successful transitions (e.g., Poland and Hungary), but that comparative insights into incomplete transitions or transitions followed by reversion to authoritarian politics have to be found elsewhere instead (e.g., changes taking place in some formerly authoritarian Latin American countries). Other attempts have been made to compare diverse trajectories—for instance, Deniz Kandiyoti's initiative to consider the development in Central Asia during the socialist and post-Soviet era in comparison with the colonial and postcolonial changes in the Middle East.[31]

The anthropologist Chris Hann is also concerned about reconciling the empirical reality in which the world of socialism on the Eurasian continent, in his words, "has now (almost everywhere) disappeared" with the analytical necessity to consider emerging new social forms in this territory according to some sort of common framework. This reconciliatory effort faces some formidable conceptual challenges. In Hann's account, postsocialist societies are defined by their common historical experience of bureaucratic socialism and at the same time by the fact that this commonality is now arguably nonexistent. Hence, the term *postsocialism* is torn between the observers' wish to hold on to a common ground and a propensity in the observed societies to break with the defined common ground. This somewhat tortuous conflict in the referential reality of post-socialism forces Hann to redefine socialism in the language of moral economy rather than in the language of political economy: "The everyday moral communities of socialism have been undermined but not replaced. Nor does lacing capitalist consumerism with increased doses of national sentiment seem to produce the desired results."[32] Following Hann, it appears that the principal objective of postsocialist studies is to chart a transitory reality that is neither formally socialist nor ideologically capitalist and to do so in critical dialogue with prevailing public discourses about encompassment by the liberal market and the inevitability of change to a market-dominated society.

A set of intriguing issues arises from this formulation of the postsocialist research agenda. One issue concerns the revival of the idea of moral economy. The notion of the "moral economy" was an important conceptual tool among certain social historians and anthropologists in the 1960s and 1970s. The British historian E. P. Thompson excavated the term from the pamphleteers of the eighteenth-century English food riots in his monumental social history of that period.[33] In its original meaning, the idea of moral economy represented the ethos of popular resistance against the ideology of free trade, particularly concerning subsistence goods. For Thompson, this idea permitted a critical review of the rising philosophy of the free market in the eighteenth century. He described the food crisis among the English workers during early industrialization, explored it in relation to Adam Smith's proposition that local food shortages in Europe would be solved only by a general, full liberalization of grain distribution, and concluded that Smith's philosophical treatise on a free market, *The Wealth of Nations*—which turned into a bible for policymakers during the time—in fact contributed to aggravating the food crisis rather than solving it. The anthropologist James Scott later studied the peasant rebellions in colonial Southeast Asia according to a related perspective and explored what he called "the moral economy of the peasant" in terms of this socioeconomic group's subsistence ethic.[34] Scott argued that peasants took to organized acts of protest when the intensity of economic exploitation reached an unbearable level, which broke their traditional ethical principles about subsistence and communal survival.

Thompson and Scott wrote about moral economies at the height of the cold war conflict, when a growing number of historians and sociologists were interested in social and political movements, stimulated by the multitude of revolutionary upheavals in the decolonizing world, and disturbed by the intensity of the countermeasures taken by Western industrial powers to quash such revolutionary movements. The idea of a moral economy therefore arose from critical intellectual engagement with cold war global politics, despite the fact that the idea was expressed in literature with reference to eighteenth-century England or nineteenth-century French Indochina. Thompson's intellectual career testifies to this connection. He was a historian who wrote about the moral economy of English food rioters, but he was at the same time a public intellectual who was deeply engaged in the predicaments of a bipolarized Europe. For Thompson, the concept of a moral economy spoke essentially of an economic and social history "from below," and he approached the divided political reality of Europe according to a related perspective that emphasized the mobilization of popular consciousness and initiatives "from below" against the Iron Curtain (see chapter 4). It is interesting to note that the idea of a moral economy, seen against this background, is revived today in the academic discourse of postsocialism, which is now identified with the negative effects of parting the curtain and everyday resistance to these effects.

Postsocialist studies' emphasis on the moral economy of everyday life is in part a reaction to the dominance of liberal macroeconomic ideas at the institutional level, both among the policymakers of the formerly Eastern bloc states and among the advisors from the Western states.[35] It is observed that the former group is sometimes a stronger believer in the assumptions about *Homo economicus* than the latter is and a more militant advocate of outright market liberalization. According to some observers, in the Eastern bloc states' radical transition from paternalistic providers of social security to aggressive pursuers of corporate freedom and economic utopianism, society has been thrown into a state of limbo because it has to deal with "the debris left over from communism as well as the chaos of the new order."[36] For the sociologist Zygmunt Bauman, postsocialism signifies a liminal condition—suspended in the uncertain state of neither being severed from the socialist past nor being integrated into a wider capitalist reality—and this condition is engendered by the prevailing forces to classify social entities in terms of either this or that social form.[37]

Following these accounts, it transpires that in passing the threshold of 1989, the duality of socialism and capitalism has changed from being a spatial notion based on geographically discrete political blocs to being a temporal notion that entails movement from one to the other form and all the repercussions that this transition involves. *Transition* is indeed a key word in postsocialist studies, being used sometimes almost synonymously with *postsocialism* and understood as "a temporary state between two fixed positions, a movement between the point of departure and that of arrival."[38] Opinions vary on what the prospective point of arrival should be and whether it will involve a full incorporation to a western European–style free-market economy and liberal democracy or rather a perpetual process of coming close to (yet never reaching) that ideal. About the point of departure, however, researchers of postsocialist social transitions seem to have a broad consensus, identifying it unambiguously with the end of the cold war.

Hann defines the cold war as the "struggle between capitalism and socialism" and writes that this struggle has been over since 1989. At the same time, he characterizes the capitalism/socialism struggle as "a long drawn out contest that decisively framed the political consciousness of most of the world's population while it lasted and continues to exercise pervasive effects a decade after it was apparently won by 'the free world.'"[39] As we try to come to terms with Hann's apparently contradictory statements about the end of the ideological struggle, on the one hand, and about the old struggle's persistent and pervasive effects on the contemporary world, on the other, we realize that the latter is in fact what he intends to address with the idea of postsocialism. Hann divides the history of Europe into two parts and places them selectively on each side of the 1989 threshold. One part is the cold war as a geopolitical order, which is placed on the pre-1989 side. The other part is the postsocialist transition after the cold war, in which the conflicts between local norms and global forces are highlighted. It may then appear that the process that Hann calls "postsocialism" corresponds with what I earlier called the "decomposition of the cold war as a social order."

However, the phrases *postsocialist transition* and *decomposition of the cold war* are not merely different ways to address the same phenomenon. The cold war was in part a struggle between two contending visions and versions of modernity that might be glossed as "socialism" and "capitalism," but this does not mean that its global history may be reduced to this abstract conceptual scheme. As discussed earlier, the reality of the global cold war was much more complex than a competition over economic ideology or strategic control: it meant the division of the world into separate blocs of states and ideological spheres, but it also included the formation of relations of domination in each sphere and the measures taken to police the threats and resistance to the hierarchical formation. In the decomposition of the cold war order, moreover, it is not possible to think of some societies as undergoing a "transition," whereas others are not. If the cold war was a global conflict, it is logical to think that at the present time every nation and every society the world over is experiencing some kind of momentous transition. The ideas relating to economic and cultural globalization discussed in the previous chapter express this global transitory condition.

Apart from the encompassment of postsocialist societies by liberal market forces, Hann highlights the rise of nativist regionalism and ethnic nationalism as a key feature of post-1989 eastern and central Europe. Observers offer various explanations for this phenomenon, among which is the role of literacy. One of the laudable achievements of the socialist polities was a comprehensive, high-level literacy rate in the population. Ernest Gellner argues, following the classical rendering of nationalism as an epiphenomenon of mass education and printing technology, that the high literacy rate, once having been an instrument to disseminate Communist internationalist ideals through printed media, now contributes to disseminating militant nationalist ideology through the same means.[40] Gellner views the fall of communism in Europe with mixed feelings: both as a positive momentum for a political integration of Europe and as a crisis that would bring about the disintegration of existing political unities into regional autonomies and interethnic rivalries. In his understanding, the eruption of ethnic nationalism in central Europe is set against a historical background in which nationalism's appeals to the population were successfully contained by the states and their socialist federalism and is identified with the breakdown of the political structure of containment. In the context of the Soviet Union, it is argued that in contradiction to the rhetoric that national questions and conflicts would disappear in an advanced Communist civilization, the Bolshevik policies actually indirectly encouraged the growth of national consciousness across Eurasia by instituting the linguistic and geographical pigeonholing of national and ethnic groupings.[41] Other socialist states also encouraged an ethnicity-based political geography rather than worked against it. Scholars emphasize how the Soviet-style nationality policies in Yugoslavia and Czechoslovakia guaranteed by constitution the rights of national groups to have their own republics, even while at the same time enshrining the Communist Party as the single institution of authority beyond these separate territorial units.[42]

Two streams of great social transformation have swept through former socialist states and societies since the late 1980s. In the former Soviet bloc, the transformation consists of radical socioeconomic changes that observers of eastern and central Europe call a "postsocialist transition." These changes have been both external and internal; they have involved not only the increasing incorporation of these societies into the Euro-Atlantic economic and political structure but also the rapid incorporation of liberal market ideas and rules of electoral democracy into these societies as new organizing principles. Other related yet different sets of changes can be associated with Asian socialist polities, notably China and Vietnam. This transformation is often called "market socialism," involving a gradual move toward market economic reform and a related political move toward a controlled social liberalization.

With two principal elements (as described earlier), economic restructuring and political fragmentation, Hann attempts to extend the comparative horizon of postsocialism, in a broad scope, to the historical terrain of what he calls "socialist Eurasia"—that is, from European to Asian socialist societies and from one to another stream of global postsocialist transformation.[43] However, his Europe-centered understanding of socialism and postsocialism presents some formidable conceptual problems when applied to other regional contexts. For instance, how can we think about the history of socialism in China, as Odd Arne Westad shows, without considering the history of the Chinese Civil War (1946–1949) and the effects of this war on the nation's political development as a whole?[44] Can we possibly understand this conflict in terms of a struggle of economic ideologies without taking into account the history of colonial threat and the humiliation it triggered?

Mark Bradley writes that the political history of Vietnam's socialist revolution is not to be considered separately from the experience of devastating wars that occurred as part of a postcolonial transition. He defines the Vietnamese revolution as the pursuit of a prevailing postcolonial vision for a fully independent, prosperous nation-state in the era of the cold war.[45] It follows that the nation's contemporary social transition, after the initiation of the *doi moi* (renovation) reform, is much more than a shift from one economic form to another, just as Vietnam's past historical struggle was not merely about realizing a particular economic order. North Korea's political system is unique in Asia in that it has largely ignored the structural changes that have swept through most other former socialist states and societies since the late 1980s. North Korea is still a solidly single-party state and still stubbornly adheres to a centrally planned and executed system of economic production and distribution, whether that system is functional or dysfunctional (although it has recently taken some limited, haphazard economic liberalization initiatives mainly in relation to China and South

Korea). The country has not followed either of the two great streams of postsocialist transition, both of which its official media sometimes accuses of being treacherous. Because of its refusal or inability to embrace the known forms of postsocialist transition, North Korea has earned the references frequently made to it as a reclusive, isolated, and anachronistic polity not only by international actors in the liberal world but also by the country's previous allies in the former Eastern bloc. In the outside world's view, today's North Korea may appear to be a highly anachronistic political entity, unable to shake off the political ethos of the cold war era and therefore incapable of joining postsocialist developmental streams. Prominent in the domestic political arena of North Korea, however, are issues of colonial and postcolonial history: the history of armed resistance activity in Manchuria against Japan's colonial occupation of Korea and northeastern China by the region's displaced population of Korean origin in the 1920s and 1930s as well as the sublimation of this history as the founding episode for the constitution of North Korea's political order in the postcolonial era.[46]

Hann's conceptions of "actually existing socialism" and "postsocialism" are based on his long-term observation of rural Hungary and Poland and draw upon a widely held view of cold war political history in Europe among political scientists, which is, according to John Young, "an era characterized by U.S.–Soviet tension, the division of Europe between communist and capitalist systems and, at the center, the existence of two Germanies."[47] A large part of the non-Western world experienced an "actually existing socialism," and a much larger part experienced political movements that hoped to achieve it. In this historical context, however, "socialism" was not merely the antithesis of "capitalism" or ethnic nationalism, but rather an integral part of general social struggles to counter the injustices and contradictions of a colonial political order and to achieve a politically independent and economically prosperous nation-state in its stead. During World War II, the United States regarded these political movements in the colonial world largely as a positive force in the prospect of the free world, but after the war it shifted its view and began to see them in a negative light, defining them as a menacing proxy force of Soviet communism (see chapter 4). This shift of perspective complicated immensely the subsequent courses of political decolonization. One would expect, therefore, that extending the comparative horizon of postsocialist studies to the postcolonial historical contexts would involve rethinking the divergent meanings of socialism across territories. If the cold war's historical milieu was much wider and more complex than a competition of economic ideologies, the transition beyond it is, likewise, not merely about the incorporation to a market economy or the resurgence of nationalism (see chapters 4 and 5). One hopes that the scholarship of postsocialism, in broadening its inquiry to the diverse decomposing processes of the cold war, would also broaden and open the defining features of the postsocialist transition to the plurality of the process. For this hopeful trajectory, however, it is imperative to recognize that the "struggle between capitalism and socialism" is a place-specific, "provincial" view of the cold war that is not to be considered emblematic of the global cold war.[48]

Hann advocates an empirical, ethnographic method in grasping the social transition from socialism—a " 'close-up' view acquired through fieldwork"—and contrasts this descriptive strategy with what he calls the bird's-eye view taken by policymakers and macroeconomists, which he rightly argues is oblivious to how ordinary people are actually experiencing the market-style deregulation of economic life.[49] The ethnographic method is indeed important, as other observers agree, for rendering the myriad local responses in eastern European economies to the uncertainty of privatization and deregulation.[50] These responses are highly variant across communities and thus not necessarily apparent to research that adheres to a sweeping, generalizing bird's-eye view. Although emphasizing an ethnographic method, however, Hann also criticizes the tradition of Western ethnographic research, which, he argues, focuses exclusively on exotic cultural forms in distant places, ignoring important social processes taking place at or near home. Although this criticism has some relevance, and the anthropology at home is certainly an important genre of research, it is important to note that anthropological research of the home territory involves confronting the dominant ideology at home.[51] The idea that the central and eastern European countries will inevitably be encompassed by the liberal market and liberal political institutions may be a familiar "rhetorical action," as some observers argue, and must be scrutinized.[52] However, this rhetorical practice is based on another hegemonic idea in Europe—that the end of the cold war is about the defeat of "actually existing socialism" by capitalism after an extended competition between the two versions of modernity. A critical engagement with the idea of inevitable encompassment, therefore, should involve a struggle over the meaning of the end of the cold war and Europe's place in that global struggle.

We may not accurately assess the current economic and political integration of Europe without considering the history of the early community-building efforts after World War II that took place as part of the global process of political bipolarization or with considering the latter separately from the history of decolonization in Europe's colonies. "Capitalist" Europe, both in its past and future horizons, has the history of the non-European world in it; the scholarship of postsocialism should recognize that if its main object of inquiry, "socialist" Europe, now faces a cultural other called "capitalist" Europe, the latter is the product of a long interaction with many other cultural others existing beyond the boundary of Europe. Moreover, Europe's place in the aftermath of cold war geopolitics far exceeds the regional interests in the enlargement of the community to the states and societies in eastern and central Europe. The community of Europe aspires to play a more active, expectantly constructive role in the international theater of balance of power and is considered to be able to do so by a number of non-Western state actors.[53] Therefore, the value of anthropological research at this level should partly be found in its capacity to inform the public and policymakers in Europe of the horizons of the lived world that may not be easily discernable from a Eurocentric political worldview.

With this discussion in mind, it is instructive to note the proposition made by Katherine Verdery about revising the focus of postsocialist studies according to "a new angle of vision." Verdery suggests that the term *post–cold war studies* is preferable to *postsocialist studies*.[54] In a recent article, she and coauthor Sharad Chari write: "It is time to liberate the Cold War from the ghetto of Soviet area studies and postcolonial thought from the ghetto of Third World and colonial studies. The liberatory path we propose is to jettison our two posts in favor of a single overarching one: the post–Cold War."[55] The main difference between these two frameworks or two "posts," the postsocialist and the post–cold war, in my interpretation of Verdery's proposition, is the cold war perspective's capacity to circumvent the referential problems of postsocialism. In the cold war framework, the analyst does not see changing everyday reality on one side of the formerly bipolarized world merely against the dominant social forms on the other side. On the contrary, it is important to emerge out of the grid of such a unilateral perspective. The post–cold war historical framework should consider both the East and the West as transitory entities rather than relegating only one side to the horizon of transition, thereby mistakenly making the other side appear to be a cohesive, unchanging entity.

Verdery's essay "Whither Postsocialism?" is crowded with persuasive ideas, some of which originate from her earlier work, which presented social changes in eastern Europe as part of global processes and as being in critical dialogue with some discourses of globalization.[56] In the essay, she observes: "The Cold War organized the world around a dichotomy different from that of post-coloniality—not colonies and metropole, 'the West' and 'the Rest,' but East and West, communism and capitalism. And it organized knowledge both by underscoring other aspects of capitalism than colonial relations and by grouping places and states differently from the center-colony groupings of European imperialism."[57] Despite these differences, Verdery argues that postsocialist studies have much to gain by interacting with colonial historiography and postcolonial studies. The latter does not privilege political economy over cultural politics, and it has developed ways to integrate analytically cultural representations with unequal economic relations (see chapters 3 and 6). Verdery anticipates that constructing an analytical connection between these two spheres of investigation will contribute to introducing fresh insights to postsocialist scholarship.[58]

Verdery's attempt to open up the analytical contours of postsocialism to a broader field of ideas consists of two interrelated approach. One approach sees cold war history from a relational perspective, incorporating both sides of the political bipolarity, and this suggestion resonates strongly with a recent discussion in the scholarship of cold war history (see chapter 4). My comparative approach to contemporary social developments in Vietnam and South Korea (see chapters 4 and 5) is in part intended to demonstrate the relevance of this relational perspective. The other approach is to reorient postsocialist studies to facilitate closer communication with postcolonial studies and to replace the East/West trajectory, as Geir Lundestad has done in his pioneering work on cold war history, with a more complex framework inclusive of the North/South trajectory.[59] I agree with Verdery that by moving in this direction, postsocialist studies may be able to engage more critically with the coexistence of the enduring pastness of socialism and the intensifying futureness of capitalism in the perceived transitional realities in eastern and central Europe.[60] It is to the critique of this temporal distance, as I explore in the next chapter, that contemporary postcolonial scholarship has made its most notable contribution. More important, Verdery's post–cold war scheme aims to bring to attention the "connections between the legacies of colonialism and socialism in contemporary empires."[61] In exploring these interconnected legacies, we need to recognize that there are actually existing connections between colonial and bipolar history and that these connections exist in local lives as well as in global forms.

If the cold war was both a globally waged and a locally experienced conflict, the tool for understanding its history should be sharpened accordingly—that is, by situating each local experience in wider relational terms to other locally specific experiences. On this point, I share Appadurai's concerns about the predicament of area studies discussed in the previous chapter, despite my reservations about the exclusion of bipolar histories from his suggested alternative scheme. In the "world after 1989," Appadurai advocates that the focus of area studies should be on relatedness between local histories and global dynamics rather than on the supposed integrity of the locale defined as against the global processes. Postsocialist transitions are a particular ramification of the decomposition of the cold war and should be considered in relation to other concrete ways in which the bipolar political structure is coming to an end elsewhere. The cold war was a global phenomenon, and so is the process beyond it. Its rise in the European theater was inseparable from the fall of Europe's colonial powers in non-European theaters; the bipolarization of Europe and the postcolonial developments in the non-European world are correlative issues in the history of the cold war. It follows that the conceptual tools with which we grasp postsocialist historical transitions should communicate with those tools that are developed for grasping postcolonial historical realities. The realization that Europe was only one province in the bipolarized world, not its exemplary center, is crucial for placing its depolarizing contemporary moments in more viable positions (see chapter 6).

The previous discussion raised two key issues with respect to the decomposition of the cold war: (1) the crosscutting dimensions of colonial history and bipolar history, which I described as two color lines (the question of time) and (2) the scale of analysis between the local and the global, which I earlier characterized as the social and geopolitical order of the cold war (the question of space). In the next chapter, I focus more sharply on the question of time and explore how the old racial color line intersected with a new ideological color line in the era of the cold war. The twentieth century's two intermingled color lines are problems for all sides of the color divides. Any understanding of the constitution of one color line and the pains it caused is incomplete without knowing the complications and turmoil caused by the other color line; any vision of an alternative future where human beings and societies are not color bound has likewise to deal with both forms of ideological polarity.

3

AMERICAN ORIENTALISM

The previous chapters raised questions about the way in which we think of and remember the cold war today. One question concerns the tendency to relegate the global cold war wholly to the past. The cultural historian John Gillis reflects on the particularity of the cold war in our collective memory: "The Cold War contributed in its own way to shifts in the forms and location of memory. The blurring of the old distinction between war and peace meant that it was very difficult to define the beginnings or endings that had previously been the focus of memory."[1] In the early 1960s, when the cold war was a collective experience rather than a memory, Hannah Arendt cautioned against any notions of a definitive historical turning point, which she believed results from a false transcendental perspective to history.[2] Arendt was one of the few political theorists of her generation who radically rejected the dualist terms of the cold war, protesting, as Jeffrey Isaac puts it, against "a monologic politics that is incapable of projecting beyond the subject [and] a polarizing politics in which the Other becomes simply a projection of one's own obsessions and fears, epitomized by the mutual balance of terror and conformity."[3] For Arendt, to live politically is to place ourselves "between past and future": to witness our suspension between "what has been" and "what is not yet," and "to live both with a history which is inescapably ours but which does not fully determine us, and with our projections of new realities[,] the pursuit of which gives meaning to our existence."[4]

The Greeks express a transitory state such as the time after the cold war or after socialism with the prefix *meta-* rather than the prefix *post-* of Latin origin. The former implies an occurrence of morphological alteration in making a spatiotemporal transition. The Koreans are greatly concerned about the future of their nation's bipolarized political systems, and they express their hope for an alternative future with the prefix *tal-*, which also indicates a morphological alteration, as in *talpi*, meaning "shedding off the skin" or "emerging from the old condition," including the phenomenon of exuviations. These local expressions, in my view, help us to think about the ending of the cold war order in a less totalizing, chronologically determined way. We need to resist the propensity to detach bipolar history from our understanding of the contemporary time and not be oblivious to the impact of bipolar politics on our view of history. I argued that the first step toward a new understanding of the cold war is to question the idea that the cold war has ended globally, to think instead about our time "between past and future," and to rethink the end of the cold war as a slowly decomposing global reality involving a multitude of emerging, locally specific moral initiatives and political actions. The cold war was a global conflict, but this truism does not mean that the conflict was experienced globally in identical terms or that it is remembered as a single entity. We need to break out of the global abstraction of the cold war and attend to its diverse, contrary historical realities across locales before we can set out to put the pictures back together to create a new image of the whole.

In this light, I have so far critically assessed modalities of cultural globalization and postsocialist social transition, which I argued adopt a mystified notion of the global, thereby failing to conceptualize the identity of the lived locality in a historically grounded way (for the former) and in a wider, relational context involving the process of social change on the formerly opposite side of the bipolar conflict (for the latter). This chapter develops these discussions, focusing on another key issue in comparative cold war social and cultural history—the conjuncture between the colonial and the bipolar political order. This inquiry is central to diversifying cold war history, and an engagement with the colonial/bipolar historical conjuncture (and disjuncture) is also important for understanding the complexity of contemporary transitions away from the bipolar order. To this end, this chapter investigates how the currently influential scholarship of postcolonial criticism assimilates cold war histories into its general scheme of ideas. In the next chapter, I examine, in turn, how the scholarship of cold war studies conceptualizes its subject matter in relation to colonial and postcolonial political history.

Focusing on the Semitic civilizations in the Near East and the ways in which they are represented in Western literature, Edward Said advances a powerful case in favor of a cultural continuity from the colonial order to the bipolar order. In the last part of his classic work *Orientalism*, published in 1978, Said narrates how the tradition of oriental studies migrated from western Europe to North America after the end of World War II, and he situates this movement in the context of the postwar shift in global political power from European colonial empires to American imperium. He documents how the development of American orientalist scholarship included the inception of Europe's prejudice-infested ideas about Near Eastern religious and cultural traditions and how these ideas influenced American foreign policy and popular imagination about the region. Early American area specialists of the Near East, according to Said, saw the region through the same looking-glass that Europeans had elaborated to make sense of and justify their imperial ambitions in the eighteenth and nineteenth centuries; this similar viewpoint is partly responsible for (and partly explains) the "parallel between European and American imperial designs on the Orient (Near and Far)."[5] On the basis of this premise of continuity, Said describes in another work how "in today's Europe and the United States what is described as 'Islam' belongs to the discourse of Orientalism, a construction fabricated to whip up feelings of hostility and antipathy against a part of the world that happens to be of strategic importance for its oil, its threatening adjacence to the Christian world, its formidable history of competitiveness with the West."[6] Although Said believes that there is strong parallelism and continuity between the European orientalist tradition and the American variety, he nevertheless points out that the latter includes a few distinctive features at a practical level. One of these features involves the disciplinary focus: the European orientalist corpus was dominated largely by philological and literary studies, whereas the American offshoot played down the importance of poetry and literature as a vehicle for understanding indigenous cultural traditions. According to Said, the early American specialists of the Near East reduced the hearts and minds of the region's population to opinions, attitudes, and trends in accordance with the new behaviorist language. He traces this change to the strong influence of the U.S. military academic establishment (where the earliest program of Arabic-language instruction was conducted) on the early American oriental studies and the general trend in post–World War II American social sciences biased in favor of quantitative methods and quantifiable social facts.[7] Said expresses a stronger objection to this behaviorist orientalist trend than to its European predecessor on the grounds that the new American-style orientalism not only distorted the cultural identity of the Orient but also made it a soulless entity with neither literary imagination nor discursive subtlety.

Since its publication in 1978, Said's critique of orientalism has led to an explosion of interest in colonial discourse and cultural constructs across disciplines. It has also provoked an array of appraisals and critical responses.[8] A notable constructive criticism pointed to the suggested structural continuity of orientalism across time and space. For instance, Dennis Porter questions how it is possible to project "a continuity of representation between the Greece of Alexander the Great and the United States of President Jimmy Carter, a claim that seems to make nonsense of history at the same time as it invokes it with reference to imperial power/knowledge."[9] Porter's critique of the continuity thesis focuses on the theoretical tools that Said brings to describing the politics of representation. Said says that his investigation of the history of orientalism draws primarily upon Michel Foucault's discourse theory and Antonio Gramsci's idea of cultural hegemony. Porter, however, believes that these two cultural theories of power, although thematically related, are analytically incompatible.[10] The idea of hegemony is effective in procedural analyses that explore changing patterns of relations of domination and cultural politics over time, according to Porter, whereas the efficacy of the discourse theory lies in its synchronic orientation to time, concerned primarily with the multiple, similar phenomena that arise at a particular period of time for the purpose of eliciting a hidden mechanism linking the simultaneous elements. Porter argues that by employing these separate theoretical approaches to politics of symbols irrespective of their crucial epistemological differences, Said turned orientalism into both a discourselike phenomenon that is diachronically conceptualized and a hegemonic phenomenon that is nonetheless unaffected by historical process. As a result, according to Porter, orientalism presented by Said has no "epistemological breaks between different periods" and appears to be "the unity and continuity of Western discourse on the Orient."[11]

As many other commentators have noted, Said's critique of orientalism, despite the problem indicated by Porter, has a lasting importance.[12] It opened a way to consider the production of racial and cultural stereotypes as a constitutive element in the making of unequal economic and political relations rather than merely as their representational byproducts. It showed the importance of knowing the past horizons of alterity and imaginations about cultural hierarchy if we wish to liberate our lives from their enduring legacies. It is argued that the expository power of Said's work lies in part in its presentation, "within a single analytical framework, [of] core elements in the European intellectual and political tradition for a very long period [and] in ways that obscured internal relations of contestation and resistance in Western cultures."[13] Commentators note that *Orientalism* might never have been written had Said been too concerned about these internal relations of contestation within the West, and its absence would have been a great "loss to the whole scholarly community."[14] In order to keep and augment the expository values of *Orientalism*, however, I also believe that it is necessary to reconsider "the unity and continuity" of orientalism and to tease out the element of rigidity from this formulation. Any rendering of regularities and patterns, which does not allow room for change and dialectics of patterned alterations, is problematic in cultural historical inquiry.[15] The effort to reconsider orientalism's degree of regularity in historical process is particularly relevant (and lacking in current debates) for the historical field of the "imperial designs" moving across the Atlantic Ocean and for the related shift of global order from the colonial to the bipolar.

Said notes that "modern American Orientalism derives from such things as the army language schools established during and after the war, sudden government and corporate interest in the non-Western world during the postwar period, [and] Cold War competition with the Soviet Union."[16] Issues of national liberation, secular nationalism and communism, and communism's compatibility with the Islamic tradition were widely discussed among intellectuals in the Middle East in the mid–twentieth century, and Said describes how these issues became important subjects of consideration in the Near East studies circles of the United States during this period. He also notes that these area-specialist groups aspired to be social and political scientists, departing from their philology-dominated European precedents. However, Said regards this shift of focus and orientation as a minor modification with no structural significance in the orientalist discourse. The political language of "good Muslim" versus "bad Muslim" emerged forcefully in certain circles of Middle East specialists during the so-called second cold war of the 1970s as well as in the aftermath of the Arab–Israeli war (1956–1967) and the civil war in Yemen (1962–1970).[17] Said finds no novelty in this classification, seeing it largely as a repetition of the old racialist image of the oriental other, nor does he explore its connectedness to the idioms of "good" moderate nationalists versus "bad" radical nationalists that were prevalent in other Asian regions and elsewhere during the earlier phase of the cold war in the 1950s and the modernization drive of the 1960s.[18]

Following Porter, we may say that Said's tendency to downplay these formal changes in the orientalist rhetoric relates to his excessive reliance on Foucault's discourse theory and his related reluctance to conceptualize hegemony in a procedural perspective.[19] When Gramsci wrote about cultural hegemony in his prison letters, he did so in the midst of a rising fascist power in 1920s and 1930s Italy and escalating political tensions in wider Europe. In addition, it was during the escalating cold war crises of the 1950s that his prison writings became widely known and popular in a host of Western countries and beyond. Gramsci advanced the idea that economic relations and ideological forms shape each other reciprocally. His insights into political coercion and moral consent, both in their inception and dissemination, reflected on the turbulent transition of the world order from the old imperial form to a new political form and on the related political crises in Europe. About what he called "Americanism," which he associated particularly with the Taylor–Ford system of labor organization, he wrote: "America does not have 'great historical and cultural traditions'; but neither does it have this leaden burden to support. [Hegemony] is born in the factory and requires for its exercise only a minute quantity of professional political and ideological intermediaries."[20] Gramsci's idea of hegemony was tied to his reflection on the invention of what he saw as a new structure of domination, such as the new "rationalized" social structure in North America in place of the old system in Europe, which he described as a system of production burdened by residues of feudalism and a conservative sexual and family life.

In his book *American Orientalism*, Douglas Little argues: "[W]ith the waning of Britain's power and the waxing of America's after 1945, something very like Said's orientalism seems subconsciously to have shaped U.S. popular attitudes and foreign policies toward the Middle East." Little also refers to Catherine Lutz and Jane Collins's critical reading of *National Geographic*, which they describe as "America's lens on the world" and present as evidence of America's distorted, orientalist view of Arabs, Africans, and Asians as "backward, exotic, and occasionally dangerous folk."[21] Little claims:

> Once the orientalist mindset of imperial Britain insinuated its way into the White House, the Pentagon, and Foggy Bottom during the late 1940s, and once the orientalist worldview epitomized by *National Geographic* found its way onto America's coffee tables and movie screens during the early 1950s, U.S. policies and attitudes toward the Middle East were shaped in predictable ways. Influenced by potent racial and cultural stereotypes, some imported and some homegrown, that depicted the Muslim world as decadent and inferior, U.S. policymakers from Harry Truman through George Bush tended to dismiss Arab aspirations for self-determination as politically primitive, economically suspect, and ideologically absurd.[22]

Following this interpretation, it appears that post–World War II international history was largely an extension of earlier European imperial history in the hands of a different player. As a result, the politics of the "American Century" became a repetition of the old imperial-age scenario of cultural and political domination.

The notion that the orientalist politics of representation is reproduced across historical epochs is also strong in contemporary political debate. In his contribution to the important edited volume *The New Crusades*, Said confronts Samuel Huntington's insistence that the framework of East/ West ideological rivalry should be replaced, after the cold war, by the framework of a clash of culture: between the West as a distinct, coherent entity of universal cultural values and liberal political norms, on the one side, and the non-West as made up of illiberal, undemocratic civilizations, in particular the Islamic and Confucian cultures, on the other. Said believes that Huntington's view is a rhetorical means of constructing a new horizon of "us versus them."[23] The editors of *The New Crusades*, Emran Qureshi and Michael Sells, write:

> The West is a relational designation; it has meaning only in contrast or opposition to an East. The self-definition of the West and its military,

economic, and ideological investment in the defense against communism need not be dismantled but could be directed toward the threat
of this newly configured East. The same West (defined as individualis-
tic, enterprising, egalitarian, peaceable, and tolerant) is pitted against an
East now embodied by Islam and characterized as fundamentalist, reactionary, terrorist, static, and oppressive of women. Anti-Western Muslim
militants construct a similarly absolute conflict between the degenerate,
repressive, soulless, hedonistic, and women-exploiting West and the justice, truth, and moral center represented by Islam.[24]

The rhetoric of culture clash, as this concept is advanced by Huntington, postulates that after the cold war a substantively different world order
emerges in which "states increasingly define their interests in civilizational
terms" rather than in ideological terms. Huntington claims:

> The West is and will remain for years to come the most powerful civiliza-
> tion. Yet its power relative to that of other civilizations is declining. As
> the West attempts to assert its values and to protect its interests, non-
> Western societies confront a choice. Some attempt to emulate the West
> and join or to "band-wagon" the West. Other Confucian and Islamic soci-
> eties attempt to expand their own economic and military power to resist
> and to "balance" against the West. A central axis of post–Cold War world
> politics is thus the interaction of Western power and culture with the
> power and culture of non-Western civilizations.[25]

Qureshi and Sells do not question the idea that the cold war is globally
over and in fact agree with Huntington that the cold war had "the vir-
tue of controlling the flow of violence."[26] Their objection to the idea of
clashing culture groups is instead based on the observation that the idea,
rather than being a constructive model for a new global reality after the
cold war, is actually an attempt to reclaim and perpetuate the old bipolar
cold war worldview. Said, too, believes that Huntington's thesis is intended
to extend "the mindset of the cold war into a different time and for a new
audience."[27] It then appears that these critics see the cold war as consisting
of two separate aspects. One aspect is the cold war as a geopolitical reality,
and on this aspect the critics of the culture clash idea share with the proponents of the idea the view that this contest of power between two superpowers is over. The other aspect is the cold war as a distinctive worldview

and "mindset." The critics argue that this aspect of the cold war, as a set of beliefs and mental constructs rather than as a material reality, reasserts its vigor in the contemporary world, creating a new image of an alien way of life and an identity whose beliefs and cultural dispositions are incompatible with and antithetical to those of the liberal world.

The critique of culture clash asserts that the bipolar worldview continues and has merely adopted a new language in order to continue and that this new language of self/other differentiation feeds on the old colonial language of the civilized self versus the uncultivated other. If we follow this argument, however, how should we understand the relationship between the old and the new languages about the other? Between the European-style colonial orientalism and the American-style orientalism of the bipolar era, which one is the schema (and which one is the facade) in the new rhetorical practice about war among civilizations? In other words, what is it that speaks through the clash of civilizations: the pre–cold war European imperial culture or the mindset of American cold war culture? Pointing to this question, Michael Hardt and Antonio Negri argue, in their influential work *Empire*, that postcolonial criticism, although effective for rereading history, is "insufficient for theorizing contemporary global power." They claim: "[Postcolonial theory] manages to condemn the current global power structures only to the extent that they perpetuate cultural and ideological remnants of European colonial rule. [Said] charges that 'the tactics of the great empires, which were dismantled after the first world war, are being replicated by the U.S.' What is missing here is a recognition of the novelty of the structures and logics of power that order the contemporary world."[28] Hardt and Negri propose that an entirely novel form of global domination (which they call an "empire of network power") was invented in the American Century, and they argue against postcolonial critics in this light, asserting that the latter regard the structure of domination and the representation of power only in retrospect.

I am not concerned here with the question of whether the preeminence of American power is to be understood ideologically in the scheme of invention or convention. The point is rather that whichever way we are inclined to lean, it is inappropriate to define the cold war, as do Qureshi and Sells, as merely a competition over spheres of influence between superpowers. To do so excuses cold war history from critical issues of cultural representation, thereby further aggravating the tendency in postcolonial literary criticism to reduce complex, changing hegemonic processes to a timeless, discursive scheme. Said locates "American orientalism" in the direct lineage of the European tradition of colonial cultural politics; Qureshi and Sells present the clash-of-civilizations rhetoric as a regression to the tradition of imperial worldview. Following these critics, cold war history appears to have no relevance for cultural criticism and to be devoid of any distinctive political culture and capacity for improvisation. This point relates to Said's perspective of orientalism as preeminently a "citational" discourse, according to Melani McAlister, in which authors and artists construct their works by drawing extensively on preexisting representations. In this system of intellectual and aesthetic production, McAlister points out, the reference to an earlier generation of ideas and images provides authority and reliability to the new expository product.[29] However, the act of citation is ultimately intended to strengthen the work of creativity, not to replicate the tradition. The conformity between the old order and the new order means, in the words of T. S. Eliot, that "the past should be altered by the present as much as the present is directed by the past."[30] The tendency to see cold war cultural politics as an analytically insignificant arena for cultural criticism closely relates to the mistaken definition of the cold war political arena in general merely in terms of a balance of military power and a competition over economic ideologies. The shift from philological to behaviorist discourse, which Said mentions with reference to "American orientalism," may give the impression that the construction of the cold war order was not a very cultured practice, if we mean by culture the artifacts of high art and literature. However, as we will see shortly, behaviorism was not only a significant aspect of the making of the cold war order but also an important instrument for making this order distinct from the colonial order.

The critique of orientalism and the wider postcolonial criticism (see chapter 6) aim broadly at resisting an essentialist, hierarchical notion of cultural difference. In my view, this resistance against the concept of culture as a timeless entity concerns not only the critique of orientalist representational tradition but also the critical understanding of the culture of orientalism. If orientalism is a form of cultural tradition and, as a way to imagine cultural others, reduces those others to a timeless entity, the critique of this cultural form must break out of the very essentialist notion of culture in representing the cultural form as well as in criticizing its representational politics. The cold war engendered some novel ways to imagine collective self-identity and the identity of the other; understanding these alterations is necessary for considering orientalism as a shifting horizon of cultural hegemony rather than merely as an unchanging textual order. The critical inquiry needs also to be self-critical of the tendency to view the West in an ahistorical perspective, to engage with alterations in the politics of representation, and to explore what elements of similarity and difference the cold war politics of identity and alterity demonstrate in comparison to the colonial precedent.

According to Said, orientalism operates on an asymmetrical binary logic, presenting the world as made up of two unequal halves, Occident versus Orient or Europeans versus Others, through myriad textual and symbolic media. The scale and complexity of these binaries were among the most distinctive features of cold war political culture (as against colonial culture). The cold war encompassed the Western metropole and its colonial peripheries, and the construction of "cold war enemies" imagined threats arising from within society as well as coming from without.

According to Melvyn Leffler, from the perspective of post–World War II U.S. administrations, "the specter of communism" was endangering the future of both western Europe and its colonial outposts in Asia, so securing both these territories against the Red menace was fundamental to safeguarding the security and economic interests of the United States.[31] For the Harry S. Truman administration (1945–1953), reconstructing the war-torn Japanese economy was therefore as strategically crucial as incorporating western Germany into a military alliance and economic unity with World War II European allies. The perceived Red perils consisted not only of the external threat from the rising Soviet power but also of the internal challenges from home-grown political oppositions in Europe and the colonial world alike. Hence, thwarting the popularity of the Communist Party in France, Italy, and Greece was a task as urgent and frustrating as dealing with the vigorous radical nationalist movements in Northeast and Southeast Asia, and the incorporation of these regions into the western political orbit and markets was considered vital for Japan's economic reconstruction. When the United States tolerated or actively took part in initiatives by some of its World War II European allies to repossess their Asian colonial territories after 1945, this collusion was intended to harness the colonial reconquest as an instrument of the global struggle against communism, to repress the indigenous radical forces and prevent the territory from falling into the Soviet orbit, not necessarily because the United States was interested in bringing back the old prewar European imperial order.

Fatema Mernissi explains how the current political crises in the Middle East are rooted in the two-pronged cold war containment politics against projected enemies within and without. The rise of radical political Islam, according to Mernissi, is unintelligible without considering "the liberal democracies' strategic support of conservative Islam, both as a bulwark against communism and as a tactical resource for controlling Arab oil." Mernissi also emphasizes how the Western powers worked against the secular Arab nationalist movements (such as in Nasser's Egypt) and supported instead what she calls the "palace fundamentalism" of theocratic states and later the "street fundamentalism" of radical Islamists, believing that these forces would make effective allies in combating Communist incursions from outside and radical nationalist claims from inside.[32] Reflecting on the Soviet–Afghan war against the aforementioned background, Leffler examines Gorbachev's initiative in the mid-1980s to withdraw Soviet troops from Afghanistan and his plea to the U.S. administration to do likewise—that is, to stop supporting and empowering the radical Islamist insurgents in that volatile country. Although U.S. officials were conscious of the growing threat of Islamic fundamentalism, according Leffler, they could not resist the opportunity to topple the Communist regime in Afghanistan and further to "incite tens of millions of Muslims in the Soviet Union."[33] U.S. secretary of state George Schultz declared in 1985 that the United States was not ready to betray and abandon the freedom fighters in Afghanistan. Central Intelligence Agency director William Casey was less diplomatic and more candid about it when he told his aides: "Here is the beauty of the Afghan operation. Usually it looks like the big bad Americans are beating up on the natives. Afghanistan is just the reverse. The Russians are beating up on the little guys. We don't make it our war. The Mujahedin have all the motivation they need. All we have to do is give them help, only more of it."[34] With respect to this background, Mahmood Mamdani is probably right to claim that the Afghan jihad was in reality an "American jihad": "to unite a billion Muslims worldwide in a holy war, a crusade, against the Soviet Union, on the soil of Afghanistan."[35] Mernissi also concludes that modern Islamic fundamentalism was originally "[a] weapon to fight communism."[36]

Looking at the modern history of Middle East from a different angle, McAlister explores the complex ways in which cold war political imaginations connected enemies within to enemies without. Particularly notable in her engrossing accounts of the history of American political and cultural interests in the Middle East is the importance of racial diversity in American society in shaping these interests. McAlister narrates how post–World War II U.S. foreign policy in relation to the Middle East advanced the idea of "benevolent supremacy." This policy aimed at keeping the region from falling under Soviet influence or falling back under British influence, and it advocated that the United States support measures to free the "formerly subject peoples" from "slavery" (or threats of slavery) under all forms of empire, whether colonial or Communist. McAlister discusses these declared policy objectives in a broad context of postwar American imaginings about declining Europe and Europe's freedom-seeking colonies, a context that also includes the intense popularity of epic biblical fictions and dramas in the 1950s, such as *The Ten Commandments* (1956) and *Ben-Hur* (1959), which depicted the struggles for freedom from slavery and tyranny in the ancient Near East. McAlister describes how the popularization of these epic dramas among the American public affected the nation's foreign policy for the region. According to her, the American public expressed their concerns about civil rights and racial equality in close interaction with the historic imagery and historical reality of the Middle East. African American civil rights leaders, the activists of the Black Power movement, and conservative white segregationists expressed their separate visions commonly with reference to biblical messages. They also observed closely and reacted differently to the critical events in the Middle East (such as the Arab–Israeli war of 1948, the Suez crisis of 1956, and the Six-Day War of 1970). As a result, the political turmoil in the Middle East and the domestic racial conflicts became increasingly interwoven in the United States. McAlister concludes: "[In postwar America,] the us–them dichotomies of Orientalism have been fractured by the reality of a multiracial nation, even if that reality was recognized only in its disavowal. In other words, there was never a simple, racial 'us' in America, even when, as was generally the case, whiteness was privileged in discourses of Americanness."[37]

McAlister argues that what Said called "American orientalism" should be considered within a tremendous shift in the politics of representation from a relatively simple scheme of racial and cultural hierarchy that characterized the colonial era to a new, more complex view in which the image of the other was no longer definable simply in terms of cultural hierarchy and in which the collective self-identity was not an unambiguous antithesis to the projected distant others.

Little places "American orientalism" within the continuum of European cultural imperial heritage. However, it is important to remember that the former belongs to the era of the cold war, whose preeminent horizon of alterity was ideological rather than cultural or racial. According to Christina Klein, America's "Cold War orientalism" and its related advocacy of "benevolent supremacy" in the postcolonial world were about encountering alien cultural worlds and inventing a new way to assimilate these alien worlds in the context of a global ideological struggle against communism.[38]

Klein explores the representations of Asia in this light, focusing on the so-called middlebrow literary world in mid-twentieth-century America. She writes: "The United States [after World War II] became the only Western nation that sought to legitimate its world-ordering ambitions by championing the idea (if not always in practice) of racial equality. In contrast to nineteenth-century European imperial powers, the captains of America's postwar expansion explicitly denounced the idea of essential racial differences and hierarchies." Klein makes a persuasive argument that in the cultural sphere, America's postwar imperial expansion was based on exclusionist rhetoric against communism (as a mode of life incompatible to the American way of life) and on ideas and ideals about tolerance (of cultural differences) and inclusion (as a cultural progress). She illustrates this changing horizon and texture of orientalism with the idiom "getting to know you"—from the title of the theme song for the colorful and hugely popular postwar American musical and motion picture The King and I.[39]

Orientalism in its American version was a two-sided complex consisting of images of cultural difference and ideas of political incompatibility. With respect to this complication, I emphasize once more that the two-sided discourse projected that the ideological enemies existed both near and afar. Two important documents of the early cold war show how the ideological "other" was imagined both from within and from without. George Kennan, an American diplomat considered the "father of containment policy," wrote in his famous "Long Telegram" sent from the U.S. Embassy in Moscow to the U.S. State Department in February 1946:

At bottom of [the] Kremlin's neurotic view of world affairs is the traditional and instinctive Russian sense of insecurity. Originally, this was the insecurity of a peaceful agricultural people trying to live on a vast exposed plain in the neighborhood of fierce nomadic peoples. To this was added, as Russia came into contact with the economically advanced West, fear of more competent, more powerful, more highly organized societies in that area. . . . For this reason they have always feared foreign penetration, feared direct contact between [the] Western world and their own, feared what would happen if Russians learned the truth about the world without or if foreigners learned the truth about the world within. And they have learned to seek security only [in] a patient but deadly struggle for total destruction of rival power, never in compacts and compromises with it.[40]

In September of the same year, J. Edgar Hoover, director of the U.S. Federal Bureau of Investigation, spoke at the San Francisco Conference of the American Legion:

During the past five years, American Communists have made their deepest inroads upon our national life. In our vaunted tolerance for all peoples the Communist has found our "Achilles' heel." . . . The Communist Party in this country is not working for the general welfare of all our people—it is working against our people. It is not interested in providing for the common defense. It has for its purpose the shackling of America and its conversion to the Godless, Communist way of life. . . . We, of this generation, have faced two great menaces in America—Fascism and Communism. Both are materialistic; both are totalitarian; both are antireligious; both are degrading and inhuman. In fact, they differ little except in name. Communism has bred Fascism and Fascism spawns Communism. Both are the antithesis of the American belief in liberty and freedom. If the peoples of other countries want Communism, let them have it, but it has no place in America.[41]

Kennan highlighted the "traditional and instinctive Russian sense of insecurity": just as their "neurotic" leaders ruthlessly destroyed all domestic oppositions to their rule, he argued, so would they act in a similar fashion toward their defined enemies abroad. Kennan's "Long Telegram" was mainly about the threats to the West's security in the international sphere, and it was Hoover who epitomized the flip side of the "two-pronged policy of containment"—the commitment to containing communism both at home and abroad.[42] In his book *A Study of Communism*, Hoover explored what he called the biggest mystery of his time: "How anyone who enjoys the rights and privileges of American citizenship [can] bring himself to join a [Communist] movement which is such an outspoken foe of our entire way of life."[43]

As the views of these influential state officials were circulated and were becoming a consensus in policy circles and public opinion, by the end of 1946 "the basic Cold War psychology" was taking hold of the U.S. administration.[44] The Soviet maneuvers in northern Iran and incursions to the Turkish border in 1946 strengthened the belief in the United States that the Russians were hell bent on expansion and that only a united, preponderant counterforce could stop it. At the same time, Stalin encouraged the idea of encirclement by hostile Western forces to justify his brutal terror campaigns against his own population. The rise of the so-called cold war security culture was to a large measure, according to Mary Kaldor, a reciprocal action between opposing powers and had an "inertial logic" of mutually reinforcing external threats and internal fears. She argues that the construction of the cold war was thus a "joint venture" between the contending political blocs.[45]

Hoover stated that "if the peoples of other countries want Communism, let them have it, but it has no place in America." It is argued in recent studies that American foreign politics in the mid–twentieth century was based on a broad bipartisan compromise between the Republican-dominated militancy against domestic labor and civil rights unrests and the largely Democrat-led initiatives to aggressively counter Communist threats in foreign soils. These studies show that although the U.S. administration perceived the threats of communism to be coming both from within the society and from overseas, the formulation of security threats was initially complicated by bipartisan politics in which contending groups lay emphasis on either the domestic dimension or the foreign dimension of containment.[46] These two dimensions of perceived Communist threats gradually merged into a rhetorical whole; the polemics against the enemy within (such as Hoover's) and the polemics against the external enemies (such as Kennan's) became increasingly indistinguishable. In the beginning of the 1960s, therefore, Hoover advocated radical measures against overseas Communist threats to Asia and Europe, whereas Kennan lamented the lack of spiritual vigilance and moral solidarity against communism within the Western world.[47] Hence, we should add to Kaldor's idea of "joint venture" another dimension—how the vision of the ideological enemy inside and the vision of the enemy outside colluded with each other, thereby augmenting the intensity of anti-Communist politics.

Dwight D. Eisenhower aptly summed up the emerging Manichean worldview in his inaugural speech in 1953: "The forces of good and evil are massed and armed and opposed as rarely before in history. Freedom is pitted against slavery; lightness against the dark."[48] This anti-Communist worldview drew on an epidemiological model of society as a vulnerable organism.[49] Hoover saw communism as "a condition akin to disease that spreads like an epidemic and like an epidemic a quarantine is necessary to keep it from infecting the nation."[50] In 1950, an important report from the U.S. National Security Council known as *NSC-68* described the Soviet Union as aiming to "contaminate" the Western world by means of its preferred technique of infiltrating "labor unions, civic enterprises, schools, churches, and all media for influencing opinion." The document argued that, in parallel with the urgency to stop domestic contagion, there was a need internationally "to quarantine a growing number of [states] infected [by the disease of communism]."[51]

NSC-68 asserted that the enemies of the liberal world were shadowy and entrenched within society as well as embodied by radical political movements and states out there in the distant geographical horizons. Referring to this way of imagining "us and them," Ron Robin writes: "American society of the 1950s was increasingly fascinated by the threat of a foreign presence within the American body politic. The political, social, and intellectual atmosphere of the period reflected concern for, and fascination with, the enemy within."[52] Robin details how during the 1950s some social scientists sought to explain the psychological process in which individuals and social groups came to assimilate the alien ideals of communism. Scientists sought to develop models applicable to diverse contexts, ranging from labor unrest and racial conflict in American cities to rebellious Communist prisoners of war in the Korean War theater. Robin's investigation of this process of scientific model making shows the remarkable popularity of behavioral methods and constructivist theories. The behaviorists sought to explain the origin of socially disruptive behavior, whether it was urban unrest at home or Communist revolt abroad, with a set of environmental and psychological factors (such as poverty, deprivation, and group pressure). They rejected the idea that cultural norms or ideological beliefs play any meaningful role in shaping human behavior and choices. Instead, they believed that human behavior is determined by the particular circumstances into which people are brought and that behavioral patterns can therefore change by altering these social and material circumstances.

The constructivist approach to human behavior in the academic estab-lishment arose within a wider social environment in which cultural or racial questions were in part subordinated to the imperative of anti-Communist moral solidarity. With reference to the McCarthy period, David Caute observes: "[Joseph McCarthy] was the first right-wing demagogue in American history who denounced no special racial, ethnic or religious group. [One] of the appeals of McCarthyism was that it offered every Amer-ican, however precarious his ancestry, the chance of being taken for a good American, simply by demonstrating a gut hatred for Commies."[53] Explor-ing the political mobilization against communism in a wider framework, Christopher Shannon also emphasizes the rhetorical power of "tolerance" for racial, ethnic, and religious differences and the rising vision of "a world made safe for [cultural] differences," citing Margaret Mead.[54] He argues that the construction of international anti-Communist solidarity involved changes in the conception of racial and religious differences: from the social-evolutionary and moral-hierarchical conception of the colonial era to something akin to what is in the present day known as "cultural plural-ism." According to Shannon, cultural differences were tolerated in cold war politics insofar as the different entities were united on the political frontier against communism, and the rhetoric of tolerance and the idea of cultural diversity, in turn, were important instruments for global political mobilization. The politically engendered cultural pluralism also justified the empowerment of theocratic or authoritarian rules as long as they fell in line with the containment of communism and on the grounds that these rules were more suited to certain cultural traditions.

Shannon probes into the geopolitics of cultural pluralism in relation to the paradigm of cultural relativism advanced in American cultural anthropology. To this end, he describes the works of Franz Boas, a found-ing figure in the discipline, who aimed to shake off the so-called Victorian anthropological tradition in Europe. Boas went against the conception of cultural differences in terms of a temporal hierarchy, or variant stages in the ladder of social evolution, and Shannon situates Boas's advocacy of a nonhierarchical, pluralistic conception of cultural forms within the broad political conditions of mid-twentieth-century America. Shannon brings into the discussion Ruth Benedict, a student of Boas and author of a clas-sical monograph on Japanese culture, *The Chrysanthemum and the Sword*; Margaret Mead; and Frances Fitzgerald, the author of an influential book on Vietnamese culture and history, *Fire in the Lake*. He argues that there is a close affinity in terms of ideas between these popular anthropological classics and the influential political documents and fictional narratives of the period, such as Arthur Schlesinger Jr.'s *The Vital Center* and William Lederer and Eugene Burdick's *The Ugly American*.[55]

One of Shannon's main propositions is that the ideas of tolerance and the paradigm of cultural pluralism were constitutive of the making of the global cold war order. The "liberal anti-communist strategy" outlined in Schlesinger's *The Vital Center*, according to Shannon, took as of supreme importance the basing of U.S. foreign policy on a broad understanding of the culturally diverse world and an in-depth understanding of the specific culture ("cultural personality" of the population) in the conflict zone. Schlesinger believed, according to Shannon, that "cultural ripening" was necessary to win the hearts and minds of the population for a sustained solidarity with the United States against the common enemy, and that it was also important for the American public to recognize their nation's need to move away from its traditional tendency toward isolationism and to embrace its new mission to spread the ideals of freedom and self-determination to peoples yet unacquainted with such ideas.[56] This mission was to proceed gradually, in sensitivity to local cultural traditions and their ways of life, and it had to involve economic and social development projects, which could "address specific local needs and enlist the active participation of the native population." Here Shannon quotes the character Harrison MacWhite, a U.S. ambassador to the fictional Southeast Asian country "Sarkhan" (Vietnam, in actuality) in the influential novel *The Ugly American* by William Lederer and Eugene Burdick. The ambassador's culturally aware character is counterpoised in fictional reality to that of his predecessor, Louis Sears. Ambassador Sears "looks on Asians as strange monkeys" and is entangled in the distorted, orientalist sense of cultural superiority, whereas MacWhite is a pragmatic person, free from the burden of prejudices from history. MacWhite believes "to the extent that our foreign policy is human and reasonable, it will be successful. The extent that it is imperialistic and grandiose, it will fail."[57]

Shannon considers these two seemingly opposite personalities, represented by MacWhite and Sears, as constituting a single identity: America as a global civilizer.[58] He argues that the pluralist discourse of culture colluded with the tough, unilateral foreign policies of containment and intervention. The former emphasized the difference between individual-focused, future-looking American culture and community-bound, past-oriented other cultures, and it presented the ability to accommodate distinct local cultural dispositions as the core aspect of successful American foreign politics. Ruth Benedict conceptualized the Japanese culture as a radical other in opposition to American culture (e.g., in terms of its tight network of ordered interpersonal obligations in contrast to the easygoing individualism of American culture), but she also believed that the two culture groups shared, according to Shannon, "a basic, fundamental human character trait."[59] Peter Mandler states that Benedict saw this shared human character as the ability and the will to change—a "flexible, change-oriented mentality to the world much as the Americans."[60] This is how Benedict's symbol of chrysanthemums works: when the Japanese put aside the wire rack that they insert into the flowers to force them to take the shape they would like to see, they are able to appreciate the flower's natural beauty thriving in freedom. Likewise, the symbol of the sword, purified of its militaristic connotations, is "a simile of ideal and self-responsible man," like the energetic leaders of the Meiji reform. Shannon concludes that Benedict's study of Japanese culture, Schlesinger's political writing, and the story of *The Ugly American* all share the same concern and idea—the concern as to how cold war international politics could accommodate "a vision of one world comprising many cultures" and the idea that cultural pluralism is a far more effective instrument of geopolitics than a hierarchical conception of cultural difference.[61]

It is doubtful whether one can discuss, as Shannon does, the pluralistic conception of culture merely in the context of a political history without taking into account its complex intellectual history.[62] In the evolution of modern concept of culture, ideas of cultural pluralism appear to have much deeper roots and wider significance than simply being instruments of American cold war politics.[63] It should also be noted that Boasian cultural relativism also influenced the critique of American power, such as that offered by William Appleman Williams, who explored the idea of "empire as a way of life" and argued that the pursuit of imperial power is a historically rooted aspect of American civilization, tracing it back to the war against Spain (1898–1899) and further to the experience of the American Civil War, rather than a historical contingency in the twentieth century caused by the breakdown of European empires. In this light, Williams explained the cold war standoff as a manifestation of America's historically enduring propensity for global dominance in confrontation with a new imperial contender.[64] Describing America's imperial pursuit as part of the nation's constitutional history, Williams intended to challenge the then dominant discourse about the origin of the cold war (blaming only the Soviet side) by relativizing and diversifying that origin (including the American side). This interpretative move among the cold war historians, according to Paul Buhle, was "part of a larger interdisciplinary paradigm shift [that] had been strongly affected by the 'cultural relativism' of the anthropologists."[65] Furthermore, it should be mentioned that the engagement of anthropology's cultural relativism with cold war politics led to frustration and disappointment. Reviewing the turbulent public career of Margaret Mead during and after the Korean War, the historian Peter Mandler describes how Mead, after having high hopes for a world development after World War II, was in the late 1950s greatly disappointed by "a fundamental incompatibility between her anthropological tradition and the international vision of the American public and policymakers." The radical militarization of the cold war political frontier, domestic and international, frustrated her hope to "bring the Boasian perspective to bear on international relations" in a constructive way and by peaceful means.[66]

The advancement of racial tolerance and cultural pluralism as an instrument of political integration and mobilization was not unique to the United States. On the other side of the bipolar border, international communism also diverted and neutralized ethnic tensions and racial hierarchy. The new post–World War II eastern European states had strong commitment to creating supraethnic society and ethnically pluralist political order. For instance, the Yugoslav People's Assembly passed, as early as in 1945, a law "prohibiting the incitement and advocacy of ethnic, religious, and racial hatred." This initiative represented the commitment of early Yugoslav Communists, led by Josip Tito, who "sought legitimacy as guardians of ethnic harmony and guarantors that the genocidal massacres of World War II would not be repeated."[67] In the Soviet Union, the respect for cultural-linguistic plurality (within the union of Soviet states) and for the principle of national self-determination (within the union as well as in regard to the colonized nations in the Third World) had been strongly present in the political agenda since the early revolutionary era. Yuri Slezkine describes how Vladimir Lenin viewed national differences as "objective" differences and how, therefore, he envisioned that "the surest way to unify in content [through communism] was diversity in form [of national cultures]." Lenin said, "We are going to help you develop your Buriat, Votiak, etc. language and culture, because this way you will join the universal culture, revolution and communism together," and Joseph Stalin believed that "[t]he triumph of ethnicity was both the cause and consequence of progress" toward a universal, common human culture (*obshchechlovecheskaya kul'tura*, in Russian).[68] Although the ethnic pluralism of Soviet politics differed in character from the cultural pluralism of American cold war politics (the former had relatively less of a racial overtone compared to the latter and was grounded in a particular conception of social evolution and historical progress), Slezkine concludes that a pluralistic understanding of national and ethnic differences was central to the political order of the Soviet Union (and to the transnational order of international communism), much more so than a class-based proletarian cosmopolitanism.

All these issues aside, I think Shannon is right to complain that our contemporary understanding of concepts such as cultural tolerance and pluralism is "in almost complete ignorance of the cold war history of these terms."[69] I might extend his argument and say the following: the view that the orientalist, hierarchical conception of human cultures continued without alteration in the critical transition from the colonial to the bipolar order ignores the fact that the rise of an opposite pluralist, liberal understanding of cultural difference was constitutive of the transition. The bipolar era inherited elements from the colonial past, yet the transition between these two forms of dominance involved the invention of a novel way to imagine cultural diversity and moral unity. This "epistemological break" may be described in terms of collusion between knowledge and power, as Shannon does, or it may be understood alternatively as having also had critical, creative potentiality, as Williams illustrates. Whichever way we choose to interpret the meaning of "culture" in the era of the cold war, it is clear that this concept cannot be considered in too rigid a framework of descent from the culture of colonialism.

Orientalism in the bipolar era was an invented tradition. It drew upon the traditional, colonial-era politics of representation, but it reshaped the conceptual parameters of cultural differences and hierarchy for the purpose of creating a united front against the "common" threat to the "American way of life" in particular and to the "free world" at large. As Williams illustrates with a quote from Dean Acheson, Truman's secretary of state, the prevailing ethos of power politics in the cold war era was that "[America is] willing to help people who believe the way we do, to continue to live the way they want to live."[70] The orientalism of this era departed from the previous

European orientalism by transforming the latter's binary vision into a more complex, multidimensional matrix of "us and them." The result was a pragmatic political culture that was tolerant of cultural diversity within a defined moral and ideological unity and within a broad framework of social development in which the specific local cultural traditions and the general modernization of political and economic relations according to the American model were believed to be reconcilable. The Marshall Plan was the most notable initiative conceived of in this light, but many more smaller-scale, less liberal, and at times less peaceful projects were undertaken in the Far East, Southeast Asia, the Middle East, and Africa.[71] The horizon of alterity in bipolar politics increasingly defined the East/West economic and political differences as a morally irreconcilable division and, in so doing, transformed the old orientalist, essentialist differentiation between the Western and the non-Western world into a largely technical issue that could be resolved by political and economic interventions. In the era of the cold war, the ideas of cultural difference were modernized in the service of a new set of political goals and ideas that shifted the domain of essentialism from the cultural to the ideological.

If the contemporary political rhetoric makes any attempts to shift the domain of essentialism from the ideological back to the cultural, these attempts should be scrutinized against the historical background of the earlier shift in the opposite direction. Even if the new discourse of culture clash may appear to resemble closely the old colonial imagination about self and other, we must not be carried away by their similitude in appearance to the extent that we relegate the important shifts to analytical irrelevance. The relationship between colonial culture and bipolar culture has been a marginalized issue in contemporary cultural criticism (see chapter 6), but it has attracted some debate in cold war scholarship. In the next chapter, I turn to existing efforts to structure the shifting historical horizons of decolonization and political bipolarization and review the idea of parallax visions invented for this purpose.

4

THE AMBIDEXTROUS BODY

The eminent British historian E. P. Thompson opens his influential pamphlet *Beyond the Cold War* with a story about his brother, an officer of the British army killed in action during World War II. In his letter from the Middle East in 1943, the officer wrote: "How wonderful it would be to call Europe one's fatherland, and think of Krakow, Munich, Rome, Arles, Madrid as one's own cities. I am not yet educated to a broader nationalism, but for a United States of Europe I could feel a patriotism transcending my love for England." Just before the officer was parachuted to a high plateau in eastern Serbia to assist a group of Bulgarian partisans, he sent another letter to his brother, in which he wrote: "My eyes fill very quickly with tears when I think what a splendid Europe we shall build (I say Europe because that's the only continent I really know quite well) when all the vitality and talent of its indomitable peoples can be set free for co-operation and creation."[1]

The recipient of these letters had his own awakening experience about Europe's changing political identity in the final years of World War II. Thompson says that as a soldier he lived through the unintelligible shift of the Allies' war effort, from the clearly legitimate antifascist struggle to much less clear-cut assaults against Communist-led uprisings in southern Europe.[2] Out of this experience, which was not uncommon for Europeans of that generation, and in memory of his brother's idealism, Thompson in subsequent decades turned into a prominent scholar-activist in the anti–cold war, antinuclear peace movement, which has arguably been the most significant sustained social movement in western Europe until recently.

The peace movement Thompson joined and led was nonaligned to political authorities on either side of the Iron Curtain and initiated, beginning in the 1970s, a series of dialogues between "minority" intellectuals in western Europe and critical thinkers and writers in the eastern and central European nations. The idea was, as Mary Kaldor explains in her reminiscences, to create a broad forum of independent actors that could cut through the national and systemic borders and, as Thompson put it, "to influence the course of history by little movement 'from below.'"[3] The objective was to end Europe's bipolar division and to challenge the root cause of this disunity, which was considered to be its separate (but related) dependence on the two superpower state actors of the time.[4] The ideal of "détente from below" or "Europe from below" was both retroactive and progressive. It kept up the war generation's aspiration for a broader transnational European identity such as Thompson's brother had hoped for, and it envisioned a cross-national civil society to replace eventually the confrontational bloc system of national societies in Europe. Kaldor has continued to elaborate on the latter after "the revolution in 1989" and has written about the idea of "global civil society" that expands the European experience of "transnationalism in practice" to a broader network of voluntary civil associational initiatives as a vital political force and an alternative framework of security at the global stage.[5]

Reading Thompson and Kaldor, one gets the impression that a cold war history "from below" is indeed quite different to a history "from above." The latter, which here refers to the voluminous historiography of the global conflict written with the focus primarily on state and interstate actions, tended to highlight politicoeconomic differences between East and West, whereas the history "from below" emphasized common moral and ethical values among individuals living in the Eastern or Western bloc. This emphasis on "the role of the individual and the importance of personal links," as Kaldor puts it, was probably inevitable, for the system that the initiatives were working against emphasized collective purposes and conformity to collective designs, but it may have also been influenced by the participating actors' particular social subjectivity, as some claim in calling it into question; these actors were mostly middle-class (in the sense previously

understood in Western bloc societies) journalists, writers, and intellectuals.[6] In any event, it is hard to underestimate the strength of the paradigm "from below," through which, according to Thompson, one could
see in the early 1980s that something dramatic was to happen. He wrote
in 1982: "There would not be decades of détente, as the glaciers slowly
melt. There would be very rapid and unpredictable changes; nations would
become unglued from their alliances; there would be sharp conflicts within
nations; there would be successive risks. We could roll up the map of the
Cold War, and travel without maps for a while."[7] Few other specialists in
international politics and history expected at that time that the Berlin Wall
would fall so swiftly and so easily and by the bare hands of the Berliners.[8]

Thompson sought to draw a road map "beyond the cold war," mainly
in response to one aspect of Europe's bipolarized history, although this
aspect is a prominent one. I argued earlier, following Stephen Whitfield,[9]
that the cold war should be considered to have had two dimensions, as a
geopolitical order and as a social order, and that these two dimensions had
different developmental cycles (see chapter 1). The program of "Europe
from below" is persuasive from the geopolitical dimension, but it comes up
against some formidable conceptual problems if seen within the parameter
of the cold war as a social order. If we take as an example a conscientious
left-wing public intellectual in England under the government of Margaret Thatcher and an oppositional journalist in Poland writing against the
undemocratic rule of his country's Communist Party, the moral consensus
between these individuals at the cross-border level must be based on their
place-specific, divergent life experience and expectations within each society and its borders. Although both actors aspire to a more democratic and
more open society, the critical expression of this aspiration points to different social structural conditions.

Thompson's *Beyond the Cold War*, as I see it, tends to circumvent this
issue and to play down its importance under the wider objective of opening up the border. His understanding of the cold war's frontier is focused
on its external form, and his vision of opening up the frontier does not
offer a way to understand this process in connection to the diverse, locally
specific social conditions and practices. This inattention to local specificity
and variability places his notion of "opposition from below" to the political
structure of divided Europe somewhat in disharmony with the analytical
concept of "history from below" that he applies to the traditional popular
culture of rural England in the eighteenth century and the moral economy

of the English working class during early industrialization. The latter studies emphasize the role of "traditional norms or rights" and "popular consensus as to what were legitimate and what were illegitimate practices" in shaping the course of historical transformation; the former, "opposition from below" thesis plays down the importance of these popular norms and consensus in social mobilization to "make history."[10] Pointing out this disparity is not in any way meant to question the merits of Thompson's important initiatives for the integration and nuclear disarmament of Europe, but rather to confront the tendency in his thesis to relegate the sites of bipolar conflicts only to the external boundaries between political communities and his failure to see them in the milieu of communal norms and obligations.

The cold war was waged within communities as well as between them and on both sides of the frontier. In order to imagine the process beyond a two-pronged conflict, it is therefore necessary to deal with the boundaries within as well as the boundary without, especially if we wish to maintain a global perspective on cold war history and include in the historical transition beyond it the experience of societies that fought the war in a way that does not fit its dominant meaning—namely, in the form of violent, "hot" military and political confrontation rather than in Europe's "long peace" or "imaginary war" of arming for war in order to avoid actual armed confrontation and maintain peace.[11] In these societies, the bipolar political structure may not be relegated to social exteriority, even for the practical purpose of mobilizing counterforce, and the weight of history may be felt within the society as strongly as without and at multiple scales of human life—from personal and domestic to local and national. I come back to the notion of "history from below" with regard to the history of the cold war (and to the related idea of cold war as a social order) at the end of this chapter. But next I explore, with reference to southern Vietnam, how to think of the transition "beyond the cold war" in a sphere of norms and practices that Thompson would have called "traditional popular culture." Before I turn to this case study, however, it is necessary to outline briefly the controversial status of Vietnam in cold war historiography.

The Vietnam War, in the outside world's dominant view at the time of the conflict, was one of the major "limited wars" of the cold war era fought between the Soviet- and Chinese-backed northern Communist forces and the U.S.-supported southern regime. In Vietnam, however, the war is referred to as "the American war" (literally, "the war against America") and, as such, is officially considered to be an extension of the collective struggle against colonial domination ("the French war") and part of the long march to achieving a fully sovereign, united nation-state. These two contradicting identities of the war, postcolonial and bipolar, have been a key issue of historical research and a point of paradigm shift.

Many distinguished scholars of modern history have delved into the contradiction. Marilyn Young begins her seminal history of the Vietnam War with the troubled episode of the U.S. Merchant Marines in 1946. While the Merchant Marine vessels were in charge of bringing home the American troops from the Pacific, they were ordered to ferry thirteen thousand French combat troops to Saigon and thus, against the protest of many sailors, to assist France's attempt to reoccupy Vietnam in the name of protecting its old colony from the threats of communism.[12] Odd Arne Westad foregrounds the dynamics of decolonization in the history of global cold war. In his account, the anticolonial, postcolonial political movements of Asia and Africa and the superpower competitions appear to have shaped each other in myriad interpenetrative ways.[13]

Bruce Cumings approaches the bipolar/postcolonial contradiction as a parallax effect embedded in modern geopolitics.[14] Parallax vision is a key concept in early astronomical sciences, and, according to Alan Hirshfeld, it addresses "the apparent shift in an object's position when viewed alternatively from different vantage points."[15] Cumings extends this principle, originally applied to gauging the distance to stars, to an understanding of mid-twentieth-century American foreign politics—in particular, the question of how it was possible, in the words of Peter Kuznick and James Gilbert, that "the United States had repudiated [after the war] the values underlying the liberal construction of World War II as the democratic war against racism, fascism, and colonialism."[16] After the end of World War II, radical political movements in Asia changed in identity from a positive force in the prospect of a postwar world of free nations to a negative, menacing force serving the expansion of Soviet power. Cumings explains that this shift of identity was a parallax effect arising from the change of position at the geopolitical center rather than from an actual change in the peripheral regions. According to him, America, alternating from member of the anti-Axis alliance to preeminent leader in a global anti-Communist crusade, imposed on the Asian political movements an illusory translocation to the Soviet side.

Cumings discusses the geopolitical parallax within the broad context of post–World War II U.S. policy toward East and Southeast Asia, including the occupation of Japan, the occupation of the southern half of the Korean Peninsula, and the intervention in Vietnam. The positional shift in U.S. foreign policy that he mentions took place in the midst of a tremendous shift in American society, according to Eugenia Kaledin, from the collective commitment to the war efforts in the 1940s to the early stirrings of the civil rights movement in the 1950s.[17] Mark Bradley explores similar ideas in early Vietnam–American diplomatic history, based on his extensive archival research in Vietnam, the United States, and Europe. He confirms that following the surrender of Japan in August 1945, the Vietnamese revolutionary leaders eagerly anticipated that their initiative for national independence would be endorsed by the United States, whose attitude to the non-Western world, they considered, was different to that of the European imperial powers. The Vietnamese revolutionaries were encouraged by Franklin Roosevelt's denunciation of French colonialism, and, with this and other related background incentives, their leader Ho Chi Minh came to declare Vietnam's independence in September 1945 with a quote from the U.S. Declaration of Independence. Bradley shows how this initial convergence in diplomatic vision between Vietnam and America concealed their leaders' radically divergent expectations, which were to become manifest in violent clashes in the following decades. He proposes that the origin of the Vietnam War is unintelligible without relating the horizon of bipolar geopolitics to the field of postcolonial visions and "the visions and assumptions of the imagined Vietnam and America of Vietnamese revolutionaries and U.S. policy-makers in a mutually constitutive fashion."[18] The Vietnam–American war, he concludes, was the pursuit of a postcolonial future in the era of the cold war.

Bradley's persuasive study shows a "postrevisionist" orientation in cold war historiography, which inherits and in part attempts to go beyond the earlier trend called "revisionism" in international history. The latter tradition, disillusioned with the "orthodox" interpretation of the origin of the cold war that put the blame for the escalation of hostility on the Soviet side, instead turned to the active role played by the U.S. side. This tradition has developed into the currently dominant "postrevisionist" approach, in part thanks to the accessibility of archival material held in the Eastern bloc countries, which attempts to reassess East–West relations as a mutually constitutive, reciprocal "joint venture" and to further decenter the cold war origins.[19] Concerning the revolutionary movements in the peripheral regions, scholars of this tradition contributed to an understanding of the rise of bipolar confrontation within the wider historical context of decolonization. Following the visual metaphor of Cumings, we may say that the core of the revisionist school in this sphere of research was to refuse analytically the positional shift that resulted in the geopolitical parallax. In other words, it sought to tell a different story of the cold war in the Third World by placing the horizon of the bipolarizing modern world firmly within the spectrum of the decolonizing traditional societies.

Although I fully endorse this approach and indeed spent part of my youth trying to digest some of the explosive ideas in Cumings's seminal work on the origins of the Korean War,[20] I also feel obliged to point out the limits of this perspective in comprehending bipolar modernity in a multidimensional, multifocal way—that is, from inside out as well as from outside in and from above as well as from below. It is ironic that the very strength of this approach, taking into account the view of peripheral actors, turns out to be its main weakness by rendering it unrealistically homogenous. In order to understand the political process in the bipolarized postcolonial periphery, our attention must be pointed in new directions, including one that is opposite to what the revisionist historians have called for—namely, to a consideration of postcolonial visions within the field of bipolarized historical experience. The cold war's parallax was not merely geopolitical or diplomatic; it created a further parallax between state and society. When a revolutionary movement turned into a revolutionary state, its postcolonial vision sometimes turned into a doctrine to be imposed on the diversity of communal experience.

In the communities of southern and central Vietnam (what was called "South Vietnam" before 1975), kinship rarely constitutes a politically homogenous entity. These communities' genealogical unity is crowded with the remains of wartime political bifurcation. In the customary practice of *ve chau to* (literally, "to gather to serve the ancestors"), people face not only the legacy of meritorious ancestors who contributed to the nation's revolutionary march to independence but also the stigmatizing genealogical background of working against the defined forward march. As in Sophocles' epic tragedy *Antigone*, which inspired Hegel in his philosophy of the modern state, many individuals and families in these regions were torn between the familial obligation to attend to the memory of the war dead related in kinship and the political obligation not to do so for those who fought against the revolutionary state. It is very common in this region for a family to have a few revolutionary martyrs from the American war to commemorate, but many also have relations who were on the opposite side of the war's frontier and who somehow have to be accounted for. The commemoration of the former group has been a legitimate organized activity highly encouraged by the state hierarchy of the unified Vietnam; the commemoration of the latter group is not. The dead in the ancestor worship of this region are thus at the same time united in kinship memory and polarized in political history.

Since the early 1990s, following the general initiatives for socioeconomic reforms later known as *doi moi* (renovation) legislated by the Sixth National Congress of the Vietnamese Communist Party in December 1986, the disparity in genealogical memory has become a critical social issue in the communities of the southern and central region. The report from the party congress focused on economic issues, including changing the organizational basis of agricultural production from collective to private units, opening the border to foreign capital investments, and raising the managerial skills of the state's political and administrative apparatus.[21] In cultural matters, it highlighted investment in education to prepare the younger generation to be a skilled industrial workforce and the continued need to oppose "vestiges of feudal, colonialist, and bourgeois cultures [as well as] superstitions and other backward customs and practices," according to William Duiker.[22] Despite this official warning, the reform has sparked off in local communities a forceful revival of ancestor worship and other ritual activities that previously belonged to the category of "feudal vestiges" and "backward customs and practices."[23]

Throughout the 1990s, Vietnamese communities were seized with an intense, sometimes competitive, mobilization of human and financial resources necessary to rebuild the family and lineage ancestral shrines (*nha tho toc*) and the village communal houses (*dinh*). This largely voluntary popular activity, *viec ho* (the work of family ancestor worship) or what Hue-Tam Ho Tai calls "the commemorative fever," was less of a return to the old "backward customs" than the rise of a distinct way to demonstrate economic development.[24]

In the villages near Danang in the central region with which I am familiar, a large number of former partisan fighters of the American war took an active role in ancestral ritual revival, and their participation contributed to the communal initiative being tolerated by the state admin-istration. In his letter to the district Communist Party office requesting permission for the construction of his lineage temple, a prominent war veteran and a senior member of the lineage argued: "It is according to the principle of our revolution to share wealth and happiness with the generations of war dead who knew nothing but poverty and suffering. The nation's prosperity should benefit all the generations of Vietnam, not merely those who are alive."[25] Ordinary Vietnamese villagers may not phrase their interests in family affairs in such an eloquent way, but those whom I knew were nevertheless cognizant of the particular idea of human rights or justice embedded in his statement: just as the liv-ing have a right to subsistence and a right to pursue economic pros-perity, so do the dead. In popular Vietnamese conception, subsistence means, for the dead, ritual commemoration, which guarantees their inalienable rights for social existence. The notion of justice in this moral economy is founded on a general social intimacy with the memory of the dead in Vietnamese cultural tradition, on the one hand, and in a critical dialogue with the militant secularism and coercive enlighten-ment drive of revolutionary state politics, on the other. The former par-tisan leader's statement offers good dialectical reasoning to these two forces—tradition and revolution—and creatively grafts traditional norms to the tree of revolutionary morality using the new, reform-era language of national economic prosperity. The art of grafting has been a princi-pal metaphor in historical imagination (about old and new, foreign and native) in modern Vietnamese intellectual history since the very early colonial era.[26]

The revival of ancestral rituals was a generalized phenomenon throughout Vietnam, but it had an added complexity in southern and central communities. Patricia Pelley highlights the importance of ritual politics in modern Vietnamese history and argues that the revolutionary Vietnamese state, after taking power in 1945 in the northern half of the country, sought to divert ancestral ritual from the family and community to the state.[27] Describing the same process, Shaun Malarney explains how the state penetrated into domestic and communal lives and turned their ritual space into an instrument of social integration and political con-trol.[28] Whether the state moved into family ritual life or the ritual moved into the hands of the state, these scholars' focus is commonly on the poli-tics of war heroes—a central, familiar element in the process of modern nation building.[29] The Vietnamese state placed a great emphasis on civic moral duty to commemorate the sacrifice of revolutionary patriots to the wars of liberation, and it invested enormous administrative resources to instituting the national memory of war. The result was, at a local level, the establishment of war cemeteries and monuments at the center of village public spaces and the substitution of hero worship for traditional ancestor worship.

In this new organization, Vietnamese villagers were encouraged to relate to the memory of young volunteer soldiers and eminent party activists in the same way as they had previously related to the founding ancestors of the community or the lineage. In domestic life, people replaced family ancestral memorabilia with state-issued death certificates of revolutionary martyrs and the mass-produced portraits of national leaders. Beyond the formal similarity, however, there was a considerable semantic difference between the old and the new "ancestor worship." In the old form, these worship practices strengthened communal solidarity on a local scale, but in the new form they were meant to contribute to integrating these parochial local relations with the sacred community of the nation.

Following the reunification of the country in 1975, the institution of hero worship was forcefully extended to the southern half. It was the principal instrument to integrate this confused region into a moral and political unity with the established revolutionary northern Vietnam. Unlike in the North, however, the imposition of ritual political institution created formidable social problems in the South. The problems are related to the political complexity of genealogical memory that I mentioned earlier and, ultimately, to the question of what George Mosse has called "the Myth of War Experience," the myth of national experience in war memory.[30] Jay Winter and Jean-Louis Robert demonstrate, extending Mosse's insights, how World War I was experienced differently by Paris and London and even by various residential districts of Paris. They suggest that the history of this war should be approached in terms of multiple "convergences" and "divergences" rather than according to a unifying, mythifying scheme of national or European experience.[31] The same is true regarding the history of the American war in Vietnam.

The institution of hero worship made relative sense in the context of northern Vietnam, where the memory of the war dead was predominantly of the "voluntary" soldiers who had left their homes to fight in the distant battlefields: the communities to which these soldiers belonged handed over to the state their precious offspring; the state brought the soldiers' bodies back to the community and honored their memory. It is not easy, however, to extend this classical relationship between civil society and the national state to the postwar situation in the southern regions. The war efforts in these regions did not consist of a clear division between the home front of war economic production and the distant horizon of actual battlefields but were instead a *xoi dau*, a "village war," as the southern Vietnamese put it, which turned the spheres of secure communal life inside out into a vicious, confusing battleground.[32]

Xoi dau is the name for a Vietnamese ceremonial delicacy made of rice flour and black beans. As a metaphor, it refers to wartime village life seized by and oscillating between two contending sides as regularly as the change of day to night. When people savor *xoi dau*, they need to eat both the white and the black part of the pastry. Likewise, survival in the village war meant accepting both sides of the dual world. I heard about many painful episodes that came from the attempt to live in "harmony" with thundering bipolarity and just as many creative stories about subverting the zero-sum logic of the situation. One very common episode involved brotherly disunity: one brother joined "this side" (*ben ta*, the revolutionary side) and another brother (usually the younger one) was dragged to "that side" (*ben kia*, the American side). The situation was tragic, and the result often painful: neither of them returned home alive, and even years later the younger one cannot return home even in memory. Yet the situation also had a creative side: for instance, the family hoped to have at least one of them survive the war by having them on different sides of the battlefield; or if the family had the extraordinary luck of seeing them both return home alive, the brother on the winner's side would be able to help the brother on the loser's side to rebuild his life.

In the home of a stonemason south of Danang, the family's ancestral altar displayed two framed pictures of young men. One man wore a military uniform and his name was inscribed on the state-issued death certificate hanging above the altar. But the other man, who also fought and died in the war, is dressed in his high school uniform, and his death certificate, issued by the former South Vietnamese authority, was carefully hidden in the closet. In 1996, the matron of this family decided to put the two soldiers together. She took down the hero and his death certificate from the wall and placed them on the right-hand side of the newly refurbished ancestral altar, the side usually reserved for seniors. She also enlarged a small picture of her younger son that she had kept in her bedroom. Then she invited some friends, her surviving children, and their children for a meal. Before the meal, she held a modest ceremony, in which she said she had dreamed many times about moving the schoolboy from her room next to his elder brother. She addressed her grandchildren:

> Uncle Kan admired Uncle Tan. Uncle Tan adored the Little Kan. And the two were sick of the thought that they might meet in a battle. I prayed to the spirits of Marble Mountains that my two boys should never meet. The goddess listened. The boys never met. The goddess carried them away to different directions so that they cannot meet. The gracious goddess carried them too far. She took my prayer and was worried. To be absolutely sure that the boys don't meet in this world, the goddess took them to her world, both of them. We can't blame the goddess. So, here we are. My two children met finally. I won't be around for much longer. You, my children, should look after your uncles. They don't have children, but they have many nephews and nieces. Remember this, my children. Respect your uncles.[33]

Another family living near Danang has a similar yet deeper history of displacement and reconciliation. The grandfather of this family was one of the numerous laborers conscripted from the central region of Vietnam by the French colonial army. In 1937–1938, these conscripts were shipped to the great Mediterranean city of Marseilles to work in the city's powdery manufacturing gunpowder for the French army and, under the Vichy regime, for the German army under French management. A number of these Vietnamese laborer-soldiers objected to their situation and joined the French resistance, whereas others continued to endure the appalling working conditions in the powdery. After sharing the destruction and humiliation of World War II with the French citizens, these foreign conscripts returned home in 1948, but there they again found themselves in a highly precarious situation: on one side, the cadres in the Vietnamese revolutionary movement distrusted them and, indeed, looked upon them as collaborators with the colonial regime; on the other, the French took no interest in their past service to the French national economy or in their contribution to the resistance movement against the German invasion. Many of these returnees perished in the ensuing chaos of war, and in the following era many of their children joined the revolutionary resistance movement, which the Vietnamese call the "war against America." The family's grand-father survived the carnage and has an extraordinary story of survival to tell: how he rescued his family in 1953 from the imminent threat of sum-mary execution by pleading to French soldiers in their language and again in 1967 thanks to the presence of an American officer in the pacification team who understood a few words of French as a result of having fought in Europe during World War II. The man's youngest brother was killed in action during the Vietnam War as a soldier of the South Vietnamese army and died unmarried and without a descendent. The man's eldest son is a decorated former partisan fighter belonging to the National Liberation Front, and he now performs periodic death anniversary rites on behalf of his deceased uncle.

This Vietnamese family has a multiple history of cooperating with the wrong side of the political divide, according to how the "wrong side" is defined by the postwar political community. The family's grandfather worked for the French colonial army, and his brother fought in opposition to the Vietnamese revolutionary movement. Yet this history of collabora-tion coexists in a family that also has a history of patriotic contribution, embodied by the grandfather's eldest son, and these two histories inter-act with each other within the family in ways that differ from how they play out in the wider society: the man's experience of working in France helped to save his family from annihilation; his son's record of revolution-ary merit helped to rescue his family from the stigmatic collaborator or "reactionary" status, which many other families have had to endure in the postwar years.

These Vietnamese generations can help each other to overcome the bipo-lar structure of enmity, even when members of one generation are dead, as in the case of the brothers of the stonemason family introduced earlier. This imaginative reciprocity has been one of the prominent aspects of the recent ritual revival in the southern regions. Just as the active involvement of revolutionary war veterans helped to legitimize the communal initiatives to reconstitute ancestral temples, so did the presence of a revolutionary death certificate at home help in assimilating the stigmatized genealogical memory to the domestic ritual space. In the greater Danang area in the second half of the 1990s, it was clear that the residents were conducting their regular ancestral rites more publicly than before and hoping to hold death commemoration rites within a more open circle of relatives than they previously were allowed. The larger circle now includes identities, in particular the war dead from "that side," who in previous times would have been labeled "counterrevolutionary" (*phan dong* in Vietnamese). In the places that I observed, this regionally specific aspect of ritual revival was first brought into action by families with a meritorious revolutionary credential (and there were many of them in the area). It was apparent to me, as I studied this domestic space, that the presence of certificates for the revolutionary dead facilitated bringing home the memory of the unrevolutionary dead into a demonstrative coexistence with the former. The former's positive moral value contributed to neutralizing the latter's negative political value.

This political economy of ancestral worship, particular to southern and central Vietnam, has not yet been properly addressed in existing studies on Vietnamese social development, but it has, in my opinion, far-reaching implications not only for Vietnam's future but also for comparative studies of cold war history and culture. Here I confine my discussion to the second question.

The Vietnamese politics of heroic war death are based largely on a prevailing postcolonial vision. The state-instituted commemorative art, including the monumental forms found in many villages or districts, clearly renders the sacrifices in the American war part of a continuum with earlier struggles against colonial occupation and often even farther back with the ancient battles against Chinese intrusion. In cold war historiography, the change of perspective from the dominant, singular cold war framework to the alternative framework of disjunctive parallax effects between decolonization and bipolarization is an important, constructive paradigm shift. The postcolonial paradigm is superior, in anthropological language, in representing "the natives' point of view" compared to the orthodox cold war paradigm proper. The relative strength of this postcolonial perspective, however, becomes a weakness when the analysis turns its attention from the domain of international history to that of local history. Although the postcolonial perspective is attentive to the intentions and historical particularities of the peripheral other, unlike the geopolitical perspective, which tends to be oblivious to them, it also has the tendency to be analytically oblivious to the fact that in cold war conflicts, the peripheral national other has itself already assimilated the bipolar geopolitical worldview and is therefore not reducible to a homogenous, unifying identity.

We must approach cautiously the idea of "global experience" of the cold war conflict.[34] The same is true, as noted earlier, about any assumption of "national experience" in the conflict. In the fields where the conflict took a violent form and involved radical bifurcation of social forces, the assumption can be especially problematic. The postcolonial historical perspective has not yet come to terms with the ironical progression of bipolar history in which the "native point of view" it tried to represent has turned into a locally hegemonic force, thereby ruling against divergent experience and memories.

The revival of ancestral and death-commemorative rituals in southern and central Vietnam should be considered partly in view of these historical questions as a creative local response to the place of the postcolonial vision in a changing global structure of power. The practice of reuniting brothers away from their bifurcated history of death is primarily a family affair, but it is at once an initiative to change the existing, towering political hierarchy of war death into a more historically accountable, socially democratic form. The voluntary cultural movement is in line with a growing intellectual movement in Vietnam, among writers in particular, that is attempting to reconfigure the history of the American war, using mainly fictional and poetic forms of communication, from a coherent, unified historical narrative of self-determination to a relatively less coherent, divergent experience of a "domestic conflict."[35] This rising "civil war" perspective on the history of the war, as Marilyn Young indicates, is not a negation of the foreign and international dimension of the conflict.[36] On the contrary, I argue elsewhere that this perspective is an expression of a civil society that is in the process of being empowered: if the war was a communal conflict as well as an international one, that means that the community should play as active a part as state actors and international organizations in bringing these conflicts finally to end.[37]

The last point brings the discussion back to the issue with which I began this chapter: the notion of "history from below" with regard to cold war history. In the southern Vietnamese context, I have located the cultural sphere of death commemoration as a site of major communal initiative for the resolution of bipolar conflicts and as the milieu of what Robert Hertz would have called morally "ambidextrous" social practices. It is in part thanks to this scholar, whose promising intellectual life ended prematurely in the fields of mass mechanical slaughter during World War I, that anthropological research has been exploring the close analytical relations between social attitudes to death and the structure of political power. Hertz was interested in how societies construct hierarchies biopolitically and explored the question through his investigation of a traditional mortuary cultural complex in Southeast Asia that expresses the moral hierarchy of "good death" versus "bad death" by means of their symbolic association with the right hand and the left hand.[38] These ideas require close examination; for the purpose of my discussion here, it suffices to introduce the notion of "symbolic ambidexterity" that Hertz coined at the end of his classic *Death and the Right Hand*,[39] as an alternative to the prevailing moral and hierarchical polarity between the symbolic properties of the right and of the left. Hertz believed that the preeminence of the right hand is the inscription of the principles of social hierarchy (including "good death" versus "bad death") on the human body, and he expressed his political vision using the same symbolic language: "The distinction of good and evil, which for long was solidary with the antithesis of right and left, will not vanish from our conscience. . . . If the constraint of a mystical ideal has for centuries been able to make man into a unilateral being, physiologically mutilated, a liberated and foresighted society will strive to develop the energies dormant in our left side and in our right cerebral hemisphere, and to assure by an appropriate training a more harmonious development of the organism."[40]

The moral symbolic bipolarity in the traditional societies that Hertz wrote about is clearly not an issue of the same nature as the ideological bifurcation of modern politics with which we are dealing here: the former relates to questions of social hierarchy within a given society, whereas the latter, in conventional wisdom, is principally about a contest between contrary social formations and ideologies. Nevertheless, we have seen how these two separate issues of bipolarity can make a critical association in the historical field of the cold war as waged in violent forms.[41] If we reduce the history of the cold war to "the test of wills" between two superpower actors and a mutual duel to deter "an alien way of life," the two forms of bipolarity will probably establish no meaningful relationship. If we confine our knowledge of the history to the narrow meaning of the "cold" war and within the centrality of the dominant Western experience of the conflict, it is difficult to imagine how the two bipolarities can be intersected. This Western experience of the cold war was more about the fear of mass annihilation of human lives than about the reality of mass death and displacement. If we attend to bipolar history elsewhere as well as herewith and include in it the experience of violent political confrontations within local and national communities, which is what the global cold war actually meant in much of the world in the past century, the political bifurcation of the human community and the moral polarization of death become closely interrelated phenomena. In the history of the global conflict in the latter sense, communities were driven to select politically "good death" from other war death and extract an ideologically coherent genealogy out of the enmeshed history of violence across the ideological border.

When we decenter our position in this way, we need also to decenter the history from a geopolitical history to the milieu of social history so that we can include in it the enduring locally specific legacies of the global conflict and the creative everyday practices for conflict resolution that have arisen from this milieu. Otherwise, the horizon of the cold war's mass death will remain only a series of tragic and unfortunate events in the past, with no transformative values meaningful to the present time. The life of the late E. P. Thompson testifies to the relevance of approaching cold war history in terms of both political structure and moral practice; we need to extend this lesson and explore ways to understand bipolar history from below as well as from above and from inside as well as from outside.

The memory of brotherhood in Thompson's peace activism is not identical to the history of brotherhood in Vietnamese ritual activity. The two instances point to variant historical backgrounds and take on different forms of manifestation. Vietnamese brotherhood is not separable from the deep-rooted cultural tradition of death remembrance or from the history of mass death in the transitional field from colonial order to bipolar order. The "ambidextrous" social practice of the Vietnamese rises from this particular background of culture and history. Beyond such differences, however, these two brotherhoods commonly raise an issue that we need to think about further: the centrality of kinship for interpreting the history of the cold war. If the question of "which cold war" is central to thinking about the origins and the end of the cold war, as Walter LaFeber shows,[42] the historical inquiry should recognize the fact that the clashes between "this side" and "that side" in the past century took place not only between political communities but also within the moral community of kinship. As Hannah Arendt wrote, the hidden forces of modern politics may be unraveled in the very realm of life that the political forces strive to reduce to privacy—that is, within the rich and manifold conditions of intimate domestic interaction.[43]

5

THE DEMOCRATIC FAMILY

The democratic family is the backbone of a successful political development beyond the conventional left and right oppositions, says the eminent sociologist Anthony Giddens in his widely mentioned book *The Third Way*. Painting an outline of social democracy in the post–cold war world, Giddens repudiates both what he calls the "rightist" idealization of the traditional, patriarchal familial order and the "leftist" view of the family as a microcosm of an undemocratic political order. He proposes in their stead a new model of family relations, which in his view can synthesize the imperative of communal moral solidarity with the freedom of individual choice, forming a unity based on contractual commitment among individual members. This social form of democratic family relations, according to him, would respect the norms of "equality, mutual respect, autonomy, decision-making through communication and freedom from violence."[1]

Giddens writes about family and kinship relations at length in a work devoted to the political history of bipolar ideologies because he believes that families are a basic institution of civil society and that a strong civil society is central to successful social development beyond the legacy of left and right oppositions.[2] His "third way" agenda is premised on the notion that new sociological thinking is demanded after the end of the cold war. According to him, political progress after the cold war depends on how societies creatively inherit positive elements from both right and left ideological legacies, and its main constituents will be "states without enemies" (as opposed to states organized along the frontline of bipolar enmity), "cosmopolitan nations" (as against the old nations pursuing nationalism), a "mixed economy" (including both capitalism and socialism), and "active civil societies." At the core of this hopeful, creative process of grafting, Giddens argues, are the "post-traditional" conditions of individual and collective life, an understanding of which requires transcending the traditional sociological imagination that sets individual freedom and communal solidarity as contrary values.[3] The post-traditional society, according to Giddens, is expressed most prominently in the social life of "the democratic family."

The idea of "the third way" was first described by E. P. Thompson (although this is not acknowledged in Giddens) as a way of expressing his hope that after the end of the cold war, efforts would be made to synthesize the cold war's bifurcated paths of modernity. Thompson emphasized, as discussed in the previous chapter, transnational civil initiatives against the divided Europe, envisaging that these initiatives would contribute to bringing together positive experiences and creative insights from both sides of the division. Thompson hoped that the laissez-faire market ideology of Western capitalism might be moderated in the political transition away from a bipolar world order. Giddens, on the contrary, advances his third-way thesis in the knowledge that the free market and freedom of capital will become a stronger, more encompassing ideology in the new world order than in the cold war era. There is another notable difference between their propositions. Thompson conceived of the end of the cold war in Europe mainly in terms of dismantling the external walls and borders of mutual opposition that existed between bounded political communities. Giddens, however, believes that this macropolitical process is interconnected with microsociological issues.

In light of the last point, I argue that Giddens's approach to political development beyond the cold war order overcomes some of the conceptual problems in Thompson's view regarding the developmental process, which, as noted in the previous chapter, ignores the social dimension of the bipolar order. The merit of Giddens's approach is that his view of the political transition from the cold war does not privilege the changes taking place in state identities and interstate relations. Instead, he relates these changes to other general issues in social structure, including individual identity and the relationship between state and society. For Giddens, "the new kinship"—based on mutual recognition of individual rights, active communal trust, and tolerance of diversity—will be a key agent in making a general break from the era of politically bifurcated modernity, which appropriated individual freedom and collective solidarity into falsely contradictory, mutually exclusive categories in the context of two tautological systems of ideas in confrontation.[4]

Giddens's discussion of the social order after the cold war is based primarily on the specific historical context of western Europe. In his accounts, the positions of "left and right" appear mainly as those with respect to visions of modernity and schemes of social ordering. According to the Italian philosopher Norberto Bobbio, "left and right" are correlative positions, like two sides of a coin, in which "[the] existence of one presupposes the existence of the other, the only way to invalidate the adversary is to invalidate oneself."[5] This privileged experience of both left and right oppositions as integral parts of the body politic, however, may not extend to other historical realities of the cold war. In these other realities, the left and right were mutually exclusive positions rather than correlative ones in the sense that taking the position of one side meant denying the other side a raison d'être or even physically annihilating the other side from the political arena.

In the situation of an ideologically charged armed conflict or systemic state violence, left and right might not be merely about antithetical political distinction, but may rather form a question that has direct relevance to the preservation of human life and the protection of basic civil and human rights. Against this historical background of the cold war experienced as the "balance of terror" rather than as the "balance of power," moreover, family and kinship relations may take on a relevance in the general social transition from the bipolar order that is different from the relevance discussed by Giddens.

In April 2004, many places on Jeju Island at South Korea's southernmost maritime border were bustling in preparation for the annual commemoration of the 4.3 (April 3) Incident. The "incident" was the Communist-led uprising triggered on April 3, 1948, in protest against both the measures undertaken by the U.S. occupying forces to root out radical nationalist forces from postcolonial Korea and the policies of the U.S. administration to establish an independent anti-Communist state in the southern half of the Korean Peninsula.[6] But "the incident" also refers to the numerous atrocities that devastated the island following the uprising and that were caused by both brutal counterinsurgency military campaigns by the government and counteractions by the Communist partisans. This violent period was in many ways a prelude to the Korean War (1950–1953).

The 4.3 Incident has only recently become a publicly acknowledged historical reality among the islanders, in contrast to past decades during which the subject remained strictly taboo in public discourse.[7] The situation has changed since the beginning of the 1990s, and the islanders are nowadays free to hold death-anniversary rites for their relatives who were killed or who disappeared in the chaos of 1948. Every April the whole island turns briefly into a gigantic ritual community consisting of thousands of separate but simultaneous family or community-based events of death commemoration.

It is now a familiar experience for visitors to the island during the month of April to encounter a ritual occasion that the South Korean anthropologist Seong-Nae Kim calls "the lamentations of the dead."[8] Presided over by local specialists in shamanic ritual, these occasions welcome the spirits of those who suffered a tragic death, offer food and money to them, and later enact the clearing of obstacles from their path to the netherworld. A key element in this long and complex ritual procedure is when the invited spirits of the dead publicly tell of their grievous feelings and unfulfilled wishes through the ritual specialists' speeches and songs.

In a family-based performance, the lamentations of the dead begin typically with tearful narration of the moment of death and the horrors of violence and with expressions of indignation against the unjust killing. The ritual performance later moves on to the stage where the spirits, now somewhat calmed down, engage with the surroundings and the participants. They express gratitude to the family for caring about their grievous feelings, and this expression is often accompanied by conversations between the dead and the living, mediated by the ritual specialist, about the family's health or its financial prospects. The spirits' expression of concern about their living family is understood to mean that they have become free from their pain and sorrow, a process that the Koreans describe as a successful "disentanglement of grievous feelings."[9]

In a ritual on a wider scale that involves participants beyond the family circle, the lamentations may include the spirits' confused remarks about how they should relate to the strangers gathered for the occasion, which later typically develop into remarks of appreciation and gratitude. The spirits thank the participants for their demonstration of sympathy to the suffering of the dead, referring to those present who have no blood ties to the invited spirits and to whom therefore the participants have no ritual obligations. If the occasion is sponsored by an organization that has a particular moral or political objective, moreover, some of the invited spirits may proceed to make gestures of support for the organization. Thus, the spirit narration from the victims of a massacre may explicitly invoke concepts such as human rights if the ceremony is sponsored by a civil rights activist group or gender equality if the occasion is supported by a network of feminist activists. The lamentations of the dead closely engage with the diverse aspirations of the living.

Several observers of Korea's modern history have noted that South Korea's recent democratic transition and the vigorous popular political mobilization since the late 1980s that enabled this transition are not to be considered separate from the aesthetic power of ritualized lamentations.[10] The country's civil rights groups disseminate the voices of the victims of state violence as a way of mobilizing public awareness and support for their cause, and they employ forms of popular shamanic mortuary processions to materialize the dead victims' messages. The lamentations of the dead are a principal aesthetic instrument in Korea's "rituals of resistance."[11] The voices of the dead are considered both as evidence of political violence and as an appeal for collective actions for justice. Political activism in South Korea is so intimately tied to the ritual aesthetics of the lamenting spirits of the dead that even an academic forum may not preclude this aesthetic form. When the annual conference of Korean anthropologists chose the cultural legacy of the Korean War as its main theme in 1999, the conference included a grand shamanic spirit consolation rite dedicated to all the spirits of the tragic dead from the war era. In these situations, the history of mass war death is more than an object of academic debate or collective social action; it takes on a vital agency of a particular kind that influences the course of communicative actions about the past. In *Beyond Good and Evil*, Nietzsche wrote, "A thought comes when 'it' wants to and not when 'I' want; thus it is a falsification to say: the subject 'I' is the condition for the predicate 'think.' It thinks: but there is ... no immediate certainty that this 'it' is just that famous old 'I.' "[12] The remembering self's incomplete autonomy and the remembered other's incomplete passivity are thus implicit in any form of commemoration. The lamentation of the dead is a radical example of this intersubjective nature of remembrance.

The lamentations of the dead constitute an important aesthetic form in Korea's culture of political protest, and this relationship should be considered in the light of the nation's historical background—most notably, its experience of the cold war in the form of a violent civil war and the related political history of anticommunism. The proliferation of the spirit narration of violent war death in recent times relates to the repression of the history of mass death in past decades. Jeju Island's rich literary tradition testifies to this intimate relationship between the grievance-expressing spirits of the dead and the living people's inability to account for their memories.

Hyun Gil-Eon's novella *Our Grandfather*, for instance, tells of a village drama caused by a domestic crisis when a family's dying grandfather is briefly possessed by the spirit of his dead son.[13] The possessed grandfather suddenly recovers his physical strength and visits an old friend of the son in the village. During the 4.3 Incident, the villager had taken part in accusing the son of being a Communist sympathizer, thereby causing the son's summary execution at the hands of counterinsurgency forces. The grandfather-son demands that the villager publicly apologize for his wrongful accusation. The villager refuses to do so and instead gathers other villagers to help him in his plot to lynch the accuser. The return of the dead in this magical drama highlights the villagers' complicity in the unjust death of the son and the long imposition of silence about past grievances. The novella's climax comes when the son's ghost realizes the futility of his actions and turns silent, at which moment the family's grandfather passes away.

Just as the silence of the dead was a prime motif in Jeju's resistance literature under the anti-Communist political regime, so the publicly staged lamentations of the dead are now a principal element in the island's cultural activity since the democratic transition. Between the past and the present, a radical change has taken place in that the living are now no longer obliged to play deaf to what the dead have to say about history and historical justice. What is continuous in time, however, is that the understanding of political reality at the grassroots level is expressed through the communicability of historical experience between the living and the dead.

The rituals displaying the lamenting spirits of the dead have become public events in Jeju since the end of the 1980s and were part of the forceful nationwide civil activism in the 1990s. In Jeju, the activism was focused on the moral rehabilitation of those people killed by government troops and paramilitary forces in the 4.3 Incident as innocent civilian victims

rather than as Communist insurgents or their sympathizers. The rehabili-
tative initiatives have since spread to other parts of the country and resulted
in the legislation in 2000 of a special parliamentary inquiry into the 4.3
Incident. This inquiry was followed by legislation passed in May 2005
on the investigation of the incidents of Korean War civilian massacres in
general. These initiatives led in subsequent years to forensic excavations
of suspected sites of mass burial on a national scale, which were widely
reported in the Korean and foreign media, including the *New York Times*
and *Science Magazine*.[14] The 2005 legislation included an investigation of
the roundup and summary execution of alleged Communist sympathizers
in the early days of the Korean War, an estimated two to three hundred
thousand civilians.[15]

These dark chapters in modern Korean history were relegated to nonhistory under the previous military-ruled authoritarian regimes, which
defined anticommunism as one of the state's prime guidelines. Since the
early 1990s, in contrast, these hidden histories of mass death have become
one of the most heated and contested issues of public debate, and observers in fact regard their emergence into public discourse as a key feature
of Korea's political democratization. The province of Jeju is exemplary in
terms of this development. It initiated an institutional basis for a sustained
documentation program for the victims of the 4.3 atrocities and province-
wide memorial events; it continues to excavate suspected mass burial sites
and plans to preserve these sites as historical monuments. The provincial
authority seeks to develop these activities to promote the province's public
image as "an island of peace and human rights."

These laudable achievements by the Jeju islanders were made possible
through sustained community-based grassroots mobilization, activated
through a network of nongovernmental organizations and civil rights
associations, including an association made up of the victims' families.
For those active in the family association, the early 1990s was a time of
sea change. Before 1990, the association was officially called the Anticom-
munist Association of Families of the Jeju 4.3 Incident Victims, and, as
such, it was dominated by the families who were related to a particular
category of victims—local civil servants and paramilitary personnel killed
by the Communist militia. This category of victims, in current estimation,
amounts to 10 to 20 percent of the total civilian casualties in the incident.
The rest of those killed at this time were the victims of government troops,
police forces, or the paramilitary groups and previously were classified as

Communist subversives or "Red elements." Since 1990, the families of the majority of victims have gradually taken over the association, relegating the family representatives from the association's anti-Communist era to a minority status within the association. This change was a "quiet revolution," a result of a long, heated negotiation between different groups of family representatives.[16]

During the transition from a nominally anti-Communist organization to one that intends to "go beyond the blood-drenched division of left and right,"[17] the association confronted several crises: some family representatives with anti-Communist family backgrounds left the association, and some new representatives with opposite backgrounds refused to sit with the former. Conflicts still exist within the provincial-level association and at the village level. Nevertheless, the association's resolute stand that its objective is to account for all atrocities by and on both sides, Communist and anti-Communist, has been conducive to preventing the conflicts from reaching an implosive level. Equally important is the fact that many family representatives (particularly from the villages in the mountain region, who suffered both government troops' pacification activity and Communist partisan groups' retributive actions) had casualties on both sides of the conflict within their immediate circle of relatives. The democratization of the family association was a liberating experience for those on the majority side, including those who were members of it before the change. Under the old scheme, some people who were actually the victims of the state's anti-Communist terror had instead been registered as victims of the terror perpetrated by Communist insurgents. This labeling was in part a survival strategy for the victims' families, but it was also in part caused by the prevailing notion that the violent "Red hunt" campaign would not have happened had there been no "Red menace" in the first place. The "quiet revolution" of the 1990s meant that these families are now free to grieve publicly for their relatives killed in 1948 and to do so in a way that does not falsify the history of their mass death.

This development has affected the islanders' ritual commemorative activities and resulted in the rise of diverse, highly inventive new ancestral shrines across communities. One new shrine is the monument in the village of Hagui, in the northwestern district of Jeju Island, completed at the beginning of 2003. The monument consists of a tall white stone situated at the center, where it is written in Chinese characters, "Shrine of spirit consolation." On each side of the central stone stand two smaller black stones. The two black stones on the left (from the observer's perspective) commemorate the patriotic ancestors from the colonial era, from the era of the Korean War, and, later, from the military expedition to the Vietnam War.[18] The two black stones on the right side commemorate the hundreds of villagers who fell victim to the protracted anti-Communist counterinsurgency campaigns waged in Jeju before and during the Korean War.

The completion of this village ancestral shrine has a complex historical background. Two important factors were the division of the village into two separate administrative units in the 1920s, which the locals understand now to have been the Japanese colonial administration's divide-and-rule strategy at the time, and the distortion of this division during the chaos following the April 3 uprising. Hagui elders recall that the village's enforced administrative division developed into a perilous, painful situation at the height of the counterinsurgency military campaigns. The logic of these campaigns set people in one part of the village, labeled then as a "Red" hamlet, against those in the other part, who then tried to dissociate themselves from the former. After these campaigns were over, Hagui was considered a politically impure, subversive place in Jeju (just as the whole island of Jeju was known as a "Red" island to mainland South Koreans). Whether from one unit or the other, villagers seeking employment outside the village experienced discrimination because of their place of origin, which aggravated the existing grievances between the two administratively separated residential clusters. People of one side felt it unjust that they were blamed for what they believed the other side of the village was responsible for, and the latter found it hard to accept that they should endure accusations and discrimination even within a close community. It was against this background that, after the end of the Korean War in 1953, some Hagui villagers petitioned the local court to give new, separate names to the two village units. Their intentions were both to bury the stigmatizing name "Hagui" and to eradicate signs of affinity between the two units. After that, in official documents the village of Hagui became separated into Dong-gui and Gui-il, two invented names that no one liked but that were nevertheless necessary.

The historical trajectory of the cold war in this case resulted in a host of problems and conflicts in the villagers' everyday life. Not only did a number of them suffer from the extrajudicial system of collective responsibility, which prevented individuals with an allegedly politically impure family and genealogical background from taking employment in public sectors or from enjoying social mobility in general, but some of them also had to endure sharing the village's communal space with others who in their view were culpable for their predicament. This last point relates to the enduring wounds of the April 3 history within the community, caused by the villagers' complex experience of the counterinsurgency actions. Such wounds included, as shown in the novella *Our Grandfather*, being coerced into accusing neighbors of supporting the enemy. These hidden histories are occasionally brought into the open and become an explosive issue in the community, as when, for instance, two young lovers protested against their families' and the village elders' fierce opposition to their relationship without giving them any intelligible reason for doing so.

The details of these intimate histories of the April 3 violence and their contemporary traces remain a taboo subject in Hagui. The most frequently recalled and excitedly recited episodes are instead placed within the context of festive occasions. Some time before the villagers began to discuss the idea of a communal shrine, the two units of Hagui joined in an intervillage sporting event and feast organized periodically by the district authority. They had done so on many previous occasions, but this time the two soccer teams of Dong-gui and Gui-il managed to reach the semifinal, each hoping to win the championship. During the competition, the residents of Dong-gui cheered against the Gui-il team , supporting the Gui-il team's opponent from another village instead, and the residents of Gui-il did the same while watching a match involving the Dong-gui team. This experience was scandalous, according to the Hagui elders I spoke to, and they contrasted the divisive situation of the village with an opposite initiative taking place in the wider world (at the time of the intervillage feast, the idea of joint national representation in international sporting events was under discussion between South and North Korea). The village was going against the stream of history, the elders stated, and the village's shameful collective representation on the district football ground created the momentum for thinking about a communal project that would help to reunite people of Hagui.

In 1990, the village assembly in Dong-gui and its counterpart in Gui-il agreed to revive their original common name and to shake off their forty-year nominal separation since the Korean War. They established an informal committee responsible for the rapprochement and reintegration of the two villages. In 2000, the Committee for Village Development proposed to the village assemblies the idea of erecting a new ancestral shrine based on

111

The Democratic Family

donations from both villagers and nonresidents. The idea attracted broad support from the villagers, including those who had come to settle in the village in recent years. It also received strong endorsement from the village elders' associations; among the most enthusiastic supporters was the elder who, as a boy, had joined the partisan group and whose elder brother had been killed by the insurgents. Donations to the project came from many elderly widows who had lost their husbands to the counterinsurgency violence during the April 3 chaos as well as from a successful businessman settled in Seoul who was the eldest son of a villager killed by the insurgents. When the shrine was completed in 2003, the Hagui villagers held a grand opening ceremony in the presence of many visitors from elsewhere in the country and from overseas (many former Hagui residents live in Japan).

As noted earlier, the black memorial stones on the left side of the white stone are inscribed with the names of patriotic village ancestors, including one hundred names from colonial times, dozens of patriotic soldiers from the Korean War and the Vietnam War, and a dozen villagers killed by Communist partisans during the April 3 chaos. The twelve villagers killed by the insurgents belonged to the village's civil defense groups hastily organized by the South Korean counterinsurgency police forces. Most of them were not equipped with firearms and had been forcibly recruited to the role. One of the most difficult, contested questions during the three-year preparation of the shrine was whether to place the names of these twelve individuals on the side of patriotic ancestors or on the other side with the victims of tragic mass death. The one hundred patriotic ancestors from the colonial era include a few persons whose dedication to the cause of national liberation was combined with a commitment to socialist or Communist ideals. The merit of these so-called left-wing nationalists was not recognized before the 1990s.

The two stones on the right commemorate 303 village victims of the anti-Communist political terror during the 4.3 Incident and dedicate the following poetic message to the victims:

When we were still enjoying the happiness of being freed from the colonial misery,
When we were yet unaware of the pains to be brought by the Korean War,
The dark clouds of history came to us, whose origin we still do not know after all these years.

Then, many lives, so many lives, were broken and their bodies were
   discarded to the mountains, the fields and the sea.
Who can identify in this mass of broken lives a death that was not
   tragic?
Who can say in this mass of displaced souls that some souls have
   more grievance than others?
What about those who could not even cry for the dead?
Who will console their hearts that suffered all those years only for
   one reason that they belonged to the bodies who survived the
   destruction? . . .
For the past fifty years,
The dead and the living alike led an unnatural life as wandering
   souls, without a place to anchor to.
Only today,
Being older than our fathers and aged more than our mothers,
We are gathered together in this very place.
Let the heavens deal with the question of fate.
Let history deal with its own portion of culpability.
Our intention is not to dig again into the troubled grave of pain.
It is only to fulfill the obligation of the living to offer a shovel of fine
   soil to the grave.
It is because we hope some day the bleeding wounds may start to
   heal and we may see some sign of new life on them . . .
Looking back, we see that we all are victims.
Looking back, we see that we all are to forgive each other.
In this spirit, we are all together erecting this stone.
For the dead, may this stone help them finally close their eyes.
For us the living, may this stone help us finally hold hands
   together.[19]

The democratization of kinship relations lies at the heart of political development beyond the polarities of left and right. This is the case not only
in a relatively advanced capitalist society such as South Korea but also in
a transitory "postsocialist" context such as southern Vietnam, despite the
apparent economic and political-structural differences between the two
places. The end of the cold war as the dominant geopolitical paradigm of
the past century has made it possible, across these communities, for people to recount publicly their lived experience of the bipolar conflict without

fearing the consequences, and it has encouraged many scholars of cold war history to turn their attention from diplomatic history to social history (see chapter 7). These two developments are interconnected and together constitute the emerging field of social and cultural studies of the cold war.[20] In societies that experienced the cold war as civil war, recent research shows how such a violently divisive historical experience continues to influence interpersonal relations and communal lives.[21] The reconciliation of ideologically bifurcated genealogical backgrounds or ancestral heritages ("Red" Communists versus anti-Communist patriots; revolutionary patriots versus anti-Communist "counterrevolutionaries") is a critical issue for individuals and for the political community. In these societies, kinship identity is a significant site of memory for past political conflicts and can also be a locus of creative moral practices.

The experience of the cold war as a violent civil conflict resulted in political crisis in the moral community of kinship. It resulted in a situation that Hegel characterizes as the collision between "the law of kinship," which obliges the living to remember their dead kinsmen, and "the law of the state," which forbids citizens from commemorating those who died as enemies of the state.[22] The political crisis was basically about a representational crisis in social memory, in which a large number of family-ancestral identities were relegated to the status that I have elsewhere called "political ghosts," whose historical existence is felt in intimate social life but is traceless in public memory.[23]

Hegel explored the philosophical foundation of the modern state with regard to the ethical questions involved in the remembrance of the war dead, drawing in particular on the legend of Antigone from Sophocles' Theban plays. Antigone was torn between the obligation to bury her war-dead brothers according to "the divine law" of kinship, on one hand, and the reality of "the human law" of the state that prohibited her from giving burial to enemies of the city-state, on the other.[24] She buried one brother, who had died as the hero of the city, and then proceeded to do the same for the other brother, who had died as an enemy of the city. Her decision to bury the latter violated the edict of the city's ruler, and she was subsequently condemned to death as punishment. Invoking this powerful epic tragedy from ancient Greece, Hegel reasoned that the ethical foundation of the modern state is grounded in a dialectical resolution of the clashes between the law of the state and the law of kinship. For Judith Butler, the question concerns the fate of human relatedness wherein the individual is suspended between life and death and forced into the tortuous condition of having to choose between the norms of kinship and subjection to the state.[25]

The epic heroine Antigone met death by choosing family law over state law; in contrast, survival for many families in postwar South Korea meant following the state's law and thus sacrificing their right to grieve and seek consolation for the death of their kinsmen. The state's repression of the right to grieve was conditioned by the wider politics of the cold war. Emerging from colonial occupation as one of two divided and hostile states, the new state of South Korea found its legitimacy partly in the performance of anti-Communist containment. Its militant anti-Communist policies included making a pure ideological breed and containing impure traditional ties, and they engendered the concept of unlawful, nonnormative kinship. In this context, sharing blood relations with an individual believed to harbor sympathy for the opposite side of the bipolar world meant being an enemy of the political community as an extension of the individual. Left or right in this political history was not merely about bodies of ideas in dispute but also about determining the bodily existence of individuals and collectives. Likewise, the later process "beyond left and right" in this society has to deal with corporeal identity. If someone is an outlawed person because he shares blood ties with the state's object of containment, that person's claim to the lawful status of citizen involves legitimizing this relatedness. This legitimation is how kinship emerges as a locus of the decomposing bipolar world in the world's outposts and as a powerful force in the making of a tolerant, democratic society.

The democratization of kinship relations is a vital part of political development beyond the age of extremes—not merely because family and kinship are elementary constituents of civil society as Giddens describes it, but primarily because kinship has actually been a locus of radical, violent political conflicts in the past century, which, by extension, means that social actions taking place in this intimate sphere of life are important for shaping and envisioning the horizon beyond the politics of the cold war. Giddens writes: "If there is a crisis of liberal democracy today, it is not, as half a century ago, because it is threatened by hostile rivals, but on the contrary because it has no rivals. With the passing of the bipolar era, most states have no clear-cut enemies. States facing dangers rather than enemies have to look for sources of legitimacy different from those in the past."[26] He then proceeds to chart what he considers the new sources of state legitimacy, highlighting the political responsibility to foster an active civil society—that is, to further democratize democracy. In this light, Giddens paints the form of the democratic family as the backbone of an active civil society after the cold war. As a new social form, the democratic family is meant to reconcile individual choice and social solidarity and to achieve a dialectical resolution between individual freedom and collective unity.

Giddens's discussion of social and political developments "beyond left and right" is based on the assumption that the end of the cold war is coeval with the advance of globalization and that these developments constitute what he sees as "the emergence of a post-traditional social order."[27] By "left and right," Giddens refers on the one side to the tradition of Soviet-style communism and the Keynesian welfare state and on the other to the neoliberal economic ideology and conservative moral worldview (family values, sanctity of possessive individualism). His idea is that although these philosophic "left and right" positions were meaningful in the context of the East–West geographical setting, they are no longer viable guidelines for structuring social and international order in the globalizing, post–cold war world environment. Based on this idea, Giddens writes about two ways to conceptualize the process of depolarization—through either fragmentation or diversification. The fragmentation perspective projects a post–cold war world composed of separate communities holding diverse truths and fundamentalist beliefs, each of which negates all other communities' truth claims; the diversification perspective envisages a strengthening of cosmopolitan solidarity among the separate communities, which acknowledge their mutual differences but do not relegate them to fundamental traits unavailable to dialogic imagination and communicative action.[28] Giddens blames Nietzsche in this regard for allegedly sowing the seeds of the fragmentation perspective in modern social thought and Hegel for advancing a teleological conception of history, which he believes was sublimated in the cold war modernity.[29] According to Giddens's history of left and right, Hegelian historicism and Nietzschean perspectivism are the notable philosophic ills to which nations and communities should be alert when pursuing a progression away from the age of extremes toward a relationally cosmopolitan and structurally democratic political and social order.

In Giddens's scheme, the social form of kinship has no direct association with the oppositions of left and right. Its role in societal development beyond the cold war is mediated by the changing identity of the state and the related reconfiguration of its relationship to the civil society. The end of the cold war, for Giddens, affects the state primarily in the sense that the state can no longer base its legitimacy on its role in safeguarding the political community against external threats only. The displacement of the state from the dualist geopolitical structure forces it to build an alternative legitimacy in an active, constructive engagement with the civil society. The picture essentially shows the substitution of a constructive internal relationship between state and society for a hostile external relationship with other states in a battle for the moral existence of the state. The idea of the "democratic family" enters this picture as a constitutive element of the civil society—that is, as an important site of post–cold war state politics.

In the composition of "new kinship" presented by Giddens, however, there is little space for kinship practices that rise from the background of a violent modern history, such as Jeju's. His account of "right and left" unfolds as if this political antithesis was principally an issue of academic paradigms or parliamentarian organizations, without mass human suffering and displacement. If the end of the cold war is at once an age of globalization, as Giddens notes, and if the "third-way" vision speaks of the morality and politics of this age, it is puzzling why this vision, claiming to speak for the global age, draws exclusively on the political history of the "long peace" of Europe's cold war and ignores the cold war's diverse ramifications across many places.[30]

Looking at the wider context, we cannot think of the history of right and left without thinking of the history of mass death. Both right and left were part of anticolonial nationalism, signifying different routes toward the ideal of national liberation and self-determination. In the ensuing bipolar era, the ideas of right and left transformed into the ideology of civil strife and war, in which achieving national unity became equivalent to annihilating one or the other side from the body politic. In this context, the political history of right and left is not to be considered separately from the history of human lives and social institutions torn by the distinction, nor is "the new kinship" after the cold war to be separated from the memory of the dead ruins of this history. Family relations are important vectors in understanding the decomposition of the bipolar world—not merely because they are an elementary constituent of civil society, as Giddens believes, but also because they were actually a vital aspect of political control and ideological oppression during the cold war. With this historical background in mind, it is misleading to define the state in the post–cold war world merely as an entity without external enemies. Rather, we have to think of it, as Hegel did, as an entity that has to deal with internal hostilities and reconcile with society, a significant part of which it condemned as unlawful. Events in Jeju since the early 1990s have taken place along this hopeful trajectory of reconciliation, and the empowerment of the right to remember and console the dead has been a central element in this important social progress beyond the left and right.

PART 3

6

RETHINKING POSTCOLONIAL HISTORY

In chapter 1, I argued that it is misleading to think of the cold war as a unitary historical reality. The cold war took diverse forms across territories, and the idea that it was an "imaginary war" between blocs of states along a clearly defined border speaks of a particular form and experience of the global conflict. The subsequent chapters addressed the partiality of this definition of the cold war by placing it against the experience of the global conflict as a real war. I reflected on the duplicity of real and imaginary violence in the history of the cold war, and, in the same light, on the presence or absence of mass human death and suffering in the collective memory of the cold war. I then proceeded to examine how in societies that experienced the cold war as a total war or other forms of organized violence, the history of political bipolarization is analytically inseparable from the social memory of mass death and the morality of death remembrance. Relating the events of mass death to the history of the cold war may make the moniker *cold war* appear somewhat odd and contradictory, yet I argued that confronting this semantic contradiction is a necessary step toward understanding the cold war from a genuinely global perspective—that is, the cold war as a globally shared but at the same time locally distinct experience.

The problem, however, is that the imaginary war, being an expression of a locally specific cold war experience, claims to be the defining paradigm for the global cold war. This confusion of historical particularity for universal history, according to Dipesh Chakrabarty, displaces a particular thought about history from its place of origin and empowers it as a universal currency of thought whose relevance is supposed to encompass all places.[1] With this in mind, I discussed a set of conceptual confusions in the reasoning about the momentousness of "the end of the cold war" and raised objections to the tendency in contemporary social science scholarship to take "the end" as a given universal chronological condition rather than as a complexity of locally specific, emergent realities. The notion of a universal temporal rupture and the related lack of analytical engagement with the diverse decomposing processes of the cold war are in large measure connected to the prevailing assumption that the cold war was primarily about a balance of power between the superpower states. Marilyn Young and Allen Hunter write: "The usual chronology and geography of the Cold War as an East–West conflict began with the end of World War II and ended in 1989. That interpretation does not provide a way of understanding decolonization, national liberation, social revolution and civil war, development and underdevelopment, and the racial and ethnic conflict seemingly endemic to the international system that followed the Cold War. . . . Every aspect of the terms 'Cold War' and 'globalization' are open to question, starting with their assumed spatial and temporal dimensions, origins, objectives, and even protagonists."[2]

In the same spirit, I tried to unsettle the Eurocentric view of the cold war as an imaginary war and the state-centric approach to its history as mainly a diplomatic history. In their stead, I suggested a conception of the cold war as a global conflict, in which the notion of the global is not bound by the centrality of Western experience or abstracted to the extent that it makes no analytical links with local histories and social processes.

In order to set the discourse of the cold war free from this limiting paradigm, it was necessary to highlight the fusion between the process of decolonization and the bipolarization of politics, for it is specifically on this historical horizon that we witness the bipolar conflicts taking on violent forms, permeating the order of social life as well as shaping that of diplomatic relations. This effort to move away from the center/periphery conception of history corresponds closely to recent initiatives in colonial history and postcolonial criticism scholarship to deal with the differences and similarities between European history and the histories of Europe's former colonies in the conception of political modernity. This chapter reviews some of these initiatives and assesses what insights they offer to cold war history. It also examines why postcolonial scholarship to date has not engaged seriously with cold war historiography and what benefits might accrue if it were to do so. If postcolonial and cold war studies are thematically interrelated, as I noted earlier on several occasions, it is necessary to think of a way to bring these two fields of inquiry into a more intimate, constructive dialogue.

In his seminal book *Provincializing Europe*, Chakrabarty confronts a set of critical issues in the cultural history of colonialism. Focusing on the literature of Bengali nationalism under British rule, he probes the tortuous terrain of political thought in the colonial society, in which the pursuit of the vision of a liberated modern polity confined those who pursued the ideal within the very system of ideas and values from which they struggled to be free. Calling this situation "the politics of historicism," he explores how the colonization of indigenous thought by historicism is as significant in the historiography of colonialism as the exploitation of indigenous labor and resources. Chakrabarty advocates "getting beyond Eurocentric histories" and emphasizes the need to dislocate the universal, linear, and evolutionist conception of time that he argues constitutes the core of these histories.

For this purpose, Chakrabarty introduces the Bengali idea of nationhood and contrasts it to the formulations of national identity developed in the European political thought of the eighteenth and nineteenth centuries. This political thought was grounded in the rise of the bourgeoisie as a distinctive social category, from which came John Locke's idea of fraternity among property-holding individuals as the foundation of modern democratic polity. According to Chakrabarty, the Lockean notion of national brotherhood as a contractual relationship among autonomous, self-interested individuals does not extend to the ideal of brotherhood advanced by the early Bengali nationalist intellectuals under British rule. He describes how Bengali understanding of political brotherhood is anchored in the traditional notion of patrilineage called *kula*, which situates a person's identity in a vertical line of male descent and under the unchallenged sanctity of patriarchal authority. The Lockean idea of the nation as a brotherhood of men assumes that the constitutive elements of this fraternity, which are men, are freed from the paternal authority through their possession of private property: "Fraternity in the Lockean schema was predicated on the emergence of private property and the political death of parental/paternal authority." By contrast, according to Chakrabarty, "[Private property] was never stipulated as a requirement in Bengali nationalist thought that the political authority of the father be destroyed before the brothers' compact could come into being. . . . Fraternity in Bengali nationalism was thought of as representing a natural rather than contractual solidarity of brotherhood. European bourgeois assumptions regarding autonomous personhood based on self-interest, contract, and private property were subordinated in Bengal to this idea of 'natural' brotherhood."[3]

In this widely acclaimed, exciting project to pluralize modern history and in related efforts to "provincialize" European experience and thought regarding political modernity, Chakrabarty also includes a discussion of religious symbols. He shows how the Bengali vision of the postcolonial nation-state was in part constituted by traditional cultural imaginaries about ancestors (and other important religious entities, such the Hindu goddess Lakshmi). Presenting a pluralistic picture of political modernity, Chakrabarty simultaneously intends to free the diversity in the project of modernity from the historicist tendency to order the differences in social formation according to an evolutionary temporal scheme in which the diversity is translated into stages in the hierarchical ladder of historical progression, where "Indians, Africans, and other 'rude' nations" are represented as lacking the property of modernity and consigned "to an imaginary waiting room of history."[4]

Chakrabarty considers Locke and Karl Marx as two sublime intellectual examples of European historicism, and he introduces Martin Heidegger as a counterexample in Western thought and a radical alternative to the paradigm of global historical time. Focusing sharply on the literature about the origins of modern nationalist ideology, Partha Chatterjee similarly confronts what he considers the tendency in existing theories of nationalism to understate the differences between nationalist imaginations in European history and the forms of anticolonial nationalism in Asia and Africa.[5] Challenging Benedict Anderson's classical work on the subject of "linguistic nationalism," which focuses on the role of printing technology and mass literacy in disseminating the political ideas of national liberation,[6] Chatterjee highlights the "spiritual" domains of nationalism rather than the "material" culture of nationalism such as the technology of printing.

Chatterjee argues that in colonial India, the British imperial power dominated the "outer" material spheres of life but left the spiritual, "inner" domains of national culture largely undisturbed, considering them outside the business of state control. It is in this relatively uncolonized domain of life, according to Chatterjee, that the early nationalist sentiments rose in India. Early Indian nationalists advanced the inner domain as the emblem of the nation's spiritual purity and set out to formulate their political agenda in terms of protecting their inner purity from Western influence. The organization of family life and the social position of women constituted the core of the inner spirit of national culture for these nationalists, who resisted the colonial state's occasional attempts to legislate reform measures in this sphere, asserting that "only the nation itself could have the right to intervene in such an essential aspect of its cultural identity."[7] In advancing this idea of spiritual nationalism, Chatterjee explains that his intention is to present the history of Indian nationalism as an authentic experience and as other than an emulation of the European historical invention of nationalism. He writes: "If nationalisms in the rest of the world have to choose their imagined community from certain 'modular' forms already made available to them by Europe and the Americas, what do they have left to imagine? History, it would seem, has decreed that we in the postcolonial world shall only be perpetual consumers of modernity. Europe and the Americas, the only true subjects of history, have thought out on our behalf not only the script of colonial enlightenment and exploitation but also that of our anticolonial resistance and postcolonial misery. Even our imaginations must remain forever colonized."[8]

Chakrabarty and Chatterjee confront the tortuous logic of decolonization: postcolonial modernity was envisioned in the colonies in terms of the political modernity learned from Europe, which made resistance to colonial domination an act of emulating the dominator rather than an authentic, creative act. They propose that the project to "provincialize" the European heritage of political modernity is a necessary step for pluralizing modernity, which is in turn an indispensable step in decolonizing the imagination. Making one's own political history distinct from the theoretical premises of historical development in European thought, in other words, is an act of obtaining freedom from colonialism in thought.

This pluralist orientation (or Heideggerean turn, according to Chakrabarty) in the historiography of colonialism is in part an epiphenomenon of the end of the cold war as a geopolitical order. Jorge Klor de Alva notes: "Numerous progressive scholars, many in search of redemptive agendas to fill the vacuum left by the collapse of Marxist programs, have been busily attempting to discover the cultural integrity and subversive presence of the oppressed in both Western narratives of the 'colonial' enterprise and in the indigenous responses or, for those working on topics closer to our time, in the record of the confrontations between 'peoples of color' and the dominant 'white' communities."[9]

Chakrabarty is much more sympathetic to Marx than to Locke when he outlines a history of modern European political thought, whereas in discussing Bengali historiography he tries to dislocate both Marxian and Lockean philosophical heritage from Bengali political history, defining them both as descendents and proponents of the totalizing European historicist tradition. He highlights the prominence of *kula* and other local particularities in the formation of the Bengali nationalist movement, basing this emphasis on the awareness that after the cold war the Marxian critical tradition of political thought is no longer an alternative to the liberal tradition and on the related idea that both the Lockean and the Marxian traditions share the common genealogy of knowledge that he calls "Western historicism." As is partly the case with Giddens's formulation of sociological knowledge "beyond left and right" (see chapter 5), Chakrabarty's and others' effort in colonial historiography to move beyond both Marxist and liberal political thought is intelligible only in the context of the breakdown of the bipolar geopolitical order and of the crisis in political theory that this breakdown caused.

The trend to transcend the left and right streams of thought can also be observed in wider scholarship. As noted earlier, Zaki Laïdi describes "the crisis of meaning in international politics" in terms of the decline of credibility, after the cold war, in both of the contending ideologies of historical progress that constituted the bipolarized world order.[10] Drawing upon insights from Walter Benjamin, Susan Buck-Morss argues that each of the mutually hostile twins of modernity, capitalism and socialism, built a "dreamworld" of mass utopia, mobilizing collective forces to a concerted and guided action toward the production of progress.[11] For Buck-Morss, the utopia of mass-commodity consumption in the United States and that of miraculous industrial production in the Soviet Union shared the same politics of value and the same infatuation with dramatizing that value. Thus, in her analysis, both American Hollywood film stars and Soviet labor heroes were expressions of a shared obsession about the spectacle of utopia. Perhaps most prominent on this matter is the interest in human rights claims. As Lynn Hunt powerfully establishes, the ideas of human rights, although described as the innate property of human nature in the 1948

Universal Declaration of Human Rights, are rooted in history and particularly in the history of revolutions. The contemporary semantics of human
rights, according to Hunt, is inseparable from the radical exposition of
Enlightenment universalism in the American and French revolutions of
1776 and 1789. All other social revolutions of modern times, including the
Russian Revolution of 1917, according to Hunt, made claims for the realization of universal suffrage and are thus actually part of the history of the
idea of human rights as we know of it.[12] The Universal Declaration defines
human rights as "inalienable rights of all members of the human family,"
yet all revolutionary claims for universal rights (whether these claims were
liberal, national, or socialist) restricted the entitlement to these rights to a
certain sector of human society and excluded others. Societies across East
and West (in the geography of the cold war) or across West and non-West
(in the atlas of colonialism) suffered from the disparity between the ideal
and the reality of human rights, and it is in part against this common,
universal historical background of violation of rights, as Marilyn Young
notes, that the concept of human rights takes on central importance in
contemporary politics.[13] The efforts to move beyond right and left, therefore, have taken on many different forms. Some of these efforts attempt
to further universalize existing claims for universality (as in human rights
discourse), whereas others move to localize and "provincialize" traditional
universality-claiming thoughts. The coexistence of these localizing and
globalizing forces, as Young points out, is one of the main paradoxes in
contemporary political thought.[14]

If we return here to Chakrabarty's postcolonial project and recall what
was discussed earlier in this chapter, however, we will notice that there
is something not quite viable in this project to provincialize the Western
experience and thought of political modernity. The idea of postcolonial
experience proposed by Chakrabarty and Chatterjee is based on a conceptual separation of colonialism into two domains, an institutional order and
a cultural schema, and on the related premise that the latter, colonialism
as culture, continues after the achievement of political self-rule and after
the end of colonialism as an institutional order. They conceptualize the
prefix *post-* in *postcolonial* as having a potent symbolic vitality in the present regarding the past experience of the actually existing colonialism. In
this rendering of historically spectral but experientially real continuity
of colonial imaginaries, however, it is somewhat astonishing to see that
their critical reflection on the postcolonial culture of colonialism makes no

analytical associations with the political history of the cold war, which apparently coincides with the suggested historical change of colonialism from an institutional structure to a cultural form.

The idea of postcolonial experience suggested by these scholars projects the historical epoch from the end of World War II to the present as an uninterrupted struggle to be free from the cultural and mental effect of colonialism after the colonies were physically freed in the 1950s and 1960s from the formal institutional grid of colonial subjugation. This conceptual scheme does not consider the momentous shift in global power relations from the colonial to the bipolar during this period or the resultant complication in nation building in the postcolonial world. The scheme is oblivious to the radical political bipolarization of postcolonial processes and treats the questions of right and left primarily in terms of an intellectual exercise that has no relevance to the structure of social life and the contours of collective identity.

In this trajectory beyond the history of left and right, as in Giddens's work on the history of left and right in European political history, we see the traces of neither violent political struggle nor mass human suffering. The idea of fraternity is presented in either the scheme of Western individualism or that of indigenous collective kinship ideology. There are no traces of the human kinship and brotherhood that were brought to bear in fratricidal war during the global cold war or stories of kinship's contemporary struggle to move beyond the violent history of extreme right and left. The bifurcation of Lockean and Marxian historicisms are rendered as forces external to the unity and authenticity of indigenous lineage and fraternity, but it was in this domain of intimate relatedness, as we saw in the previous two chapters, that people experienced the clash between militant visions of left and right as naked violence and systemic political coercion.

Chatterjee regrets that "the leaders of the African struggles against colonialism and racism had spoiled their records by becoming heads of corrupt, fractious, and often brutal regimes; Gandhi had been appropriated by such marginal cults as pacifism and vegetarianism; and even Ho Chi Minh in his moment of glory was caught in the unyielding polarities of the Cold War. Nothing, it would seem, was left in the legacy of nationalism to make people in the Western world feel good about it."[15] In this impassioned observation, however, we do not see the immense complications in the decolonization of African nations caused by the U.S. and Soviet interventions in the process as they pursued their ambitions for "the empire of liberty" or "the empire of justice," respectively.[16]

Chatterjee conceptualizes the cold war merely in terms of external constraints against seemingly autonomous postcolonial struggles, oblivious to the fact that nationalist struggles in the postcolonial world were in fact constitutive of the development of the patterns of superpower competition. It is true that postcolonial Vietnam was entangled in the escalating polarization of global politics, yet the cold war as a global conflict developed in the way we know of it now precisely because there were sustained, formidable challenges from the decolonizing nations, including the Vietnamese, to the imposed hegemonic designs of global modernity.

The scholarship of postcolonial criticism understands the construction of colonial rule as a complex process that dominated the colony's culture, the political imaginations of its intellectuals, as well as its political structure and economic material basis. Based on this notion, postcolonial criticism advances decolonization as a multivariate process that involves "cultural decolonization," "intellectual decolonization," and "decolonization of imagination," not merely the momentum of "political decolonization" (national independence) and the process of "economic decolonization" (growth and development).[17] The ways to decolonize the imagination are understood varyingly among scholars. The institutional aspect of decolonization empowers nationalism and nativism, according to Jan Pieterse and Bhikhu Parekh; a genuine postcolonial critique, therefore, according to them, must confront nativist ideologies critically, which are in part a product of the colonial rule (in the sense of being a mimetic practice of European nationalism and racial exclusion).[18] Chatterjee, however, finds this critique of nativism problematic and sets out to chart an authentic, uncolonized, "inner" domain of nationalist imagination. Chakrabarty similarly establishes an authentic domain with the Bengali notion of *kula* and contrasts this indigenous lineage paradigm of personhood and political brotherhood to the individuated, property-based notion of fraternity that constitutes European political modernity. In these imaginative efforts to authenticate postcolonial modernity and to dethrone the universality of Europe's colonizing idea of modernity, it is confounding to see how postcolonial criticism relegates the history of bipolar modernity to an analytical margin, thereby dehistoricizing the object of the inquiry it calls "postcolonial history."

The externalization of bipolar history from both colonial and postcolonial history not only distorts the theoretical contours of postcolonial criticism but also results in a misrepresentation of the main object of the critique. In Chakrabarty's otherwise forceful rendering of European ideas of political modernity and their historical particularity, there are no traces of a modern Europe as we know of it—that is, the Europe that, after experiencing a catastrophic war, was divided into mutually hostile forces in an undeclared ideological war. His depiction of Europe's political modernity focuses on its traditional, imperial past with no consideration of its recent history of political fragmentation and bifurcation. Melvyn Leffler writes in his most recent work on the cold war Europe:

> Almost forty million Europeans had perished during [World War II], but the suffering did not end when the gun fell silent. The anguish, the turmoil, the hunger, the upheaval, were just beginning for millions and millions. As Europeans yearned for a better future, communism and communists competed vigorously for their allegiance, especially in France and Italy. . . . For Stalin, opportunity beckoned in Western Europe; for Truman there was peril—in the prospect not that Soviet armies would march to the Atlantic but that demoralized peoples would choose alternative ways of organizing their societies.[19]

Europe in the second half of the twentieth century was not the same entity as the Europe we know from colonial history, and the transition from one to the other was coincidental with some of the most violent events experienced in Asia and Africa. Whereas decolonization and political bipolarization were concurrent processes in much of the non-Western world and the violent postcolonial struggles took place within the context of the cold war, the scholarship of postcolonial criticism relegates the political history of the cold war to an analytical void. As a result, it fails to place in proper historical context both its critical aim of cultural decolonization and the main object of its cultural criticism—European political modernity.

Chakrabarty introduces "translation" as the principal element of postcolonial criticism. According to him, understanding Bengali history means not simply staging it according to the developmental logic of European historicism. Rather, it requires attending to the indigenous logic and language of development and, on this basis, engaging critically with the differences between this local language and the theoretical, universalizing language of European origin.[20] Homi Bhabha also presents *translation* as a key word for the postcolonial intellectual project. Like Chakrabarty, Bhabha conceptualizes translation as a communicative process between local histories and the universality-claiming theoretical language of European modernity. Furthermore, he associates the practice of cultural translation with what he calls "the transnational dimension," by which he refers to the condition of "migration, diaspora, displacement, relocation," conceptualized in contrast to the "natural(ized), unifying discourse of 'nation,' 'peoples,' or authentic 'folk' tradition, those embedded myths of culture's particularity."[21] These transnational conditions and "translational" practices constitute "the location of culture" in the globalizing contemporaneous time, according to Bhabha, and, as such, they call for the relocation of the culture concept from a set of taken-for-granted values to the process of mixing different sets of normative values. A transnational social life, he concludes, is a translational cultural life.

Bhabha focuses on what he calls liminal forms of existence that go beyond the traditional cultural polarities of self and other, East and West. He also sees transnational migration as the material condition of the rising translational cultural forms and the migrants who lead "border lives" or "unhomely lives" away from their place of birth as the main agents for the making of these forms. He writes: "What is theoretically innovative, and politically crucial, is the need to think beyond narratives of originary and initial subjectivities and to focus on those moments or processes that are produced in the articulation of cultural differences. These 'in-between' spaces provide the terrain for elaborating strategies of selfhood—singular or communal—that initiate new signs of identity, and innovative sites of collaboration, and contestation, in the act of defining the idea of society itself."[22] Bhabha calls this nonoriginary, in-between subjectivity a "hybrid identity" and defines it as a subaltern agent that rises in the interstices of colonialism's disciplinary functions. "The margin of hybridity" is where cultural differences "contingently touch," according to him, and as such it "resists the binary opposition of racial and cultural groups [as] homogenous polarized political consciousness."[23]

Several observers have identified an overt textualism in this trend in postcolonial theory and an excessive reliance on the metaphor of translation.[24] For the purpose of my discussion, the problem with the theoretical posturing lies not in rendering movements across bounded cultural entities as translations, but in the attempt to understand these movements across what I earlier called the "colonial color line" without taking into consideration the intertwining of this border with a new, ideologically constituted frontier in the bipolarized, bipolarizing postcolonial history.

Christina Klein argues that the transnational migrations of the past century were intimately connected to the geopolitics of the cold war, and she explores how their connectedness in part took the form of transcending racial and cultural differences through an invention of particular kinship practices. Focusing on the policy documents and middlebrow mass-educational materials of the mid-twentieth-century United States, Klein traces in this light how the adoption of orphaned children from the troubled regions of Asia developed into a powerful geopolitical practice. Advancing the political objective to contain communism globally, she argues, U.S. policymakers were worried that America's leadership in this moral crusade lacked a positive substantive quality. Anticommunism was not an ideology with an authentic vision; liberal individualism and benevolent capitalism were hard to sell to the Asian populations who associated such ideologies with European colonialism. A way had to be found, Klein explains, to mobilize unconnected groups of people—Asians who were wary of Western imperialism and Americans who were wary of expensive overseas commitment—to a common struggle against communism. The solution was the idiom of kinship, which rendered the problem of America's political obligation to Asia as a problem of family.[25] With this background, the prominent U.S. educational media began to disseminate the extension of kinship relations as a prime civic obligation of Americans in the global struggle against communism.

In the 1950s, American families were encouraged to adopt homeless children in Calcutta and Bombay, the abandoned "GI babies" in Japan, the refugees from Communist East Germany, and war orphans in Korea. The media propagated the idea that these hungry children of the world were more dangerous to Americans than the Soviet atom bomb, that unless they were brought into the paternal care of the benign American power, they would become "the most powerful weapon in the hands of the communists." Klein's careful analysis of this period presents the practice of adoptive kinship as a two-way process of learning: the American "parents" learned about the misery and inhumanity caused by communism in the wide world, and the adopted Asian "children" learned about "the material abundance and personal generosity that the free world offered." The political ethos of adoptive parental love, according to Klein, was meant to distinguish America's cold war civilizing mission from European nations' imperial practices as well as to mobilize the American public to the aggressive battle against communism by letting them participate in this geopolitical activity in their familiar, intimate domains of family norms and religious charity. Klein concludes that through this development of cold war political kinship, the horizon of transnational ties and mass immigration began to change dramatically in American society, which had restricted immigration from Asia on racial grounds since 1875.[26]

If Chakrabarty is oblivious to the fragmented, broken mid-twentieth-century Europe in his depiction of European political modernity, Bhabha's understanding of human diasporas and cultural dislocations is equally oblivious to the aforementioned history of mass human displacement during the construction of the bipolar world. Large-scale human displacement was common in the mid–twentieth century, and it occurred not only in Asia but also in large parts of Europe under the circumstances, although such displacements varied locally, relating to the onslaught of cold war conflict. In the Soviet Union, entire populations of several ethnic groups were forcibly relocated from one end of the Eurasian continent to the other. A large population of eastern and central Europeans moved to the West, and some of these immigrant communities have exercised considerable influence, after the fall of the Berlin Wall, in political developments in their native countries. In the decolonizing world, some western European nations' anachronistic attempts to reclaim their colonial territories under the pretext of fighting communism generated a whirlwind of social crisis in which displacement became a generalized experience of the population, and the dislocation of human lives was exacerbated in the ensuing era when nationalist struggle evolved to full-scale civil war with prolific international intervention.

The transnational migrants of the past century often brought troubling questions of political identity from one home to another rather than taking themselves out of the enclosed boundary of the political community to a translational cultural space. Gesèle Bousquet describes how the Parisian Vietnamese community in the 1980s was divided between the pro-Hanoi and anti-Communist factions. Rooted in the history of political and military conflicts in their homeland, these factional divisions were constitutive of the identity of the overseas Vietnamese, crosscutting their awareness as an ethnic minority in France. The generation of immigrants who arrived in France before 1975 tended to be sympathetic to the unified Vietnam and defined themselves as "liberals," but they appeared to be "Communists" to some of the new immigrants who arrived in France after 1975 as war refugees. Political division affected family relations and kin networks among the Parisian Vietnamese. It was not uncommon for the members of a single family to support different factions, and kinsmen who had contrary political views avoided one another. Bousquet goes on to describe how bipolar politics within the Parisian Vietnamese community affected the community's ethnic identity in relation to wider French society.[27]

Sonia Ryang's study of Koreans in Japan demonstrates similar predicaments of a minority community seized by both racial discrimination and political polarization.[28] The Korean community in Japan has been divided between the pro–North Korea group and the group who has maintained close ties with South Korea. This divided loyalty is strong among members of the older generation, whereas their children, in particular those from the pro-North group, are torn between familial obligation to share their parents' loyalty and their individual need to integrate into Japanese society, which is generally hostile to North Korea. Ryang is at pains to draw an optimistic picture for these children, one that goes beyond the double grid of the racial inequality of colonial origin and the political bifurcation of the postcolonial era.

Postcolonial history and bipolar history can crosscut a traditional village as well as a migrant community. I began reading about cold war history when, while trying to write about a village in central Vietnam, I realized that I could not write the village history without contextualizing it in global history. My historical research led me to learn about North Africa as well as about French colonialism in Indochina after I heard the villagers tell of their wartime experience and their memories of colonial conscripts from Algeria and Morocco. My research also came to involve not only U.S. foreign policy but also a political history of South Korea as I learned that the village had lost many lives to the Vietnam War pacification activity by America's close East Asian ally in the transnational struggle against communism. The village history project also led me to learn about World War II in Europe after some elderly villagers told me about their experience there. These villagers were among the thousands of Vietnamese conscripted by the French colonial authority in the 1930s to work in the munitions factory in a French city, and some of them later fought against the Germans as part of the French resistance. Having contributed to France's vital economy and shared its humiliation of foreign occupation, these laborer soldiers were shipped back to Vietnam soon after World War II was over. Most of the returnees perished in the ensuing chaos of war between the French and the Vietnamese resistance forces, and those who survived later had problems with the Vietnamese revolutionary authority because of their past "collaboration" with imperial France. Meanwhile, some of the few labor soldiers who managed to stay in France after World War II turned into what Bousquet might call "pro-Hanoi" activists and, alongside French activists, campaigned against the Vietnam War.

The village's modern history implicated a world history, and the transition from the colonial to the bipolar order was central to the village's global historical experience. This example and the others given here show the complicated intertwining of colonial and bipolar history in the postcolonial experience of dislocation and transmigration. Why, then, is bipolar history excluded from postcolonial historical criticism? How should we make sense of the removal of this history from the contemporary critique of imperial culture, the state, nationalism, and political modernity—all of which are unthinkable, from the perspective of the present, without considering the dislocation of global power from Europe after World War II? What is this thing called "the postcolonial process" if it is not anchored in the transformation of the global order from an imperial to a bipolar form, through which we have come to inhabit the so-called globalizing world?

Some answers may be found in the regional focus taken in many works of postcolonial criticism, which address, in the main, the experience of British rule in South Asia. P. R. Kumaraswamy argues that South Asia as a region "was not actively involved in cold war power politics." He points out that the main political tensions in South Asia were of an ethnic and religious nature, rooted in colonial experience and exacerbated by inadequate policies of the postcolonial states. However, Kumaraswamy also presents a set of issues that contradicts his claim regarding the relative irrelevance of the cold war in South Asia. For example, he describes how India and Pakistan developed close ties with Moscow and Washington, respectively, for security reasons and how their ongoing mutual hostilities evolved into a nuclear crisis in the 1990s, thus emulating the global-level geopolitics of deterrence at a regional level. Kumaraswamy writes: "The post-war ideological division of Europe had little relevance for South Asia [but rivalry] between India and Pakistan brought the region closer to rival blocs."[29]

Kumaraswamy also points out that the political communities of South Asia led or had active interests in the Non-Aligned Movement (NAM), developed during the cold war as an alternative to the dual bloc system of international relations.[30] It is probably with tacit reference to these particular historical situations in South Asia during the cold war that Bhabha is able to say: "Postcolonial criticism bears witness to the unequal and uneven forces of cultural representation involved in the contest for political and social authority within the modern world order. Postcolonial perspectives emerge from the colonial testimony of Third World countries and the discourses of 'minorities' within the geopolitical divisions of East and West, North and South."[31] I do not know what Bhabha means by the position of minorities within the division of North and South, but it seems clear that the equivalent status within the division of East and West is the nonpositioning in bipolar terms, such as that once advocated by the NAM. The NAM was a forum of newly independent postcolonial nations that attempted to create an independent global force separate from the Western industrial powers (referred to as the First World) and the Communist bloc (the Second World) through the stated objective of nonalignment with the United States or the Soviet Union. India played a pivotal role in founding the movement in 1961, together with Yugoslavia, Egypt, and Indonesia. In its early days, the NAM focused on issues of political independence, the eradication of poverty and economic development, and opposition to colonialism and neocolonialism (i.e., dependence on cold war superpowers). In the 1960s and 1970s, "NAM" was an almost equivalent term for the Third World and considered to represent the voice of the postcolonial nations in the global arena. Bhabha's comment indicates that "the postcolonial perspective" derives in significant measure from this important tradition of political neutrality in the geopolitics of the cold war.

However, the problem is that the idea of "the postcolonial" that rests on the spirit of nonalignment within the bipolar structure of global power is limited in accounting for actual postcolonial histories. In the latter, as Bhabha himself notes, the principle of political nonalignment was the discourse of "minorities," which implies that the majority of postcolonial states were obliged, in one way or another, to participate in bipolar politics. India was no exception on this matter, as Kumaraswamy indicates; otherwise, how can we explain the present-day communal ritual festivities taking place in northern India in which participants carry mock nuclear warheads as part of their religious procession? The culture of the cold war, as I explore in the next chapter, may manifest itself in diverse material symbols and social practices across societies, and one cannot ignore its enduring existence in writing about local histories or transnational movements.

Moreover, political nonalignment was by definition a reactive principle that existed only in conceptual and practical relationship with bipolarizing politics. If this was the case, it is reasonable that the concept of "the postcolonial," whether in historical research or cultural criticism, should be considered in similar, relational terms to the background of political bipolarity within which the concept actually evolved. Only in this rigorously relational perspective to the postcolonial process, inclusive of political bipolarity, can we place postcolonial theory in proper historical context and strengthen its capacity to interact with contemporary transitions.

In a recent essay, Bhabha, Chakrabarty, and other specialists in South Asia raise the question: "Do we live in a post–Cold War world *tout court*, or in the long shadow of that disastrous postwar experience of superpower collusion and competition that deformed the development of the rest of the world?"[32] In order to explore this important question, which was also noted in chapter 1, we can no longer keep bipolar history as a voiceless subaltern dominated by the preeminence of postcolonial discourses. There is another, more fundamental issue at stake in the disengagement of bipolar history from postcolonial theory. As indicated in the phrasing of the question, postcolonial theorists tend to view the cold war merely as a balance-of-power affair—that is, according to the paradigm of the imaginary war. As discussed earlier, this view is problematic in many ways. First, it excludes the dynamics of decolonization from the constitution and development of the bipolar global order. Second, the paradigm of the imaginary war marginalizes the experience of the bipolar conflict in large parts of the postcolonial world as a civil war or other forms of organized violence. Finally, the paradigm is incapable of considering the social and cultural dimensions of the cold war because it privileges exclusively the perspective of the state and the sphere of interstate actions. The uncritical acceptance of this paradigm constitutes a critical problem in contemporary postcolonial discourse.

Why is the reality of bipolar history excluded from the project of postcolonial historical criticism? The answer is that this project, although aiming to free historical thought on political modernity from the grip of European political thought, approaches cold war modernity, the flip side of postcolonial modernity, from a predominantly Europe-centered perspective of this historical process. These definitional problems regarding the cold war are not unique in postcolonial studies but exist even in the academic field that specializes in cold war history. In the next chapter, I turn to a recent debate about "the culture of the cold war" and review how this debate accounts for the enduring effects of the violent postcolonial cold war.

7

COLD WAR CULTURE
IN PERSPECTIVE

The location of culture is an important issue for cold war political history, just as it is for colonial history and postcolonial criticism. I discussed earlier how the transition of the global order from the colonial to the bipolar formation involved a significant change in the concept of culture—from an evolutionary, hierarchical scheme of thought to a relatively egalitarian, pluralistic notion (see chapter 3). The advance of cultural pluralism, as discussed with reference to the impact of behaviorism, also involved a subtle semantic change in the concept of culture, from a deterministic notion referring to given and inherited traits to a malleable system of norms that can be appropriated and changed by concerted intervention in the life conditions of the individual culture bearers.[1] This development projected that it was possible to bring together diverse cultural entities for a common moral and political objective.

Another idea of culture permeates the literature of cold war history, however, and it appears to be more about conformity (the construction of political cultural uniformity) than diversity.[2] During the cold war, even the most seemingly culture-free, technological objects such as the atomic bomb and the means to deliver it were described in reference to a wider, prevailing culture of "anxiety" or "paranoia."[3] The idea of a culture of paranoia in part refers to the inquisitional militancy of the radical right in mid-twentieth-century American domestic politics against "un-American activities," whereby issues of national security (such as protecting bomb-making technology from being leaked to enemy countries) were firmly linked with apparently unrelated preoccupations such as the purging of nonheterosexuals from the state bureaucracy. How national security was imagined at the time in biological and epidemiological terms such as "contamination (by Communist viruses)" and "quarantining (the unstable states from ideological infection)"; how this imagination affected not only foreign policy but also the norms of family life and the contours of personal identity; how in this context containment was both a material political practice and a prevailing cultural metaphor; how television functioned as a "brain-washing" instrument; how the construction of tough and liberal "American manhood" was at the vital center of the making of the American Century; and how there were "extraordinary connections between seemingly disconnected cultural currents and political events"—these are among the many provocative questions raised by the rising scholarship of American cold war cultural history.[4]

The idea of culture in the sense of engendering conformity is laid out explicitly in Stephen Whitfield's pioneering work *The Culture of the Cold War*, in which he argues that the cold war should be approached as both a question of social order and a question of international order.[5] By introducing the concept of culture to the history of the cold war, Whitfield explores the East–West conflict of the past century in the context of the symbolic and material culture that developed within a specific society as part of its engagement with the global conflict. This research turns away from the previously dominant approach to cold war history, which focused on diplomatic history and anchored itself in notions such as power (as in balance of power), behavior (as in foreign-policy behavior or enemy behavior), impacts (as in defense-policy impacts), or sphere (as in security sphere). It suggests that the inception of a culture concept to cold war historiography has resulted in a major paradigm shift in this field of studies. In this perspective, the idea of culture in "the culture of the cold war" does not refer merely to the impact of global bipolar conflict on the structure of social life. Instead, it is instrumental in bringing the milieu of intimate social norms and subtle shifts in the patterns of organizational life during the cold war era to the foreground of descriptive and analytical projects focused on the cold war, which have hitherto been narrowly focused on policy documents and profiles. This reorientation in cold war studies, sometimes called "the culture turn," is a deliberate move away from the questions of "causation and agency," which have been central to the previous realist approach to cold war history. It instead aims to reconsider the political process in the bipolar order as a "cultural system" in a sense that echoes anthropologist Clifford Geertz's definition of the semiotics of culture in the early 1970s.[6]

Studies of the cold war social order after "the culture turn" are heavily concentrated on American political culture, although some informative works focusing on Italy, Greece, and other European historical contexts after World War II have recently appeared.[7] There are also some notable initiatives to widen the comparative scope of cold war culture studies to non-Western contexts.[8] In the course of writing this book, I read a number of these informative works written by cultural and social historians, and I learned a great deal from them. They are diverse in thematic choice: middle-class domestic life in 1950s East Coast America; the politics of child adoption from peripheral cold war allies to American families; the role of mass consumption in building the so-called consensus culture; the pathology of tough manhood in political liberalism and the related question of social containment of female sexuality; the psychology of the nuclear bomb and the related issue of permeability between household and national security; the role of the Voice of America in disseminating the benevolence of American power; and the role of poetry, film, dramas, and television in consolidating public opinion in accordance with geopolitical objectives.[9] Also noteworthy are the attempts to assess the collaboration between policy institutions and academic communities in constructing the enemies of the cold war. Ron Robin's analysis of the prisoner-of-war (POW) controversies from the Korean and Vietnam wars delves into the complex process of identifying nonbelievers in Communist ideology from the mass of Communist POWs, relating this classificatory technique to some of the key assumptions in the disciplines of behavioral and experimental psychology at the time the wars took place.[10] Bruce Franklin's investigation of the issue of Vietnam War POWs and those missing in action points in another direction, revealing how the Reagan-era politics of imaginary American POWs in Indochina and the reinvigorated antagonism against the Third World Communists (the alleged captors of American combatants) that it instigated were instrumental in the self-legitimization of the administration's prolific counterinsurgency activities and low-intensity warfare waged in South and Central America.[11] In this context, the memory of a war against communism was employed as an instrument of waging another war.

Some scholars take a broader view of "American cold war culture" and explore the process of its diffusion to other parts of the world. David Ryan writes in his informative study of the reconstruction of western Europe after World War II: "The culture of the Cold War provided the atmosphere and the tools that enabled Washington to enhance its consensus, achieve its objectives and largely win the battle for the hearts and minds of West Europeans. But far from the idea of a passive transfer of culture, Washington initiated numerous programmes designed to bring about its desired ends. And, although US culture was renegotiated in Europe, in broad outline US policy was largely a success: a new West was created in which old inconsistencies were forgotten and new identities were advanced."[12] Ryan does not employ quotation marks for "American cold war culture," as I do here, and he is more liberal about imagining the formation and diffusion of a culture than a contemporary anthropologist might be, for whom, according to James Clifford, thinking about culture today involves questioning the very idea of culture.[13] Immediately after his conclusive remark about the transnational migration of cold war culture across the Atlantic, Ryan introduces a quote from an anthropologist: "The power of a metaphor derives precisely from the interplay between the discordant meanings it symbolically coerces into a unitary conceptual framework and from the degree to which that coercion is successful in overcoming the psychological resistance such semantic tension inevitably generates in anyone in a position to perceive it." He is quoting Clifford Geertz's seminal essay "Ideology as a Cultural System."[14] Ryan is interested in the formation of the modern idea of the West, and he approaches this formation in part as the product of an active dissemination of "the US culture" to postwar Europe as part of the cold war's East–West duality. Other recent studies focus on the dissemination of the "American way of life" to postwar western Europe and elsewhere. Wendy Wall investigates the "Letters to Italy" campaign launched among Italian Americans in 1948 during the crucial run-up to the national election in Italy, where the Socialist and Communist party candidates stood strong. The campaign urged Italian Americans to write letters to their relatives in Italy describing the personal freedom and material wealth they enjoyed in America and highlighting the threat of communism to traditional Italian family and religious values. This campaign was subsequently expanded to "Letters from America," extending to other ethnic groups in America. Wall explains that the letter campaign was intended not only to "sell America" to the rest of the world but also to "solidify the allegiance of millions of Americans to a particular vision of the 'American Way.' "[15]

As Elaine May describes, the containment of communism was both a policy directive to restrain the spread of communism in the international sphere and "a metaphor for the cold war on the [American] homefront," shaping familial ideology and patterns of domestic life.[16] According to Kyle Cuordileone,

> Communism inspired an animus in American society that was largely absent in democratic, capitalist nations in Europe with their longstanding welfare states and established Socialist and Communist parties. The fear and hatred of Communism has a long history in American life; its ideological roots go back to the nineteenth century, while the repression of Communists and other left-wing radicals in the late 1940s and the 1950s was foreshadowed by the red scare of 1919–1920. The United States was unique not just in its intolerance and persecution of Communists but in its obsessive demonization of them.[17]

In this understanding, anticommunism appears to have different historical backgrounds, even among Western nations. However, one of Wall's main points is that the America-led postwar anti-Communist cultural struggles constituted a two-pronged activity that took place simultaneously at home and abroad: the "American way" was in the making on the domestic front exactly at the same time that it was being disseminated elsewhere as if it were a given reality. Hence, we can rephrase Ryan's statement about "transfer of culture" and note that the "American way" delivered to western Europe was an entity invented through the process of dissemination rather than a preexisting entity ready to be exported elsewhere.

Ryan emphasizes the contest between "symbolic coercion" and "psychological resistance" in the construction of cold war cultural consensus in the West.[18] In this view, the political culture of the cold war is primarily a question of rhetorical efficacy. Geertz advances a semiotic theory of culture based on rhetorical power of symbols and metaphors. In his essay "Ideology as Cultural System," he does so in broad reference to the totalitarian politics of the Communist bloc, the nationalist politics of the postcolonial states including Indonesia, and the American political process. One of Geertz's main points is that symbolic coercions and ideological sways apply to both Western democracies and totalitarian societies. In this respect, he takes a critical look at Daniel Bell's claim for "the end of ideology" in developed commercial societies and argues instead that cultural life, whether in liberal or authoritarian political systems, is not free from ideological forces; in the same light, he refutes the claim that scientific knowledge is a value-free, nonideological knowledge of the world.[19]

Geertz wrote about the culture concept in the late 1960s and early 1970s, in part as a reaction to the prevailing political atmosphere in the United States, which explains why his definition of culture is attractive to the contemporary scholarship of cold war cultural history. Also relevant is his suggestion that symbolic coercion operates across traditional and modern societies, across the bipolar border, and across scientific and political practices. Geertz later developed his semiotic theory of culture and rhetoric-based understanding of culture process into a theory of power. Discussing the royal rituals in a precolonial Balinese state, Negara, Geertz argues that power works as "systems of interacting symbols, as patterns of interworking meanings."[20] Geertz's professed theoretical interest in this work is to challenge the classical Weberian definition of state power as the monopoly of coercive forces (army, police, and bureaucracy) and to pluralize the concept of political power. To this end, he argues that the political authority of the Negara kingship in nineteenth-century Bali was built on periodic ritualized demonstrations of the king's social and cosmological centrality rather than on control of coercive capabilities. Geertz calls his approach "theatrics of power" or "poetics of power."[21]

It is important to note that a few years before Geertz published his essay on ideology as symbolic coercion (1973) and, later, his monograph on power as spectacle (1980), a large territory of Indonesia (Geertz's main research field) had succumbed to a whirlwind of organized political terror that resulted in more than one million human casualties. The gruesome events of 1965–1966 were triggered by an alleged coup attempt by a group of army officers sympathetic to the Indonesian Communist Party, which then provided the pretext for the anti-Communist army leaders, led by General Suharto, to step in to frustrate the coup and subsequently launch an offensive against the Left. As a means of purifying the Indonesian nation and ridding it of the pollutants of alien ideology and belief, this offensive against the Communist Party quickly evolved into a widespread death campaign against segments of the population believed to be harboring Communist sympathizers. The bloodbath of 1965, according to

Leslie Dwyer and Degung Santikarma, "has soaked into Indonesia's social landscape, shifting cultural, religious and political topographies, and shaping possibilities for speech and social action," and its history has been a taboo subject in Indonesia until recently.[22]

The anthropologist Robert Lemelson's remarkable documentary film *40 Years of Silence: An Indonesian Tragedy* (2009) movingly shows how the Balinese landscape is indeed soaked in the painful, unresolved memories of 1965. The film follows several Balinese survivors and their post-1965 lives. One of them is a daughter of an ethnic Chinese family in Java whose father was involved in radical democratic political movement during the Sukarno era. The brutal death of her father in 1965 led to the social stigmatization and economic hardship of the surviving family after the massacre. In the subsequent era of democratization leading to the fall of Suharto's rule in 1998, the family's daughter became a locally prominent human rights activist. She struggled to lay to rest and move beyond the painful memory of the family's past sufferings; her tireless effort included the moving scene of her mobilizing aid and charity for the victims of a recent natural disaster in her old natal homeland. Some of these victims were the perpetrators of the violence in 1965 that had killed her father.

The film also features a man who returns to his home village after years of absence since childhood. The village is silently yet bitterly divided in its memory of the chaos of 1965, and the returnee has to face neighbors who were directly responsible for the death of his father and his other close relatives. His attempt to make peace with one of the culpable fails, and he faces instead bitter disapproval from his surviving relatives; he also tries to reconcile his memory of being abandoned by his mother with what really happened. The man learns, slowly and painfully, how his mother decided to marry one of the killers of her late husband, which forced her to leave her child behind, her only option to save him at the time.

Another survivor appearing in the film did not leave home after the mass killing of 1965, which he narrowly escaped by hiding in a tree, but which he witnessed from the top of the tree. He suffers from having witnessed the extreme violence and has sought help from traditional healers in the hope of being freed from the visions and voices that trouble him. While working in the field, he wears an army uniform that he purchased from the marketplace. The field abounds with spirits, the man believes, and based on his past experience, he knows they will not dare to approach him to cause burning pains in his heart if he is dressed in the military uniform and combat helmet. The villager believes that the many Communist spirits in the village field are still frightened of the military.

Despite the seismic impact the massacres of 1965 had on Balinese lives, they failed to attract much attention from the area specialists of Bali either at the time or later, in whose writings, according to Geoffrey Robinson, Bali continued to be presented as a "harmonious, exotic, and apolitical" space, a cultural paradise that entertains fascinating traditional arts and aesthetically rich religious performances. Robinson challenges Geertz in this context, accusing him of failing to engage with Bali's modern political history and thus unwittingly contributing to the apolitical orientation in Balinese studies.[23] Robinson writes bitterly of the fact that in Geertz's seminal work *The Interpretation of Cultures*, which includes his essay "Ideology as Cultural System," Geertz allocates a single sentence to the massacres: "[After the 1965 coup] there followed several months of extraordinary popular savagery—mainly in Java and Bali but also sporadically in Sumatra—directed against individuals considered to be followers of the Indonesian Communist Party."[24] Robinson's disappointment concerns Geertz's apparent lack of serious consideration of Bali's turbulent modern history. In his challenge to the "myth" of an apolitical Balinese culture, Robinson quotes Marshall Green, the U.S. ambassador to Indonesia at the time of the massacres, who said: "The bloodbath visited on Indonesia can be largely attributed to the fact that communism, with its atheism and talk of class warfare, was abhorrent to the way of life of rural Indonesia, especially in Java and Bali, whose cultures placed great stress on tolerance, social harmony, mutual assistance . . . and resolving controversy through talking issues out in order to achieve an acceptable consensus situation." Robinson argues that this "myth" was a distortion of the history of anti-Communist violence and a concealment of the state's responsibility in the mass killing. Against the myth making, he sets out to paint "the reality of Bali" with the layers of conflicts that were rooted in the region's colonial history and postcolonial transition and to trace the origin of the anti-Communist horror in Bali and elsewhere in Indonesia to "certain structural features of the broader political environment . . . rather than in the character, temper, or cultural makeup of a given political community."[25]

It is somewhat unfair of Robinson to assign Geertz academic culpability for the myth making of an apolitical Bali. In *The Interpretation of Cultures*, Geertz discusses extensively the nationalist politics of Sukarno's Indonesia (before the massacres) as an exemplary case of symbolic coercion, in part drawing upon George Kahin's classical work on the topic. Robinson, too, relies substantially on Kahin's work.[26] In his discussion, Geertz writes about "a polity as a concentrated center of pomp and power"—the theme that he later develops in an analysis of the public power of a precolonial theater state in Bali as "the ordering force of display, regard, and drama."[27] What Geertz is trying to achieve here is to establish certain continuity between precolonial, traditional local states in Bali and Java and the postcolonial, centralized national state of Indonesia in terms of aesthetics of power. Just as the power of the traditional state was performative in nature rather than institutional, based as it was on pompous religious rituals, so too is the power of the modern secular state as against the conventional wisdom drawn from Weberian sociological tradition, which relied heavily on ritualized symbols of power, such as the spectacles of military might and public speeches of secular political leaders made according to the order of traditional religious oratory. Geertz's objective here is to make a case for cultural continuity of state formation in Indonesian history and to bring the idea of "theater state" to a critique of the Weberian theory of state power as the monopoly of coercive institutions. Hence, it is not true that Geertz is as oblivious to Indonesia's modern political history as Robinson claims. On the contrary, Geertz is engaged with presenting the history as an "Indonesian history"—that is, in the terms that, he believes, show how politics are made in a culturally distinctive way. For him, the fundamental problem with postcolonial Indonesian politics is that Sukarno's charismatic rule under the slogans of "guided democracy" and "socialism à la Indonesia" was based on the traditional politics of spectacle, which failed to consolidate the complex, secular, and modern Indonesian society of the postcolonial era. What Geertz has in mind with his phrase "ideology as cultural system" is in fact that the *ideology* of Suharto's guided democracy is intelligible only if it is seen within the context of a *cultural system* such as the ritualized universe of Negara. It is this specific concern with cultural continuity and a particular commitment to a particular theory of culture as a historically enduring, encompassing, organizing scheme of human affairs that makes it hard for Geertz to engage with the events of 1965–1966. The massacres in 1965 may be understood according to what Hannah Arendt calls "administrative massacres"—the eruption in modern politics of a structure that administers mass death as routine state business—or perhaps as an exemplar of what Giorgio Agamben calls "exemplary exception"—the suspension of the rule of law as part of a construction of state sovereignty.[28] From whichever angle of political theory we choose to see the massacres, it is practically impossible to consider these catastrophic events as the work of a theater state or to interpret them in the scheme of "symbolic coercion" against "psychological resistance." It is true that organized mass destruction of human life may also be conceived of as a form of symbolic practice, as shown in Tzvetan Todorov's depiction of the Spanish conquest of Mexico and the Caribbean as manipulation of signs.[29] However, there is a wide gap in philosophical orientation between the latter sphere of semiotic analysis and the politics of symbols and metaphors advanced by Geertz as part of a semiotic definition of culture.

If considered in this manner, Robinson's complaint about Geertz's representation of Bali is relevant for thinking about cold war culture in comparative perspective. The idea of symbolic coercion may be an appropriate concept for describing the politics of anticommunism experienced in midcentury America and post–World War II Europe. The diffusion of the "American way" to postwar western Europe, which Ryan relates to the construction of the modern West as we know it now, relied heavily on expressive and demonstrative means. The economic assistance under the Marshall Plan accompanied the U.S. administration's efforts to propagate the superiority of American material culture to postwar Europe. In this context, the fitted kitchens and affordable automobiles were not merely material goods readily available in American society; they were powerful rhetorical devices for selling American political ideals overseas. Diplomat George Kennan emphasized in his public speeches the efficacy of talking politics with commodities,[30] and it is argued that consumer goods were as powerful a weapon as nuclear warheads in the superpower competition. In this light, May describes the so-called Kitchen Debate between Richard Nixon and Nikita Khrushchev, in which Nixon compared the superiority of the American way of life to the Soviet way of life in terms of the quality of kitchen appliances produced, arguing that these items liberated American women from the drudgery of domestic work and freed them to pursue personal interests.[31]

In other theaters of the cold war, however, the dissemination of the "American way" was not always so subtle and civilized as it was in Europe, nor was the demonstration of its promise of affluence always so peaceable and constructive. In Indonesia, as Robinson describes, the dissemination involved the empowerment of an ultraconservative military elite and radical Islamic forces, which the U.S. administration viewed would prevent the nation from falling under the Soviet sphere of influence by seizing political power and purifying the national community from the "viruses" of communism. Although the circumstances in which the massacres in South Korea in 1948–50 took place were somewhat different from the circumstances of the Indonesian experience, they, too, speak to the fact that the viability of postcolonial states in bipolar geopolitics was determined according to the quality of their performance in anti-Communist militancy. The diffusion of the "American way" to these places, in contrast to the equivalent process in the West, involved the proliferation of physical coercive measures and related incidents of mass civilian killing. Understanding the culture of the cold war, therefore, calls for a theory of culture that embraces these contradictory manifestations of the cold war construction, not for a language of culture and power that is incapable of accounting for the violent side of bipolar history even when describing a region that suffered a notable episode of such violence.

However, my suggestion that a cold war with mass human casualties and a cold war without them are different entities should not be taken to mean that these two histories are not comparable or commensurable. On the contrary, it is precisely for the purpose of making them comparable that it is necessary to clarify key features of their disparities. Dissecting the whole of the global cold war into different constituent parts is for the purpose of creating a new image of the whole rather than dismantling the image of the whole. History of mass death is one element that I emphasize consistently in this book to argue why the existing image of the cold war needs to be questioned, and there must be other elements with which we can pluralize and decenter bipolar history. Even within the history of mass death, moreover, there are elements of diversity. The U.S. experience of the cold war does not collapse to the paradigm of the "imaginary war" or the "long peace" as easily as does the dominant European experience. Indeed, the United States has a memory of mass sacrifice of American lives from the era of the cold war mainly in relation to the Korean and Vietnam conflicts. This collective memory of mass sacrifice, however, is not the same as the memory of other sacrifices discussed in this book. Consisting principally of the heroic death of armed soldiers, the American memory distinguishes the United States from the rest of the West, whose dominant memory of the cold war encompasses a painful but largely deathless confrontation between political communities, but it is also distinct from the collective memories of death in the wider world during the cold war, chiefly the tragic mass death of ordinary civilians. In the sphere of death commemoration, therefore, we cannot easily say that Europe and America constitute a single community of shared collective memory called "the West." But nor can we easily reconcile America's memory of heroic death and sacrifice in the struggle against communism with the memories of mass tragic death associated with the same struggle in the rest of the world. The world does not look back on the era of the cold war with a single, united perspective; nor can we say, for that matter, that the world is experiencing the ending of the bipolar world in an identical way. How people think about bipolar history is conditioned by how they experienced it, which in turn shapes what they make of the future.

Furthermore, these conflicting views of bipolar political history do not exist merely between different geographical regions and different political communities in the international sphere. Contradictory memories of either heroic death or tragic death can coexist in a single political community or even in a single local community and a single field of social actions. The initiatives to tell the truth about the Bali massacre, for instance, must confront not only the myth of apolitical and peaceable Bali, as Robinson claims, but also the legacy of Suharto's political rule that propagated the state's violence against society as a legitimate, heroic act of patriotism to save the nation from the threat of a Communist takeover. The same is true for the Jeju islanders in South Korea, whose public space includes patriotic memorials for anticommunism, the hidden traces of Communist insurgents, and the rising sites of memory for ordinary islanders whose history of tragic death struggles to be free from the left/right antithesis. For the villagers in coastal central Vietnam, both death in the struggle against communism and death in the struggle against the imperial ambition conducted in the name of anticommunism are constituents of their genealogical identity. And their assertion of this double, communal self-identity is in conflict with the predominant national memory of the past, which selectively celebrates only the traces of heroic, revolutionary death, thus relegating the numerous other traces of death from the Vietnam–American war to nonhistory.

Remembering the history of tragic mass death in the cold war era is an important part of social development in the regions mentioned. Thinking of the global cold war in terms of this history and in relation to the rising moral practices of remembrance is one of this book's main objectives. My intention is to show how the global cold war actually consisted of not only locally diverse but also mutually contradictory experiences of bipolarizing politics. If we take "culture" in the "culture of the cold war" to mean the webs of significance in which human beings invent and entrap themselves, following Geertz, it is important to recognize that this definition of culture is rooted in part in the experience of the cold war as and within a particular social order.[32] Geertz writes: "Each of the leading notions of what the state 'is' that has developed in the West since the sixteenth century— monopolist of violence within a territory, executive committee of the ruling class, delegated agent of popular will, pragmatic device for conciliating interests—has had its own sort of difficulty assimilating the fact that this force [the ordering force of display, regard, and drama] exists. None has produced a workable account of its nature."[33] Geertz's understanding that political power can be about "display, regard, and drama" originates, in my view, in part from his observation of cold war politics as spectacle and drama in 1950s and 1960s America (and this is why his theory of symbolic power appeals to students of America's cold war culture), not merely from his excavation of the premodern political system in Bali and certainly not from a systematic investigation of the turbulent development of modern Indonesian politics. Geertz, as a scholar of anthropology and according to the method of investigation called "participant observation" that was canonized in the particular social science discipline to which he belonged, was unable to conduct such an investigation. He could not engage with the terrible force of the cold war unleashed in the place where he built his career as an eminent ethnographer. Adam Kuper observes:

In the second half of the 1960s, Geertz began to change course. The confused but promising initial period of Indonesian independence had come to a bloody end. . . . The Cold War introduced new priorities. America became embroiled in Southeast Asia, no longer as a liberator but as a quasi-imperial power. The war in Vietnam escalated. It was now that Geertz moved his field site from Indonesia to Morocco, where the politics were stable, if not very interesting or attractive to the democrat. At home, a civil war began to take hold on the campuses, from which Geertz was alienated.[34]

Despite this estrangement, however, Geertz did continue to observe and reflect on the propensity of cold war politics in another place with which he was also familiar and deeply concerned—his home country. He was able to do so not only because he was a tireless, acute observer and a great interpreter of diverse cultural forms but also because he was a firm believer in democratic and pluralistic values. In an essay called "Anti Anti-Relativism," Geertz explains how his defense of cultural pluralism, in its origin, involved a struggle against antirelativism: "At the height of the cold war days was [this thing] called 'anti anti-communism.' Those of us who strenuously opposed the obsession, as we saw it, with the Red Menace were thus denominated by those who, as they saw it, regarded the Menace as the primary fact of contemporary political life, with the insinuation—wildly incorrect in the vast majority of cases—that, by the law of the double negative, we had some secret affection for the Soviet Union."[35] Throughout his distinguished career, Geertz was fond of mentioning theater as a metaphor for knowledge, at times being scornful of the trend in the political science of his time, which, in his view, failed to see how symbols were integral to realpolitik and which imagined instead that real power politics belonged to the backstage rooms hidden behind the theater of symbols. He resisted all forms of the "it all comes down to" attitude (including, in political analysis, "it all comes down to power"), thereby providing important insights to the study of cold war politics.[36] He did so because he believed this attitude violates the pluralistic nature of human life.

The inception of the culture concept to cold war history is for the purpose of telling the history as a process of concrete social ordering and of elucidating the multiplicity of this ordering. On this matter, the semiotic theory of culture is worth thinking about not merely because it is useful for understanding the making of modern Western political culture, but because we must acknowledge its limits in grasping the reality of the cold war as a "death-world."[37] Geertz, in the condition of his time, was not able to confront and overcome these limits. He was not alone; many other anthropologists who worked in the newly independent nations in Asia were obliged to stay away from certain social and political questions that the authoritarian political rulers of these national states did not want to see raised. The avoidance was mostly unavoidable, not only so they could conduct fieldwork in such places but also so they could protect the lives of native friends and informants. Conditions have changed since then, and the students of cold war culture today are no longer excused from facing up to this culture's different faces. In order to come to terms with the diversity of cold war culture, it is important to retain and advance Geertz's intellectual legacy—his deep concern with human plurality in the age of the cold war, which was, in fact, what actually drove him to study the coercive power of metaphors and symbols.

CONCLUSION

Each morning you have to break through the dead rubble afresh so as to reach the living warm seed.

—Ludwig Wittgenstein, *Culture and Value*

In December 1955, the U.S. Gallup Polls ran a survey on the meaning of the cold war, asking Americans, "Will you tell me what the term 'COLD WAR' means to you?" The responses to this survey question were diverse and revealing.[1] The correct answers were: "war through talking, not down and out fighting; not a hot war; a subtle war, without arms—a diplomatic war; state of enmity between countries but will not total an all out war; war without actual fighting; political war; battle of words among powers to gain prestige among their nations; like a bloodless war." They also included: "doing what you want to do and disregarding the other country's opinion; war of nerves; peaceful enemies; propaganda to agitate the reds against democracy; nations can't agree among themselves—bickering back and forth; uncertainty between foreign countries and this country; battle of wits." The pollsters classified other responses as incorrect: "little children being parents and going without; too many people feathering their own nest; cold weather; war is cold to everybody—we don't like it." The incorrect answers included: "cold war just like a hot war—as in Korea just as many boys being killed—that was supposed to be a cold war; fighting slow—no one knows what they are doing; war where no war is declared; fighting for nothing; real war all over the world; it means my brothers' lives as they are in the service; where everybody was at war; like a civil war."

This book has shown that some of these "incorrect" responses were actually far from inaccurate and that what was truly wrong was instead the tendency to assign the understanding of the cold war as a "real war all over the world" or a global "civil war" to the category of misunderstanding. The history of the cold war told in this book is principally about the cold war that was "just like a hot war," "where everybody was at war," and, indeed, "meaning my brothers' lives." It has been one of this book's principal claims that we need to pay attention to this history of the global conflict and, for a deeper and clearer understanding of the human experience of the twentieth century, that we should no longer relegate the understandings of the cold war as a real war to the status of a categorical mistake or to oblivion. How then is it possible to remember the bipolar political history of the past century in terms of a "war of nerves" or "battle of wits" and, at the same time, as a "real war all over the world"? What is required to reconcile these radically contradictory images of our common past?

The cold war was a highly unconventional war. There was no clear distinction between war and peace; there was no declaration of war or a ceremonial secession of violence.[2] The cold war was neither a real war nor a genuine peace, and this uncertainty explains why some call it an imaginary war, whereas others associate it with a long peaceful time. The cold war was fought mainly with political, economic, ideological, and polemical means; the powerful nations who waged this war kept building arsenals of weapons of mass destruction in the hope that they would never have to use them; the threats of mutually assured total destruction assured one of the longest times of international peace: these strange features that constitute our collective memory of the cold war make it difficult to come to terms with its history according to the conventional antinomy of war and peace. George Orwell's *Nineteen Eighty-Four* expressed this absurdity with the widely cited paradoxical slogan, "War is Peace."[3]

Against this background, Mary Kaldor states: "The Cold War kept alive the idea of war, while avoiding its reality. [No modern conventional warfare] broke out on European soil. At the same time, many wars took place all over the world, including Europe, in which more people died than in the Second World War. But because these wars did not fit our conception of war, they were discounted." Kaldor believes that these "irregular, informal wars of the second half of the twentieth century" took place "as a peripheral part of the central conflict," and she argues that these "informal wars" are becoming the source of new, post–cold war bellicosity.[4] If we follow Kaldor, it appears that cold war history has a concentric conceptual organization, consisting of a "formal" history of relative peace in the center and "informal" violence on the periphery. The cold war was both an *idea* of war in the exemplary center and a *reality* of revolutionary war and chaotic violence in the peripheral terrains: the center experienced the conflict as an imaginary war and actually as a peaceful time; the periphery underwent it as a violent time and as an informal war. At the center, the end of the cold war was a largely peaceful event and opened a constructive development of transnational integration, whereas in the periphery this "end" gave birth to a new age of aggression. In this view of the cold war and what comes after it, it was not only an ambiguous phenomenon, being neither war nor peace, but also a contradictory phenomenon, experienced as an idea of war for some and as a reality of prolific organized violence for others.

The comment from Kaldor, an eminent historian of modern Europe, demonstrates that our collective memory of the cold war is not a modern memory. The idea of modern memory developed from the radical changes in how societies remembered their pasts after experiencing the mass slaughter of human lives in World War I and the consequent, generalized, universal bereavement. As such, the idea highlights the breakdown of the center/periphery spatial hierarchy in the traditional mode of representation. Before World War I, public accounts of war experience were predominantly about the aristocratic heroes and their romantic or stoic attitudes to duty and honor, relegating the experience of ordinary combatants to an invisible margin. The mechanical mass slaughter suffered on the Western Front opened a chasm between the reality experienced in the trenches and the sentimental heroism that prevailed in war narratives. This chasm triggered a vigorous search for an alternative way to relate the reality of war and to commemorate mass death.[5]

Stephen Kern describes this process in his book *The Culture of Time and Space, 1880–1918* with reference to the idea of "positive negative space" developed in the theory of art after World War I. According to Kern, the notion of "positive negative space" was a radical departure from the traditional view of art in which representing the landscape consists of a division between positive space and negative space. "Positive space" refers to the objects that come to the painter's view, whereas "negative space" refers to the background with which the painter locates the central object in his representation. The new art movement at the turn of the twentieth century changed the status of the negative space.[6] In the Cubists' pictorial language in particular, the background became as positive and equally important as the foreground, thereby bringing to an end a long Western artistic tradition that had begun as far back as the fifteenth century.[7] Kern writes about this aesthetic revolution: "One common effect of this transvaluation was a leveling of former distinctions between what was thought to be primary and secondary in the experience of space. It can be seen as a breakdown of absolute distinctions between the plenum of matter and the void of space in physics, between subject and background in painting, between figure and ground in perception, between the sacred and the profane space of religion."[8] Kern suggests that the aesthetics of transvaluation is intimately related to the reality of mass violence and mass death. He quotes Gertrude Stein, who considered World War I and the art of cubism as having the same composition, "of which one corner was as important as another corner": the war, she said, departed from the composition of previous wars in which "there was one man in the center surrounded by a lot of other men," and, likewise, the composition of modern art broke down the traditional rule that rendered the negative space an inert void, empty of aesthetic relevance.[9]

In a similar light, this book argues that confronting the center/periphery concentric hierarchy in the conception of the cold war is critical to a grounded understanding of the political history of the bipolar era. In the history of the cold war as an imaginary war, the history of man-made mass death existed mainly in the form of disturbing memory and a disturbing possibility; being haunted by the morbid events in Auschwitz and Hiroshima and overshadowed by the threat of thermonuclear destruction. As the philosopher Edith Wyschogrod argues in her book *Spirit in Ashes: Hegel, Heidegger, and Man-Made Mass Death*, the "life-world" in the second half of the twentieth century was suspended between the death events of the immediate past and the fear of an apocalyptic end of the "life-world" in the uncertain future.[10] Beyond the horizon of the imaginary war, however, death events were not a possibility but an actual "unbridled reality," in the words of Gabriel García Márquez, who notes that the continent of Latin America had "not had a moment's rest" from mass death during the so-called cold war.[11]

Delving into the history of mass death in cold war–era Latin America, including the experience of the Q'eqchi' Mayan communities in Guatemala, Greg Grandin shows how political terror and routine killings were "emblematic of the power of the Cold War" on this continent.[12] The political history of the cold war is inseparable from the history of atrocious mass death in this context, according to Grandin, as well as from the vigorous claims for social justice and related democratic political developments that have risen recently there. Repressive anti-Communist politics in Guatemala and elsewhere not only destroyed human lives but also relegated a significant part of the national community to the status of noncitizens; remembering the victims of anti-Communist violence and reconstructing civil order and the rule of law are interconnected activities.[13] These assertions of civil rights and the revitalization of political life are not unique to Latin America, as I show in this book, and their transnational character is in part a manifestation of how, in global terms, the cold war world was in fact a "death-world."

If the global cold war was both an imaginary war and at the same time a generalized experience of political terror and mass death, we need to tell its history accordingly, inclusive of the seismic death events experienced by communities, rather than considering the latter only perfunctory, marginal episodes in an otherwise peaceful, balanced contest of power. The general concept of the cold war resists this effort, but we must not allow this deceptively named struggle for power to continue to deceive us and to shield us from seeing that it left behind countless dead, many of whom are still unaccounted for. The end of the cold war, therefore, signifies much more than the end of a particular political order. It means an end to the traditional way of centering this political order on the paradigm of imaginary war; it means revitalizing the semantic struggle against the dominant meaning of the cold war and beginning to think of it in an alternative, more modern way, free from a hierarchical center/periphery composition.

"The other cold war," the title of this book, refers to this field of semantic struggle and the decomposition of representational hierarchy. It is also a salutatory gesture to the multitude of courageous human deeds arising in many corners of the present world, however humble they may be, that struggle to remember and mourn the lives broken by the forces of organized violence unleashed in the second half of the twentieth century under the deceptive name "cold war." The story of the cold war is not going to find an end unless we are willing to attend to the histories of these tragic lives and their decomposing remains. If we attend to these histories with care, however, we may find, amidst the dead ruins of cold war culture, not only a heap of cold rubble but also the living warm seed of a faith in history, as Wittgenstein hoped, and even, as Hannah Arendt believed, the germ of creative, genuine politics.

NOTES

Introduction

1. See, for example, Melvyn P. Leffler and David Painter, eds., *The Origins of the Cold War: An International History* (New York: Routledge, 2005), and Allen Hunter, ed., *Rethinking the Cold War* (Philadelphia: Temple University Press, 1998).
2. For a notable exception, see Michael J. Hogan, ed., *The End of the Cold War: Its Meaning and Implications* (New York: Cambridge University Press, 1992).
3. Quoted in Odd Arne Westad, *The Global Cold War: Third World Interventions and the Making of Our Times* (New York: Cambridge University Press, 2005), 2.
4. Peter Lowe, *Origins of the Korean War* (New York: Longman, 1986).
5. Bruce Cumings, *The Origins of the Korean War: The Roaring of the Cataract, 1947–1950* (Princeton: Princeton University Press, 1990).
6. Kye-Dong Kim, *The Partition of Korea and the Korean War* (Seoul: Seoul National University Press, 2000).
7. Melvyn P. Leffler, *The Specter of Communism: The United States and the Origins of the Cold War, 1917–1953* (New York: Hill and Wang, 1994); William A. Williams, *Empire as a Way of Life* (New York: Oxford University Press, 1980).
8. Williams, *Empire as a Way of Life*, 133–35.
9. Ralph B. Levering, Vladimir O. Pechatnov, Verena Botzenhart-Viehe, and C. Earl Edmondson, eds., *Debating the Origins of the Cold War: American and Russian Perspectives* (Lanham, Md.: Rowman and Littlefield, 2002).

10. Steven H. Lee, *Outposts of Empire: Korea, Vietnam, and the Origins of the Cold War in Asia, 1949–1954* (Liverpool: Liverpool University Press, 1995); Michael Hardt and Antonio Negri, *Empire* (Cambridge, Mass.: Harvard University Press, 2000); Chalmers Johnson, *The Sorrows of Empire: Militarism, Secrecy, and the End of the Republic* (New York: Verso, 2004); Lloyd C. Gardner and Marilyn B. Young, eds., *The New American Empire* (New York: New Press, 2005); Noam Chomsky, *Imperial Ambitions* (New York: Metropolitan, 2005).

11. Francis Fukuyama, *The End of History and the Last Man* (New York: Penguin, 1992).

12. The term *triumphant liberalism* is from John L. Gaddis, *The United States and the End of the Cold War: Implications, Reconsiderations, Provocations* (New York: Oxford University Press, 1992), 179–86.

13. Zygmunt Bauman, *Globalization: The Human Consequences* (Cambridge: Cambridge University Press, 1998); Johnson, *The Sorrows of Empire*. See also Ian Clark, *The Post–Cold War Order: The Spoils of Peace* (New York: Oxford University Press, 2001), 22–28.

14. Clark, *The Post–Cold War Order*, 39.

15. Ibid., 38.

16. Zaki Laïdi, *A World Without Meaning: A Crisis of Meaning in International Politics* (New York: Routledge, 1998), 17, 15, 25.

17. Christian G. Appy, "Introduction: Struggling for the World," in Christian G. Appy, ed., *Cold War Constructions: The Political Culture of United States Imperialism, 1945–1966* (Amherst: University of Massachusetts Press, 2000), 3.

18. The expression "the long peace" is from John L. Gaddis, *The Long Peace: Inquiries Into the History of the Cold War* (New York: Oxford University Press, 1987), and John L. Gaddis, "The Cold War, the Long Peace, and the Future," in Hogan, *The End of the Cold War*, 21–38. The expression "unbridled reality" is from the novelist Gabriel García Márquez, quoted in Greg Grandin, *The Last Colonial Massacre: Latin America in the Cold War* (Chicago: University of Chicago Press, 2004), 169.

19. The quote about consensus culture is from Lary May, "Introduction," in Lary May, ed., *Recasting America: Culture and Politics in the Age of Cold War* (Chicago: University of Chicago Press, 1989), 9, and the quote about anxiety culture is from both Susan Sontag, "The Imagination of Disaster," in *Against Interpretation* (New York: Farrar, Straus and Giroux, 1986), 209–25, and Michael Rogin, *Ronald Reagan, the Movie, and Other Episodes in Political Demonology* (Berkeley: University of California Press, 1987), 263. About the juridicopolitical idea of "the state of exception" and its conceptual relationship to civil war, see Giorgio Agamben, *The State of Exception*, translated by Kevin Attell (Chicago: University of Chicago Press, 2005). For an ethnographic account of the suspension

of the rule of law as a rule of the political order, see Michael Taussig, *Law in a Lawless Land: Diary of a Limpieza* (New York: New Press, 2003).

20. See Heonik Kwon, *Ghosts of War in Vietnam* (Cambridge, U.K.: Cambridge University Press, 2008), 64–82.

21. Walter LaFeber, "An End to Which Cold War?" in Hogan, *The End of the Cold War*, 13–14.

22. Geir Lundestad, ed., *East, West, North, South: Major Developments in International Politics, 1945–1990* (Oslo: Norwegian University Press, 1991); Westad, *The Global Cold War*.

23. Mark Mazower, *Dark Continent: Europe's Twentieth Century* (New York: Penguin, 1999); Mark Mazower, "Introduction," in Mark Mazower, ed., *After the War Was Over: Reconstructing the Family, Nation, and State in Greece, 1943–1960*, 1–22 (Princeton: Princeton University Press, 2000).

24. Bruce Cumings, "The Wicked Witch of the West Is Dead. Long Live the Wicked Witch of the East," in Hogan, *The End of the Cold War*, 88. See also LaFeber, "An End to Which Cold War?" 13.

25. LaFeber, "An End to Which Cold War?" 14.

26. Cynthia Enloe, *The Morning After: Sexual Politics at the End of the Cold War* (Berkeley and Los Angeles: University of California Press, 1993).

27. Hannah Arendt, *Between Past and Future: Eight Exercises in Political Thought* (New York: Viking, 1961), 11. See also Philip B. Hansen, *Hannah Arendt: Politics, History, and Citizenship* (Cambridge, U.K.: Polity, 1993), 5, 12.

28. Mary Douglas, *Implicit Meanings: Essays in Anthropology* (New York: Routledge, 1975).

1. The Idea of the End

1. See Riki van Boeschoten, "The Impossible Return: Coping with Separation and the Reconstruction of Memory in the Wake of the Civil War," in Mark Mazower, ed., *After the War Was Over: Reconstructing the Family, Nation, and State in Greece, 1943–1960* (Princeton: Princeton University Press, 2000), 127.

2. Author's interview with a family originally from this village located on the Bulgarian border, Brussels, February 2006.

3. The term *international civil war* is from André Gerolymatos, *Red Acropolis, Black Terror: The Greek Civil War and the Origins of Soviet–American Rivalry, 1943–1949* (New York: Basic Books, 2004), 187–228.

4. Paul G. Pierpaoli Jr., *Truman and Korea: The Political Culture of the Early Cold War* (Columbia: University of Missouri Press, 1999), 8.

5. Quoted in Gerolymatos, *Red Acropolis*, 231.

6. See Taik-Lim Yun, *Red Village: A History* (in Korean) (Seoul: Historical Criticism Press, 2003).

7. Author's interview with the adopted son in Andong, South Korea, June 2004.

8. Steven H. Lee, *Outposts of Empire: Korea, Vietnam, and the Origins of the Cold War in Asia, 1949–1954* (Liverpool, U.K.: Liverpool University Press, 1995), 11–16.

9. Shaun K. Malarney, "Return to the Past? The Dynamics of Contemporary and Ritual Transformation," in Hy Van Luong, ed., *Postwar Vietnam: Dynamics of a Transforming Society* (New York: Rowman and Littlefield, 2003), 234–42.

10. Heonik Kwon, *After the Massacre: Commemoration and Consolation in Ha My and My Lai* (Berkeley and Los Angeles: University of California Press, 2006), 161–64.

11. John L. Gaddis, *The Long Peace: Inquiries Into the History of the Cold War* (New York: Oxford University Press, 1987).

12. Walter LaFeber, "An End to Which Cold War?" in Michael J. Hogan, ed., *The End of the Cold War: Its Meaning and Implications* (New York: Cambridge University Press, 1992), 13–14.

13. The term *imaginary war* is from Mary Kaldor, *The Imaginary War: Interpretation of East–West Conflict in Europe* (Oxford, U.K.: Blackwell, 1990).

14. LaFeber, "An End to Which Cold War?" 13.

15. Bruce Cumings, *Parallax Visions: Making Sense of American–East Asian Relations at the End of the Century* (Durham: Duke University Press, 1999), 51.

16. Gerolymatos, *Red Acropolis*, 53–98; William J. Duiker, *Vietnam: Revolution in Transition* (Boulder, Colo.: Westview, 1995), 30–56; Bruce Cumings, *The Origins of the Korean War: Liberation and the Emergence of Separate Regimes, 1945–1947* (Princeton: Princeton University Press, 1981); Bruce Cumings, *Korea's Place in the Sun: A Modern History* (New York: Norton, 1997), 202–9.

17. Alexander Wendt, *Social Theory of International Politics* (New York: Cambridge University Press, 1999).

18. Dianne Kirby, "Religion and the Cold War—An Introduction," in Dianne Kirby, ed., *Religion and the Cold War* (New York: Palgrave, 2003), 2.

19. Ibid., 1.

20. Elaine T. May, *Homeward Bound: American Families in the Cold War Era* (New York: Basic Books, 1999), 10–29; Deborah Nelson, *Pursuing Privacy in Cold War America* (New York: Columbia University Press, 2002), 74–111.

21. Mark Mazower, "Introduction," in Mazower, *After the War Was Over*, 16.

22. Geoffrey Robinson, *The Dark Side of Paradise: Political Violence in Bali* (Ithaca, N.Y.: Cornell University Press, 1995), 304–7, 18.

23. The first quote is from Anthony Giddens, *The Third Way: Renewal of Social Democracy* (Cambridge, U.K.: Polity, 1998), 137. The second quote is from

Anthony Giddens and Will Hutton, "In Conversation," in Will Hutton and Anthony Giddens, eds., *Global Capitalism* (New York: New Press, 2000), 8.

24. Giddens and Hutton, "In Conversation," 9.

25. Arjun Appadurai, "Grassroots Globalization and the Research Imagination," in Arjun Appadurai, ed., *Globalization* (Durham: Duke University Press, 2001), 14.

26. Arjun Appadurai, *Modernity at Large: Cultural Dimensions in Globalization* (Minneapolis: University of Minnesota Press, 1996), 16.

27. Philip G. Roeder, "The Revolution of 1989: Postcommunism and the Social Sciences," *Slavic Review* 58 (1989), 743.

28. Appadurai, *Modernity at Large*, 18.

29. Appadurai, "Grassroots Globalization," 16–20, 4. It is clear in Appadurai's proposal that his idea of "globalization from below" inherits the notion of "history from below," which was popular among historians and anthropologists in the 1960s, prompted by the intense political unrests and mobilizations at the time (see chapter 4). See Eric R. Wolf, *Peasant Wars of the Twentieth Century* (New York: Harper and Row, 1969); Eric R. Wolf, *Europe and the People Without History* (Berkeley and Los Angeles: University of California Press, 1982); E. P. Thompson, *The Making of the English Working Class* (London: Gollancz, 1963); Frederik Krantz, *History from Below: Studies in Popular Protest and Popular Ideology* (New York: Blackwell, 1988); James C. Scott, *The Moral Economy of the Peasant: Rebellion and Subsistence in Southeast Asia* (New Haven, Conn.: Yale University Press, 1976).

30. See, for example, his work published posthumously: Robert Hertz, *Death and the Right Hand*, translated by Rodney Needham and Claudia Needham (Aberdeen, U.K.: Cohen and West, [1915] 1960).

31. Edmund Leach, *Political Systems of Highland Burma: A Study of Kachin Social Structure* (London: Bell, 1964).

32. Max Gluckman, *Custom and Conflict in Africa* (Oxford, U.K.: Blackwell, 1955), 4–5.

33. Appadurai, *Modernity at Large*, 18.

34. Alfred E. Eckes Jr. and Thomas W. Zeiler, *Globalization and the American Century* (New York: Cambridge University Press, 2003), 1–8.

35. John Borneman, *Subversions of International Order: Studies in the Political Anthropology of Culture* (Albany: State University of New York Press, 1998), 3.

36. Odd Arne Westad, *The Global Cold War: Third World Interventions and the Making of Our Times* (New York: Cambridge University Press, 2005).

37. Borneman, *Subversions of International Order*, 3.

38. Westad, *The Global Cold War*, 396.

39. Ibid., 3.

40. LaFeber, "An End to Which Cold War?" 13.

41. Bruce Cumings, "The Wicked Witch of the West Is Dead. Long Live the Wicked Witch of the East," in Hogan, *The End of The Cold War*, 88–89.

42. Ron Robin explores the close relationship between certain key assumptions in midcentury U.S. behavioral science and the political process that he calls "the making of the cold war enemy." Christina Klein and Christopher Shannon review the notion of cultural personality and cultural pluralism popular in the post–World War II American anthropological studies community in connection with U.S. anti-Communist and development policies regarding East Asia. Melani McAlister similarly explores the American "cultural history of interest" in the Middle East. Rebecca Lowen investigates the so-called military–intellectual complex of the midcentury United States, focusing on a particular higher-education institute and exploring how that institute's research agendas systematically colluded with the objectives of government funding agencies.

According to these authors, the academic division of labor between area studies and strategic studies implied that the two fields developed in close coordination with each other at the policy level and from the perspective of funding agencies, but apart from each other at the practical level and in the view of academic specialists. The specialists of strategic studies advanced systems theory, game theory, and other abstract modalities of containment and deterrence, whereas specialists in area studies enriched the understanding of locally specific cultural traditions and social processes. Both were largely unaware of how these two different bodies of knowledge coalesced in the actual making of foreign policies. The study of local cultures, in actuality, was as important a part of geopolitics as balance of military power, according to Shannon, but this reality remained largely invisible under the division of labor in knowledge production that relegated the language of the global to the exclusive possession of strategic studies.

See Ron Robin, *The Making of the Cold War Enemy: Culture and Politics in the Military–Intellectual Complex* (Princeton, N.J.: Princeton University Press, 2001); Christina Klein, *Cold War Orientalism: Asia in the Middlebrow Imagination, 1945–1961* (Berkeley and Los Angeles: University of California Press, 2003); Melani McAlister, *Epic Encounters: Culture, Media, and U.S. Interests in the Middle East Since 1945* (Berkeley and Los Angeles: University of California Press, 2001); Rebecca S. Lowen, *Creating the Cold War University: The Transformation of Stanford* (Berkeley and Los Angeles: University of California Press, 1997); Christopher Shannon, *A World Made Safe for Differences: Cold War Intellectuals and the Politics of Identity* (New York: Rowman and Littlefield, 2001).

43. Appadurai, *Modernity at Large*, 30.

44. Borneman, *Subversions of International Order*, 4.

45. Kaldor, *Imaginary War*.

46. Mark P. Bradley, *Imagining Vietnam and America: The Making of Postcolonial Vietnam, 1919–1950* (Chapel Hill: University of North Carolina Press, 2000).

47. Marilyn B. Young, *The Vietnam Wars, 1945–1990* (New York: HarperPerennial, 1991), 1–2.

48. Ibid., 23–24.

49. Jonathan Nashel, *Edward Lansdale's Cold War* (Amherst: University of Massachusetts Press, 2005), 144.

50. Ibid., 146–89; see William J. Lederer and Eugene Burdick, *The Ugly American* (New York: W. W. Norton, 1958). The epilogue of *The Ugly American* says: "We have been offering the Asian nations the wrong kind of help. We have so lost sight of our own past that we are trying to sell guns and money alone, instead of remembering that it was the quest for the dignity of freedom that was responsible for our own way of life. All over Asia we have found that the basic American ethic is revered and honored and imitated when possible. We must, while helping Asia toward self-sufficiency, show by example that America is still the America of freedom and hope and knowledge and law. If we succeed, we cannot lose the struggle" (Lederer and Burdick, *The Ugly American*, 284–85).

51. Bradley, *Imagining Vietnam and America*, 3–4; Hy Van Luong, *Revolution in the Village: Tradition and Transformation in North Vietnam, 1925–1988* (Honolulu: University of Hawai'i Press, 1992), 129.

52. Lee, *Outposts of Empire*, 11.

53. Westad, *The Global Cold War*, 5.

54. John Borneman, *After the Wall: East Meets West in the New Berlin* (New York: Basic Books, 1991).

55. Alan Nadel, *Containment Culture: American Narratives, Postmodernism, and the Atomic Age* (Durham: Duke University Press, 1995); Kenneth D. Rose, *One Nation Underground: A History of the Fallout Shelter* (New York: New York University Press, 2001).

56. May, *Homeward Bound*, x–xi.

57. In places such as China and North Korea, however, vast subterranean territory and mountain areas were transformed into a complex network of nuclear shelters.

58. Rose, *One Nation Underground*, 9.

59. This also explains why the few existing anthropological studies of cold war material culture highlight radically different forms across territories. Borneman, who specializes in Germany, writes: "The [Berlin] Wall was a symbol, and its fall marked the collapse of a symbolic system" (*After the Wall*, 10). In the context of the United States, however, Hugh Gusterson chooses nuclear weapons

laboratories as a main site for exploring cold war cultural history (*Nuclear Rites: Weapons Laboratory at the End of the Cold War* [Berkeley and Los Angeles: University of California Press, 1998]).

60. John Borneman, *Belonging in Two Berlins: Kin, State, Nation* (New York: Cambridge University Press, 1992); David F. Crew and Jean-Sebastian Marcoux, eds., *Consuming Germany in the Cold War* (Oxford, U.K.: Berg, 2003).

61. The quote is from Mazower, "Introduction," 14; see also p. 13. And see Gwi-Ok Kim, *Divided Families: Neither Anti-Communist Warriors nor Red Communists* (in Korean) (Seoul: Historical Criticism Press, 2004), 203–6; Yun, *Red Village*, 214–19.

62. See Greg Grandin, *The Last Colonial Massacre: Latin American in the Cold War* (Chicago: University of Chicago Press, 2004); Steve J. Stern, *Remembering Pinochet's Chile*, vol. 1 (Durham: Duke University Press, 2004).

63. See Westad, *The Global Cold War*, 207–49.

64. See Heonik Kwon, "North Korea's Politics of Longing," *Critical Asian Studies* 42, no. 1 (2010): 10–12.

65. Janice Boddy, *Wombs and Alien Spirits: Women, Men, and the Zār Cult in Northern Sudan* (Madison: University of Wisconsin Press, 1989), 165; Heike Behrend, "Power to Heal, Power to Kill," in Heike Behrend and Ute Luig, eds., *Spirit Possession: Modernity and Power in Africa* (Oxford: James Currey, 1999), 25–26.

66. George Mosse, *Fallen Soldiers: Reshaping the Memory of the World Wars* (Oxford, U.K.: Oxford University Press, 1990).

67. Jay Winter and Jean-Louis Robert, *Capital Cities at War: Paris, London, Berlin, 1914–1919* (New York: Cambridge University Press, 1997), 20–24.

68. Christian G. Appy, "Introduction: Struggling for the World," in Christian G. Appy, ed., *Cold War Constructions: The Political Culture of the United States Imperialism, 1945–1966* (Amherst: University of Massachusetts Press, 2000), 3.

69. John L. Gaddis, *We Know Now: Rethinking Cold War History* (New York: Oxford University Press, 1998); Eric Hobsbawm, *Age of Extremes: The Short Twentieth Century, 1914–1991* (London: Abacus, 1995), 236.

70. George P. Shultz, *Turmoil and Triumph* (New York: Macmillan, 1993); Colin Powell, *A Soldier's Way: An Autobiography* (London: Hutchinson, 1995).

71. Stephen J. Whitfield, *The Culture of the Cold War* (Baltimore: Johns Hopkins University Press, 1991), 3, vii.

72. Cynthia Enloe, "Women After Wars: Puzzles and Warnings," in Kathleen Barry, ed., *Vietnam's Women in Transition* (New York: St. Martin's, 1996), 299.

73. Perhaps it should come as no surprise, therefore, why, describing the events of the past century, many of today's political theorists and historians take to the

metaphor of the ghost in communication with the geist of our living moment: "the specter of communism" in American culture during the first half of the twentieth century, "the ghost of Stalin" in postsocialist Russia, "the specter of Marx" in contemporary social and cultural theories, "the specter of ideology" in the so-called postideological society, "the ghost of the Vietnam War" in American culture, and "the specter of genocide" in the contemporary semantics of human rights.

See Melvyn P. Leffler, *The Specter of Communism: The United States and the Origins of the Cold War, 1917–1953* (New York: Hill and Wang, 1994); Adam Hochschild, *The Unquiet Ghost: Russians Remember Stalin* (New York: Penguin, 1995); Jacques Derrida, *Specters of Marx* (New York: Routledge, 1994); Slavoj Žižek, "The Spectre of Ideology," in Slavoj Žižek, ed., *Mapping Ideology*, 1–33 (London: Verso, 1994); Arnold R. Isaacs, *Vietnam Shadows: The War, Its Ghosts, Its Legacy* (Baltimore: Johns Hopkins University Press, 1997); Robert Gellately and Ben Kiernan, eds., *The Specter of Genocide: Mass Murder in Historical Perspective* (New York: Cambridge University Press, 2003).

74. Žižek, "The Spectre of Ideology," 7–15.
75. Sheldon Pollock, Homi K. Bhabha, Carol A. Breckenridge, and Dipesh Chakrabarty, "Cosmopolitanisms," *Public Culture* 12, no. 3 (2000): 580.
76. Peter J. Kuznick and James Gilbert, "Introduction: U.S. Culture and the Cold War," in Peter J. Kuznick and James Gilbert, eds., *Rethinking Cold War Culture* (Washington, D.C.: Smithsonian Institution Press, 2001), 13.
77. Marilyn Strathern, *Reproducing the Future: Essays on Anthropology, Kinship, and the New Reproductive Technologies* (New York: Routledge, 1992), 245.
78. Ibid. See also Debbora Battaglia, *On the Bones of the Serpent: Person, Memory, and Mortality in Sabarl Island Society* (Chicago: University of Chicago Press, 1990).

2. Two Color Lines of the Twentieth Century

1. W. E. B. Du Bois, *The Souls of Black Folk* (New York: Hackett, 1994 [1903]), 9, 34–35.
2. Max Gluckman, *Custom and Conflict in Africa* (Oxford: Blackwell, 1955), 164.
3. See Robert K. Murray, *Red Scare: A Study in National Hysteria, 1919–1920* (New York: McGraw-Hill, 1955); John E. Haynes, *Red Scare or Red Menace: American Communism and Anti-communism in the Cold War Era* (Chicago: Dee, 1996). On anti-Communist polemics in South Africa, which translated moral and political challenges to the apartheid order into the language of Red menace, see Thomas Borstelmann, *Apartheid's Reluctant Uncle: The United*

States and Southern Africa in the Early Cold War (New York: Oxford University Press, 1993).

4. Christopher J. Vermaak, *Red Trap: Communism and Violence in South Africa* (Johannesburg: A. P. B., 1966).

5. Borstelmann, *Apartheid's Reluctant Uncle*, 143, 139.

6. Mary L. Dudziak, *Cold War Civil Rights: Race and the Image of American Democracy* (Princeton: Princeton University Press, 2000), 29.

7. Odd Arne Westad, *The Global Cold War: Third World Interventions and the Making of Our Times* (New York: Cambridge University Press, 2005), 135.

8. Ann Stoler, "Mixed-Bloods and the Cultural Politics of European Identity in Colonial Southeast Asia," in Jan Naderveen Pieterse and Bhikbu Parekh, eds., *The Decolonization of Imagination*, 128–48 (London: Zed, 1995), 143, 130; see also Ann Stoler, "Sexual Affronts and Racial Frontiers: European Identities and the Cultural Politics of Exclusion in Colonial Southeast Asia," in Frederick Cooper and Ann Laura Stoler, eds., *Tensions of Empire: Colonial Cultures in a Bourgeois World*, 198–237 (Berkeley and Los Angeles: University of California Press, 1997).

9. Benedict Anderson, *Language and Power: Exploring Political Cultures in Indonesia* (Ithaca: Cornell University Press, 1990), 6.

10. Leslie Dwyer and Degung Santikarma, "'When the World Turned to Chaos': 1965 and Its Aftermath in Bali, Indonesia," in Robert Gellately and Ben Kiernan, eds., *The Specter of Genocide: Mass Murder in Historical Perspective*, 289–306 (New York: Cambridge University Press, 2003); Geoffrey Robinson, *The Dark Side of Paradise: Political Violence in Bali* (Ithaca: Cornell University Press, 1995).

11. Heonik Kwon, *After the Massacre: Commemoration and Consolation in Ha My and My Lai* (Berkeley: University of California Press, 2006).

12. Melvyn P. Leffler, *The Specter of Communism: The United States and the Origins of the Cold War, 1917–1953* (New York: Hill and Wang, 1994), 15.

13. Hue-Tam Ho Tai, *Radicalism and the Origins of Vietnamese Revolution* (Cambridge, Mass.: Harvard University Press, 1992), 57–87; Patricia Pelley, *Postcolonial Vietnam: New Histories of the National Past* (Durham: Duke University Press, 2002), 3.

14. Robinson, *The Dark Side of Paradise*, 300; see also Dwyer and Santikarma, "'When the World Turned to Chaos,'" 295.

15. Jeff Woods, *Black Struggle, Red Scare: Segregation and Anti-communism in the South, 1948–1968* (Baton Rouge: Louisiana State University Press, 2004).

16. Douglas Field, "Passing as a Cold War Novel: Anxiety and Assimilation in James Baldwin's *Giovanni's Room*," in Douglas Field, ed., *American Cold War Culture* (Edinburgh, U.K.: Edinburgh University Press, 2005), 88.

17. James S. Olson and Randy Roberts, *My Lai: A Brief History with Documents* (Boston: Bedford, 1998), 11, 16. See also Kwon, *After the Massacre*, 52–53.

18. Taik-Lim Yun, *Red Village: A History* (in Korean) (Seoul: Historical Criticism Press, 2003), 214–22.

19. Robinson, *The Dark Side of Paradise*, 294, 300.

20. Peter Wade, *Race, Nature, and Culture* (London: Pluto, 2002).

21. David Ryan, "Mapping Containment: The Cultural Construction of the Cold War," in Field, *American Cold War Culture*, 51.

22. Reinhold Wagnleitner, "The Irony of American Culture Abroad: Austria and the Cold War," in Lary May, ed., *Recasting America: Culture and Politics in the Age of Cold War*, 285–300 (Chicago: University of Chicago Press, 1989). See also James J. Carafano, *Waltzing Into the Cold War: The Struggle for Occupied Austria* (Austin: Texas A&M University Press, 2002).

23. Campaign quoted in Walter L. Hixson, *Parting the Curtain: Propaganda, Culture, and the Cold War, 1945–1961* (New York: St. Martin's, 1997), 134.

24. Robert E. Osgood, *America and the World: From the Truman Doctrine to Vietnam* (Baltimore: Johns Hopkins University Press, 1970).

25. Jacques Derrida, *On Cosmopolitanism and Forgiveness* (New York: Routledge, 2001), 40.

26. Ibid., 30. About the question of Nazi collaborators in postoccupation Greece, see Mark Mazower, "Three Forms of Political Justice: Greece, 1944–1945," in Mark Mazower, ed., *After the War Was Over: Reconstructing the Family, Nation, and State in Greece, 1943–1960*, 24–41 (Princeton: Princeton University Press, 2000). About the failed break with the fascist past in postwar Italy, see Christopher Duggan, "Italy in the Cold War Years and the Legacy of Fascism," in Christopher Duggan and Christopher Wagstaff, eds., *Italy in the Cold War: Politics, Culture, and Society, 1948–58*, 1–24 (Oxford, U.K.: Berg, 1995).

27. Caroline Humphrey, "Does the Category 'Postsocialist' Still Make Sense?" in Chris M. Hann, ed., *Postsocialism: Ideals, Ideologies, and Practices in Eurasia* (New York: Routledge, 2002), 12.

28. Caroline Humphrey, *The Unmaking of Soviet Life: Everyday Economies in Russia and Mongolia* (Ithaca: Cornell University Press, 2001).

29. Philip G. Roeder, "The Revolution of 1989: Postcommunism and the Social Sciences," *Slavic Review* 58, no. 4 (1999): 744–45.

30. Charles King, "Post-postcommunism: Transition, Comparison, and the End of 'Eastern Europe,'" *World Politics* 53 (2000), 145–46, 154, 166, 168.

31. Deniz Kandiyoti, "Post-colonialism Compared: Potentials and Limitations in the Middle East and Central Asia," *International Journal of Middle East Studies* 34 (2002): 279–97.

32. Chris M. Hann, "Farewell to the Socialist 'Other,'" in Hann, *Postsocialism*, 11, 10.

33. E. P. Thompson, *The Making of the English Working Class* (London: Gollancz, 1963).

34. James C. Scott, *The Moral Economy of the Peasant: Rebellion and Subsistence in Southeast Asia* (New Haven: Yale University Press, 1976).

35. Christopher G. A. Bryant and Edmund Mokrzycki, "Theorizing the Changes in East–Central Europe," in Christopher G. A. Bryant and Edmund Mokrzycki, eds., *The New Great Transformation? Change and Continuity in East–Central Europe*, 1–14 (New York: Routledge, 1993).

36. Frances Pine and Sue Bridger, "Introduction: Transitions to Post-socialism and Cultures of Survival," in Sue Bridger and Frances Pine, eds., *Surviving Post-socialism: Local Strategies and Regional Responses in Eastern Europe and the Former Soviet Union* (New York: Routledge, 1997), 1.

37. Zygmunt Bauman, "After the Patronage State: A Model in Search of Class Interests," in Bryant and Mokrzycki, eds., *The New Great Transformation?* 14–35.

38. Pine and Bridger, "Introduction," 3.

39. Hann, "Farewell to the Socialist 'Other,'" 10, 1.

40. Ernest Gellner, *Anthropology and Politics: Revolutions in the Sacred Grove* (Oxford, U.K.: Blackwell, 1995).

41. Ronald Suny, *The Revenge of the Past: Nationalism, Revolution, and the Collapse of the Soviet Union* (Stanford: Stanford University Press, 1993).

42. Katherine Verdery, "Transnationalism, Nationalism, Citizenship, and Property: Eastern Europe Since 1989," *American Anthropologist* 25, no. 2 (1998), 293–94. See also Yuri Slezkine, "The USSR as a Communal Apartment, or How a Socialist State Promoted Ethnic Particularism," *Slavic Review* 53, no. 2 (1994): 414–52.

43. Hann, "Farewell to the Socialist 'Other,'" 8.

44. Odd Arne Westad, *Decisive Encounters: The Chinese Civil War, 1946–1950* (Stanford: Stanford University Press, 2003).

45. Mark P. Bradley, *Imagining Vietnam and America: The Making of Postcolonial Vietnam, 1919–1950* (Chapel Hill: University of North Carolina Press, 2000).

46. Heonik Kwon, "North Korea's Politics of Longing," *Critical Asian Studies* 42, no. 1 (2010): 2–25.

47. John W. Young, *Cold War Europe, 1945–1991: A Political History*, 2d ed. (London: Edward Arnold, 1996), 1.

48. The use of the term *provincial* in this context comes from Dipesh Chakrabarty, *Provincializing Europe: Postcolonial Thought and Historical Difference* (Princeton: Princeton University Press, 2000), 254. See also chapter 6 in the present volume.

49. Hann, "Farewell to the Socialist 'Other,'" 2.

50. Michael Burawoy and Katherine Verdery, eds., *Uncertain Transition: Ethnographies of Change in the Postsocialist World* (Lanham, Md.: Rowman and Littlefield, 1999).

51. Roy Wagner notes, "[The act of] making the strange [ideas and practices of other cultures] familiar always makes the familiar [precepts and assumptions of one's own culture] a little bit strange. And the more familiar the strange becomes, the more and more strange the familiar will appear" (*The Invention of Culture* [Chicago: University of Chicago Press, 1981], 16). The anthropology at home is an act of making the familiar strange and, as such, may not be independent from the act of making the strange familiar in the anthropology outside home.

52. Frank Schimmelfennig, *The EU, NATO, and the Integration of Europe: Rules and Rhetoric* (New York: Cambridge University Press, 2003).

53. Geir Lundestad, "The End of the Cold War, the New Role for Europe, and the Decline of the United States," in Michael J. Hogan, ed., *The End of the Cold War: Its Meaning and Implications*, 195–206 (New York: Cambridge University Press, 1992).

54. Katherine Verdery, "Whither Postsocialism?" in Hann, *Postsocialism*, 15, 17.

55. Sharad Chari and Katherine Verdery, "Thinking Between the Posts: Postcolonialism, Postsocialism, and Ethnography After the Cold War," *Comparative Studies in Society and History* 51, no. 1 (2009): 29.

56. See Katherine Verdery, *What Was Socialism, and What Comes Next?* (Princeton: Princeton University Press, 1996); Verdery, "Transnationalism, Nationalism, and Property."

57. Verdery, "Whither Postsocialism?" 17.

58. See also Daphne Berdahl, Matti Bunzi, and Martha Lampland, eds., *Altering States: Ethnographies of Transition in Eastern Europe and the Former Soviet Union* (Ann Arbor: University of Michigan Press, 2000).

59. See, for example, the essays in Geir Lundestad, ed., *East, West, North, South: Major Developments in International Politics, 1945–1990* (Oslo: Norwegian University Press, 1991).

60. Sibelan Forrester, Magdalena Zaborowska, and Elena Gapova write about "post-Communist Orientalism" and argue that the problem of time in contemporary eastern and central Europe is much more than a transitional self-identity in relation to the supposedly advanced Western neighbors. They argue that the post-Communist Europe is western Europe's own local "Orient"—a largely undifferentiated locale that requires "Western attention, reconstruction, even redemption." Within the East, however, things are much more complicated, they argue: "Regardless of geography, Hungary was more 'Western' than Czechoslovakia, while Albania, just across the Adriatic from Italy, was

most 'Eastern' of all. Many Poles considered themselves to be 'Western' and resented being lumped together with the 'peasant' Bulgarians and saw Russians as even worse, with no taste and fashion sense at all. . . . Romanians felt that they were completely 'Western'; they loved America and hoped that President Clinton would help them get into NATO" ("Introduction: Mapping Postsocialist Cultural Studies," in Sibelan Forrester, Magdalena Zaborowska, and Elena Gapova, eds., *Over the Wall/After the Fall: Post-Communist Cultures Through an East–West Gaze* [Bloomington: Indiana University Press, 2004], 10, 12). If these sweeping characterizations are part of the lived reality in the region, the situation indeed calls to mind the issue of identity and power debated in postcolonial critique since Franz Fanon, and it appears, as Forrester, Zaborowska, and Gapova advocate, that the intellectual horizons of postcolonialism and postsocialism have much in common.

61. Chari and Verdery, "Thinking Between the Posts," 12.

3. American Orientalism

1. John R. Gillis, *Commemorations: The Politics of National Identity* (Princeton: Princeton University Press, 1994), 13.

2. Hannah Arendt, *Between Past and Future: Six Exercises in Political Thought* (New York: Viking, 1961).

3. Jeffrey C. Isaac, "Hannah Arendt as Dissenting Intellectual," in Allen Hunter, ed., *Rethinking the Cold War* (Philadelphia: Temple University Press, 1998), 284.

4. Quoted in Philip B. Hansen, *Hannah Arendt: Politics, History, and Citizenship* (Cambridge, U.K.: Polity, 1993), 5.

5. Edward W. Said, *Orientalism: Western Conceptions of the Orient* (New York: Penguin, 1991 [1978]), 295.

6. Edward W. Said, "The Clash of Definitions," in Emran Qureshi and Michael A. Sells, eds., *The New Crusades: Constructing the New Muslim Enemy* (New York: Columbia University Press, 2003), 84.

7. See Ron Robin, *The Making of the Cold War Enemy: Culture and Politics in the Military–Intellectual Complex* (Princeton: Princeton University Press, 2001), 19–37.

8. See Meyda Yeğenoğlu, *Colonial Fantasies: Towards a Feminist Reading of Orientalism* (New York: Cambridge University Press, 1998); Nicholas B. Dirks, ed., *Colonialism and Culture* (Ann Arbor: University of Michigan Press, 1992); Carol A. Breckenridge and Peter van der Veer, eds., *Orientalism and the Postcolonial Predicament* (Philadelphia: University of Pennsylvania Press, 1993).

9. Dennis Porter, "Orientalism and Its Problems," in Patrick Williams and Laura Chrisman, eds., *Colonial Discourse and Post-colonial Theory: A Reader* (Hemel Hempstead, U.K.: Harvester Wheatsheaf, 1993), 152.

10. See Rosalind O'Hanlon and David Washbrook, "After Orientalism: Culture, Criticism, and Politics in the Third World," *Comparative Studies in Society and History* 34, no. 1 (1992): 155–58.

11. Porter, "Orientalism and Its Problems," 152–53.

12. See Johannes Fabian, *Time and the Other: How Anthropology Makes Its Object* (New York: Columbia University Press, 1983); Nicholas Thomas, *Colonialism's Culture: Anthropology, Travel, and Government* (Cambridge, U.K.: Polity, 1994); Patrick Williams, "Kim and Orientalism," in Williams and Chrisman, *Colonial Discourse and Post-colonial Theory*, 480–97.

13. O'Hanlon and Washbrook, "After Orientalism," 157.

14. Ibid.

15. Emiko Ohnuki-Tierney, *Culture Through Time: Anthropological Approaches* (Stanford: Stanford University Press, 1990), 8.

16. Said, *Orientalism*, 291.

17. Mahmood Mamdani, *Good Muslim, Bad Muslim: America, the Cold War, and the Roots of Terror* (New York: Pantheon, 2004); Fred Halliday, *The Middle East in International Politics: Power, Politics, and Ideology* (Cambridge, U.K.: Cambridge University Press, 2005), 99–101.

18. Nils Gilman, *Mandarins of the Future: Modernization in Cold War America* (Baltimore: Johns Hopkins University Press, 2004).

19. Porter, "Orientalism and Its Problems," 152–53.

20. Antonio Gramsci, "Americanism and Fordism," in David Forgacs, ed., *The Antonio Gramsci Reader* (New York: New York University Press, 2000), 278–79.

21. Douglas Little, *American Orientalism: The United States and the Middle East Since 1945* (Chapel Hill: University of North Carolina Press, 2002), 10–11, quoting Catherine A. Lutz and Jane L. Collins, *Reading National Geographic* (Chicago: University of Chicago Press, 1993).

22. Little, *American Orientalism*, 11.

23. Said, "The Clash of Definitions," 86; see also Samuel P. Huntington, *The Clash of Civilizations and the Remaking of World Order* (London: Simon and Schuster, 1997), 183–206.

24. Emran Qureshi and Michael A. Sells, "Introduction: Constructing the Muslim Enemy," in Qureshi and Sells, *The New Crusades*, 12.

25. Huntington, *The Clash of Civilizations*, 34, 29.

26. Qureshi and Sells, "Introduction," 11.

27. Said, "The Clash of Definitions," 86.

28. Michael Hardt and Antonio Negri, *Empire* (Cambridge, Mass.: Harvard University Press, 2000), 146.

29. Melani McAlister, *Epic Encounters: Culture, Media, and U.S. Interests in the Middle East Since 1945* (Berkeley and Los Angeles: University of California Press, 2001), 9.

30. T. S. Eliot, *Selected Essays* (London: Faber, 1951), 15.

31. Melvyn P. Leffler, *The Specter of Communism: The United States and the Origins of the Cold War, 1917–1953* (New York: Hill and Wang, 1994).

32. Fatema Mernissi, "Palace Fundamentalism and Liberal Democracy," in Qureshi and Sells, *The New Crusades*, 52, 58–59.

33. Melvyn P. Leffler, *For the Soul of Mankind: The United States, the Soviet Union, and the Cold War* (New York: Hill and Wang, 2007), 403–14, 414.

34. Quoted in ibid., 405–6.

35. Mamdani, *Good Muslim, Bad Muslim*, 135, 128.

36. Mernissi, "Palace Fundamentalism and Liberal Democracy," 59. For a theory of political Islam as a third way beyond the bifurcated pathways of Western liberalism (and colonialism) and Soviet communism, see Khalifa Abdul Hakim, *Islam and Communism* (Lahore: Institute of Islamic Culture, 1951).

37. McAlister, *Epic Encounters*, 11.

38. Christina Klein, *Cold War Orientalism: Asia in the Middlebrow Imagination, 1945–1961* (Berkeley and Los Angeles: University of California Press, 2003).

39. Ibid., 11, 191–222.

40. The "Long Telegram" excerpted in George Kennan, *Memoirs, 1925–1950* (Boston: Little, Brown, 1967), 547–59. See also Walter LaFeber, *The American Age: United States Foreign Policy at Home and Abroad Since 1750* (New York: Norton, 1989), 449–52.

41. Quoted in Walter LaFeber, *The Origins of the Cold War, 1941–1947* (New York: John Wiley, 1971), 163–64.

42. See Ralph B. Levering and Verena Botzenhart-Viehe, "The American Perspective," in Ralph B. Levering, Vladimir O. Pechatnov, Verena Botzenhart-Viehe, and C. Earl Edmondson, eds., *Debating the Origins of the Cold War: American and Russian Perspectives* (Lanham, Md.: Rowman and Littlefield, 2002), 47–49.

43. Edgar Hoover, *A Study of Communism* (New York: Holt, Rinehart, and Winston, 1962), 3.

44. Vladimir O. Pechatnov and C. Earl Edmondson, "The Russian Perspective," in Levering et al., *Debating the Origin of the Cold War*, 123–24. These authors define "basic cold war psychology" as consisting of a vision of the world split into two opposing systems and a propensity to discipline society according to this vision.

45. Mary Kaldor, *Global Civil Society: An Answer to War* (Cambridge, U.K.: Polity, 2003), 62.

46. Leffler, *The Specter of Communism*, 59–60, 83.

47. Ibid., 61–62.

48. Quoted in Arthur Herman, *Joseph McCarthy: Reexamining the Life and Legacy of America's Most Hated Senator* (New York: Free Press, 2000), 208; see also Douglas Field, "Introduction," in Douglas Field, ed., *American Cold War Culture* (Edinburgh, U.K.: Edinburgh University Press, 2005), 4.

49. Field, "Introduction," 7.

50. Quoted in Cynthia Hendershot, *Anti-communism and Popular Culture in Mid-century America* (Jefferson, N.C.: McFarland, 2003), 13.

51. Quoted in Field, "Introduction," 3–4.

52. Robin, *The Making of the Cold War Enemy*, 168.

53. David Caute, *The Great Fear: The Anti-Communist Purge Under Truman and Eisenhower* (New York: Simon and Schuster, 1978), 21; Caute is quoted in Field, "Introduction," 5.

54. Christopher Shannon, *A World Made Safe for Differences: Cold War Intellectuals and the Politics of Identity* (New York: Rowman and Littlefield, 2001).

55. Ruth Benedict, *The Chrysanthemum and the Sword: Patterns of Japanese Culture* (Boston: Houghton Mifflin, 1946); Frances Fitzgerald, *Fire in the Lake: The Vietnamese and the Americans in Vietnam* (Boston: Little, Brown, 1972); Arthur Schlesinger Jr., *The Vital Center* (Cambridge: Da Capo Press, 1988 [1949]); William Lederer and Burdick, *The Ugly American* (New York: Norton, 1958).

56. Shannon, *A World Made Safe for Differences*, 15, 7.

57. Lederer and Burdick, *The Ugly American*, quoted in Shannon, *A World Made Safe for Differences*, 17.

58. In a similar way, Gananath Obeyesekere scrutinizes the representation of Captain Cook in European literature in his book *The Apotheosis of Captain Cook: European Mythmaking in the Pacific* (Princeton: Princeton University Press, 1993).

59. Shannon, *A World Made Safe for Differences*, 7.

60. Peter Mandler, "One World, Many Cultures: Margaret Mead and the Limits to Cold War Anthropology," *History Workshop Journal* 68 (2009), 163.

61. Shannon, *A World Made Safe for Differences*, 151.

62. See George W. Stocking Jr., *Race, Culture, and Evolution: Essays in the History of Anthropology* (Chicago: University of Chicago Press, 1982), 195–233.

63. See Adam Kuper, *Culture: The Anthropologists' Account* (Cambridge, Mass.: Harvard University Press, 1999).

64. William A. Williams, *Empire as a Way of Life* (New York: Oxford University Press, 1980).

65. Paul Buhle, "William Appleman Williams: Grassroots Against Empire," in Hunter, *Rethinking the Cold War*, 295.

66. Mandler, "One World, Many Cultures," 151, 167.

67. Vjekoslav Perica, *Balkan Idols: Religion and Nationalism in Yugoslav States* (New York: Oxford University Press, 2002), 27–28.

68. Yuri Slezkine, "The USSR as a Communal Apartment, or How a Socialist State Promoted Ethnic Particularism," *Slavic Review* 53, no. 2 (1994): 420, 423.

69. Shannon, *A World Made Safe for Differences*, xi.

70. Acheson quoted in Williams, *Empire as a Way of Life*, 183.

71. See David C. Engerman, Nils Gilman, Mark H. Haefele, and Michael B. Latham, eds., *Staging Growth: Modernization, Development, and the Global Cold War* (Amherst: University of Massachusetts Press, 2003).

4. The Ambidextrous Body

1. E. P. Thompson, *Beyond the Cold War* (London: Merlin, 1982), 4, 5.

2. E. P. Thompson, "Ends and Histories," in Mary Kaldor, ed., *Europe from Below: An East–West Dialogue* (London: Verso, 1991), 20.

3. Mary Kaldor, *Global Civil Society: An Answer to War* (Cambridge, U.K.: Polity, 2003), 53–71; Thompson, "Ends and Histories," 24.

4. Mary Kaldor, "After the Cold War," in Kaldor, *Europe from Below*, 35.

5. Kaldor, *Global Civil Society*, vii, 69, 95–108.

6. Ibid., 56 (for the quote). For the criticism of Kaldor's notion of civil society, see Chris Hann, "Introduction: Political Society and Civil Anthropology," in Chris Hann and Elizabeth Dunn, eds., *Civil Society: Challenging Western Models* (London: Routledge, 1996), 1–4.

7. Thompson, *Beyond the Cold War*, 34.

8. See John Borneman, *After the Wall: East Meets West in the New Berlin* (New York: Basic Books, 1991), 20–37.

9. Stephen J. Whitfield, *The Culture of the Cold War* (Baltimore: Johns Hopkins University Press, 1991). See also Heonik Kwon, *After the Massacre: Commemoration and Consolation in Ha My and My Lai* (Berkeley: University of California Press, 2006), 158.

10. E. P. Thompson, *Customs in Common* (New York: New Press, 1993), 188.

11. For the idea of the "long peace," see John L. Gaddis, *The Long Peace: Inquiries Into the History of the Cold War* (New York: Oxford University Press, 1987), and for the expression "imaginary war," see Mary Kaldor, *The Imaginary War: Interpretation of East–West Conflict in Europe* (Oxford, U.K.: Blackwell, 1990).

12. Marilyn B. Young, *The Vietnam Wars, 1945–1990* (New York: HarperPerennial, 1991), 1–2.

13. Odd Arne Westad, *The Global Cold War: Third World Interventions and the Making of Our Times* (New York: Cambridge University Press, 2005).

14. Bruce Cumings, *Parallax Visions: Making Sense of American–East Asian Relations at the End of the Century* (Durham, N.C.: Duke University Press, 1999).

15. Alan Hirshfeld, *Parallax: The Race to Measure the Cosmos* (New York: W. H. Freeman, 2001), xii.

16. Peter J. Kuznick and James Gilbert, "Introduction: U.S. Culture and the Cold War," in Peter J. Kuznick and James Gilbert, eds., *Rethinking Cold War Culture* (Washington, D.C.: Smithsonian Institution Press, 2001), 4.

17. Eugenia Kaledin, *Daily Life in the United States, 1940–1959* (Westport, Conn.: Greenwood, 2000).

18. Mark P. Bradley, *Imagining Vietnam and America: The Making of Postcolonial Vietnam, 1919–1950* (Chapel Hill: University of North Carolina Press, 2000), 4, 178; see also Hy Van Luong, *Revolution in the Village: Tradition and Transformation in North Vietnam, 1925–1988* (Honolulu: University of Hawai'i Press, 1992), 129–31.

19. The expression "joint venture" is from Kaldor, "After the Cold War," 36. On decentering the origins of the cold war, see Allen Hunter, "Introduction: The Limits of Vindicationist Scholarship," in Allen Hunter, ed., *Rethinking the Cold War* (Philadelphia: Temple University Press, 1998), 8–16.

20. Bruce Cumings, *The Origins of the Korean War: Liberation and the Emergence of Separate Regimes, 1945–47* (Princeton: Princeton University Press, 1981).

21. Lewis M. Stern, *The Vietnamese Communist Party's Agenda for Reform: A Study of the Eighth National Party Congress* (Jefferson, N.C.: McFarland, 1998).

22. William Duiker, *Vietnam: Revolution in Transition* (Boulder, Colo.: Westview Press, 1995), 189.

23. On ritual revival in contemporary Vietnam, see Hy Van Luong, "Economic Reform and the Intensification of Rituals in Two North Vietnamese Villages, 1980–90," in Bore Ljunggren, ed., *The Challenge of Reform in Indochina*, 259–91 (Cambridge, Mass.: Harvard Institute for International Development, 1993); Philip Taylor, *Goddess on the Rise: Pilgrimage and Popular Religion in Vietnam* (Honolulu: University of Hawai'i Press, 2004).

24. On the activity of *viec ho*, see Viet Tan, *Viec ho* (The Work of Family Ancestor Worship) (Hanoi: Nha Xuat Ban Van Hoa Dan Toc, 2000). The quote "the commemorative fever" is from Hue-Tam Ho Tai, "Introduction: Situating Memory," in Hue-Tam Ho Tai, ed., *The Country of Memory: Remaking the Past in Late Socialist Vietnam* (Berkeley: University of California Press, 2001), 1. About the described interpretation of ritual revival, see Shaun K. Malarney, "Return to the Past? The Dynamics of Contemporary Religious and Ritual Transformation,"

in Hy Van Luong, ed., *Postwar Vietnam: Dynamics of a Transforming Society*, 225–56 (New York: Rowman and Littlefield, 2003).

25. Quoted in Kwon, *After the Massacre*, 114.

26. See Neil Jamieson, *Understanding Vietnam* (Berkeley and Los Angeles: University of California Press, 1993).

27. Patricia Pelley, *Post-colonial Vietnam: New Histories of the National Past* (Durham, N.C.: Duke University Press, 2002), 168.

28. Shaun K. Malarney, *Culture, Ritual, and Revolution in Vietnam* (Surrey: RoutledgeCurzon, 2002), 56–72.

29. Benedict Anderson, *Imagined Communities: Reflections on the Origin and Spread of Nationalism* (London: Verso, 1991); John R. Gillis, ed., *Commemorations: The Politics of National Identity* (Princeton: Princeton University Press, 1994); Jay Winter and Emmanuel Sivan, eds., *War and Remembrance in the Twentieth Century* (New York: Cambridge University Press, 1999); Michael Rowlands, "Remembering to Forget: Sublimation as Sacrifice in War Memorials," in Adrian Forty and Susanne Küchler, eds., *The Art of Forgetting*, 129–46 (Oxford, U.K.: Berg, 1999); Richard Werbner, ed., *Memory and the Postcolony* (London: Zed, 1998).

30. George Mosse, *Fallen Soldiers: Reshaping the Memory of the World Wars* (Oxford, U.K.: Oxford University Press, 1990), 7–11.

31. Jay Winter and Jean-Louis Robert, *Capital Cities at War: Paris, London, Berlin, 1914–1919* (New York: Cambridge University Press, 1997), 20–24.

32. James W. Trullinger, *Village at War: An Account of Conflict in Vietnam* (Stanford: Stanford University Press, 1994).

33. Quoted in Heonik Kwon, *Ghosts of War in Vietnam* (Cambridge. U.K.: Cambridge University Press, 2008), 60.

34. John Borneman, *Subversions of International Order: Studies in the Political Anthropology of Culture* (Albany: State University of New York Press, 1998), 3.

35. Bradley, *Imagining Vietnam and America*, 189–92; Duiker, *Vietnam*, 191; Jamieson, *Understanding Vietnam*, 321–22.

36. Marilyn B. Young, "Epilogue: The Vietnam War in American Memory," in Marvin Gettleman, Jane Franklin, Marilyn B. Young, and H. Bruce Franklin, eds., *Vietnam and America: A Documented History* (New York: Grove, 1995), 516.

37. Kwon, *After the Massacre*, 174–75.

38. Robert Hertz, "The Pre-eminence of the Right Hand: A Study in Religious Polarity," in Rodney Needham, ed., *Right and Left: Essays on Dual Symbolic Classification*, 3–31 (Chicago: University of Chicago Press, 1973).

39. Robert Hertz, *Death and the Right Hand*, translated by Rodney Needham and Claudia Needham (Aberdeen, U.K.: Cohen and West, 1960 [1915]).

40. Hertz, "The Pre-eminence of the Right Hand," 22.

41. The "ambidextrous" commemorative practice in central Vietnam has a further dimension relating to the Vietnamese people's ritual organization that is constituted by gods and ancestors placed in the interior of the house and by anonymous ghosts commemorated in the exterior. The typical ritual action in this concentric-dualist structure consists of kowtowing to the placed identities and turning to the opposite side to repeat the action on behalf of the placeless beings that are imagined to wander about in the exterior environment. This organization makes the identities unassimilated to the interior ritual space, including the politically troubled memory of the dead discussed in this chapter, categorically ghosts. A proper understanding of the relationship between moral conceptual polarity and political bipolarity in the Vietnamese context, therefore, ought to include the people's complex beliefs and imaginations about ghosts of war, with which this chapter does not deal. For more on this topic, see Kwon, *Ghosts of War in Vietnam*.

42. Walter LaFeber, "An End to Which Cold War?" in Michael J. Hogan, ed., *The End of the Cold War: Its Meaning and Implications*, 13–19 (New York: Cambridge University Press, 1992).

43. Hannah Arendt, *The Human Condition*, 2d ed. (Chicago: University of Chicago Press, 1998 [1958]), 71–73.

5. The Democratic Family

1. Anthony Giddens, *The Third Way: Renewal of Social Democracy* (Cambridge, U.K.: Polity, 1998), 90–93.

2. Ibid., 89.

3. Anthony Giddens, *Beyond Left and Right: The Future of Radical Politics* (Cambridge, U.K.: Polity, 1994), 13.

4. Ibid., 14.

5. Norberto Bobbio, *Left and Right: The Significance of a Political Distinction* (Chicago: University of Chicago Press, 1996), 14.

6. Bruce Cumings, *The Origins of the Korean War: Liberation and the Emergence of Separate Regimes, 1945–1947* (Princeton: Princeton University Press, 1981).

7. Institute of 4.3 Studies, *The April Third Incident and History*, vol. 3 (in Korean) (Jeju City, South Korea: Kak, 2003).

8. Seong-Nae Kim, "Lamentations of the Dead: Historical Imagery of Violence," *Journal of Ritual Studies* 3, no. 2 (1989): 251–86.

9. Heonik Kwon, "The Wealth of Han," in Michel Demeuldre, ed., *Sentiments doux-amers dans les musiques du monde,* (Paris: L'Harmattan, 2004), 47–55.

10. Kwang-Ok Kim, "Rituals of Resistance: The Manipulation of Shamanism in Contemporary Korea," in Charles F. Keys, Laurel Kendall, and Helen Hardacre, eds., *Asian Visions of Authority: Religion of the Modern States of East and Southeast Asia*, 195–220 (Honolulu: University of Hawai'i Press, 1994); Seong-Nae Kim, "Chronicles of Violence, Rituals of Mourning: Cheju Shamanism in Korea," Ph.D. diss., University of Michigan, 1989.

11. Kwang-Ok Kim, "Rituals of Resistance."

12. Quoted in Bruno Bettleheim, *Freud and Man's Soul* (New York: Random House, 1989), 61.

13. Hyun Gil-Eon, *Our Grandfather* (Seoul: Koryŏwŏn, 1990).

14. Richard Stone, "Forensic Finds Add Substance to Claims of War Atrocities," *Science Magazine* 325, no. 24 (2009): 374–75; Sang-Hun Choe, "Time Presses on Koreans Digging Up a Dark Past," *New York Times*, September 4, 2009; Sang-Hun Choe, "South Korea Admits Civilian Killings During War," *New York Times*, November 26, 2009.

15. People were massacred on the wooded hills or in remote valleys by panicking South Korean security forces during the hurried evacuation from their regional bases before the advancing northern Communist army entered them. The rationale for the slaughter was the prevention of collaboration with the Communist occupiers. It is an established view among historians in Korea that the killing triggered a vicious cycle of retaliatory violence during the war: when the Communist army was forced to retreat with the intervention of the United Nations forces, the families of the victims of the initial massacre assaulted the families of the southern police force and civil service, which in turn ignited violent retaliation by the advancing southern police and military forces against the collaborators with the Communist occupation.

16. Family Association of the Victims of the Jeju April Third Incident, *The Chronicle of the Family Association of the Victims of the Jeju April Third Incident* (in Korean) (Jeju City, South Korea: Onnuri, 2005), 20.

17. Ibid.

18. The Republic of Korea (South Korea) sent three divisions to the combat zones in central Vietnam: a total of 312,853 men over a twelve-year period beginning on September 22, 1963, but primarily in the years 1966 to 1969. Their participation in the war contributed significantly to the economic takeoff of South Korea as an Asian industrial force. For the U.S. administration, the South Korean divisions' participation was crucial not only for justifying the war by internationalizing it, but also for easing the burden on the U.S. ground forces. See Heonik Kwon, *After the Massacre: Commemoration and Consolation in Ha My and My Lai* (Berkeley: University of California Press, 2006).

19. My translation.

20. Christian G. Appy, "Introduction: Struggling for the World," in Christian G. Appy, ed., *Cold War Constructions: The Political Culture of United States Imperialism, 1945–1966*, 1–8 (Amherst: University of Massachusetts Press, 2000).

21. Mark Mazower, ed., *After the War Was Over: Reconstructing the Family, Nation, and State in Greece, 1943–1960* (Princeton: Princeton University Press, 2000); Hue-Tam Ho Tai, ed., *The Country of Memory: Remaking the Past in Late Socialist Vietnam* (Berkeley: University of California Press, 2001); Taik-Lim Yun, *Red Village: A History* (in Korean) (Seoul: Historical Criticism Press, 2003).

22. See the discussion in Robert Stern, *Hegel and the Phenomenology of Spirit* (New York: Routledge, 2002), 135–45.

23. Heonik Kwon, *Ghosts of War in Vietnam* (Cambridge, U.K.: Cambridge University Press, 2008).

24. Stern, *Hegel and the Phenomenology of Spirit*, 135–45.

25. Judith Butler, *Antigone's Claim: Kinship Between Life and Death* (New York: Columbia University Press, 2000), 5.

26. Giddens, *The Third Way*, 70–71.

27. Ibid, 5.

28. Ibid., 251–53.

29. Ibid., 53–59, 252.

30. Even in Europe, the political history of "left and right" takes on a different intensity and scale. According to the Italian scholar Norberto Bobbio, "Fascism and communism still represent the great antithesis between right and left [in the twentieth century]" (*Left and Right*, 26).

6. Rethinking Postcolonial History

1. Dipesh Chakrabarty, *Provincializing Europe: Post-colonial Thought and Historical Difference* (Princeton: Princeton University Press, 2000), 6–11.

2. Quoted in the outline of the 2001–2004 project Cold War as a Global Conflict, directed by Marilyn Young and Allen Hunter at the International Center for Advanced Studies, New York University. Available online at http://www.nyu/gsas/dept/icas/cold_war.htm.

3. Chakrabarty, *Provincializing Europe*, 217–18.

4. Ibid, 8.

5. Partha Chatterjee, *The Nation and Its Fragments: Colonial and Post-colonial Histories* (Princeton: Princeton University Press, 1993).

6. Benedict Anderson, *Imagined Communities: Reflections on the Origin and Spread of Nationalism* (London: Verso, 1991).

7. Chatterjee, *The Nation and Its Fragments*, 9.

8. Ibid., 5.

9. J. Jorge Klor de Alva, "The Postcolonization of the (Latin) American Experience: A Reconsideration of 'Colonialism,' 'Post-colonialism,' and 'Mestizaje,'" in Gyan Prakash, ed., *After Colonialism: Imperial Histories and Post-colonial Displacements* (Princeton: Princeton University Press, 1995), 241.

10. Zaki Laïdi, *A World Without Meaning: A Crisis of Meaning in International Politics* (New York: Routledge, 1998).

11. Susan Buck-Morss, *Dreamworld and Catastrophe: The Passing of Mass Utopia in East and West* (Cambridge: MIT Press, 2000).

12. Lynn Hunt, "The Paradoxical Origins of Human Rights," in Jeffrey N. Wasserstrom, Lynn Hunt, and Marilyn B. Young, eds., *Human Rights and Revolutions* (New York: Rowman and Littlefield, 2000), 4, 3.

13. Marilyn B. Young, "Preface," in Wasserstrom, Hunt, and Young, *Human Rights and Revolutions*, vii–xii.

14. Ibid., vii–viii.

15. Chatterjee, *The Nation and Its Fragments*, 3.

16. Odd Arne Westad, *The Global Cold War: Third World Interventions and the Making of Our Times* (New York: Cambridge University Press, 2005), 8–72.

17. Jan Naderveen Pieterse and Bhikhu Parekh, "Shifting Imaginaries: Decolonization, Internal Decolonization, Post-colony," in Jan Naderveen Pieterse and Bhikhu Parekh, eds., *The Decolonization of Imagination: Culture, Knowledge, and Power* (London: Zed, 1995), 3.

18. Ibid., 7–9.

19. Melvyn P. Leffler, *For the Soul of Mankind: The United States, the Soviet Union, and the Cold War* (New York: Hill and Wang, 2007), 454.

20. Chakrabarty, *Provincializing Europe*, 17.

21. Homi Bhabha, *The Location of Culture* (New York: Routledge, 1994), 172–73.

22. Ibid., 1–2.

23. Homi Bhabha, "In the Spirit of Calm Violence," in Prakash, ed., *After Colonialism*, 338.

24. See E. San Juan Jr., *Beyond Postcolonial Theory* (New York: St. Martin's Press, 1998), 27–30, 265–67.

25. Christina Klein, *Cold War Orientalism: Asia in the Middlebrow Imagination, 1945–1961* (Berkeley and Los Angeles: University of California Press, 2003), 37.

26. Ibid., 47–48, 50, 37.

27. Gesèle Bousquet, *Behind the Bamboo Hedge: The Impact of Homeland Politics in the Parisian Vietnamese Community* (Ann Arbor: University of Michigan Press, 1991), 6, 104–5.

28. Sonia Ryang, *North Koreans in Japan: Language, Ideology, and Identity* (Boulder: Westview, 1997).

29. P. R. Kumaraswamy, "South Asia After the Cold War: Adjusting to New Realities," in Louise Fawcett and Yezid Sayigh, eds., *The Third World Beyond the Cold War: Continuity and Change* (Oxford: Oxford University Press, 1999), 171, 198.

30. Ibid., 171–74.

31. Bhabha, *The Location of Culture*, 171.

32. Sheldon Pollock, Homi K. Bhabha, Carol A. Breckenridge, and Dipesh Chakrabarty, "Cosmopolitanisms," *Public Culture* 12, no. 3 (2000): 580.

7. Cold War Culture in Perspective

1. Ron Robin, *The Making of the Cold War Enemy: Culture and Politics in the Military–Intellectual Complex* (Princeton: Princeton University Press, 2001).

2. Alan Brinkley, "The Illusion of Unity in Cold War Culture," in Peter J. Kuznick and James Gilbert, eds., *Rethinking Cold War Culture* (Washington, D.C.: Smithsonian Institution Press, 2001), 69–71.

3. K. A. Cuordileone, *Manhood and American Political Culture in the Cold War* (New York: Routledge, 2005), 101–5.

4. The quote about containment as both a material practice and a metaphor is from Deborah Nelson, *Pursuing Privacy in Cold War America* (New York: Columbia University Press, 2002), xii. The quote about the connection between cultural currents and political events is from Cuordileone, *Manhood and American Political Culture in the Cold War*, ix. The idea of brainwashing is explored in Alan Nadel, "Cold War Television and the Technology of Brainwashing," in Douglas Field, ed., *American Cold War Culture*, 146–63 (Edinburgh, U.K.: Edinburgh University Press, 2005).

5. Stephen J. Whitfield, *The Culture of the Cold War* (Baltimore: Johns Hopkins University Press, 1991).

6. On the transition from causal questions to questions of meaning, see Mark Bradley, "Slouching Toward Bethlehem: Culture, Diplomacy, and the Origins of the Cold War in Vietnam," in Christian G. Appy, *Cold War Constructions: The Political Culture of United States Imperialism, 1945–1966* (Amherst: University of Massachusetts Press, 2000), 12–13. On the idea of a cultural system, see Clifford Geertz, *The Interpretation of Cultures* (New York: Basic Books, 1973). The quote "the culture turn" is from Robert Griffith, "The Cultural Turn in Cold War Studies," *Reviews in American History* 29, no. 1 (2001): 150–57; see also Peter J. Kuznick and James Gilbert, "Introduction: U.S. Culture and the Cold War," in Kuznick and Gilbert, *Rethinking Cold War Culture*.

7. See, for instance, Christopher Duggan and Christopher Wagstaff, eds., *Italy in the Cold War: Politics, Culture, and Society, 1948–58* (Oxford, U.K.: Berg, 1995);

Mark Mazower, ed., *After the War Was Over: Reconstructing the Family, Nation, and State in Greece, 1943–1960* (Princeton: Princeton University Press, 2000).

8. Christian G. Appy, "Introduction: Struggling for the World," in Appy, *Cold War Constructions*, 1–8.

9. The works I read include: Elaine T. May, *Homeward Bound: American Families in the Cold War Era* (New York: Basic Books, 1999); Christina Klein, "Family Ties and Political Obligation: The Discourse of Adoption and the Cold War Commitment to Asia," in Appy, *Cold War Constructions*, 35–66; David F. Crew and Jean-Sebastian Marcoux, eds., *Consuming Germany in the Cold War* (Oxford, U.K.: Berg, 2003); Robert D. Dean, *Imperial Brotherhood: Gender and the Making of Cold War Foreign Policy* (Amherst: University of Massachusetts Press, 2001); William M. Tuttle Jr., "America's Children in an Era of War, Hot and Cold: The Holocaust, the Bomb, and Child Bearing in the 1940s," in Kuznick and Gilbert, *Rethinking Cold War Culture*, 14–34; David F. Krugler, *The Voice of America and the Domestic Propaganda Battles, 1945–1953* (Columbia: University of Missouri Press, 2000); Thomas Doherty, *Cold War, Cool Medium: Television, McCarthyism, and American Culture* (New York: Columbia University Press, 2003); Cyndy Hendershot, *Anti-communism and Popular Culture in Mid-century America* (Jefferson, N.C.: McFarland, 2003); Thomas H. Schaub, ed., *American Fiction in the Cold War* (Madison: University of Wisconsin Press, 1991); Bruce McConachie, *American Theater in the Culture of the Cold War: Producing and Contesting Containment, 1947–1962* (Iowa City: University of Iowa Press, 2003); and Steve Nicholson, *British Theatre and the Red Peril: The Portrayal of Communism, 1917–1945* (Exeter, U.K.: University of Exeter Press, 1999).

10. Robin also argues that the behavioral science assumptions contributed to reinforcing a social pathological orientation in policies against Communist insurgencies. Robin, *The Making of the Cold War Enemy*, 64–69.

11. Bruce Franklin, *Vietnam and Other American Fantasies* (Amherst: University of Massachusetts Press, 2000).

12. David Ryan, "Mapping Containment: The Cultural Construction of the Cold War," in Field, *American Cold War Culture*, 51.

13. See James Clifford, *The Predicament of Culture: Twentieth-Century Ethnography, Literature, and Art* (Cambridge: Harvard University Press, 1988).

14. Ryan, "Mapping Containment," 51, quoting Clifford Geertz, "Ideology as a Cultural System," in *The Interpretations of Culture*, 193–233.

15. Wendy L. Wall, "America's 'Best Propagandists': Italian Americans and the 1948 'Letters to Italy' Campaign," in Appy, *Cold War Constructions*, 109.

16. May, *Homeward Bound*, xxv.

17. Cuordileone, *Manhood and American Political Culture in the Cold War*, xii–xiii.

18. Ryan, "Mapping Containment," 51.

19. Geertz, "Ideology as a Cultural System," 199; see Daniel Bell, The *End of Ideology: On the Exhaustion of Political Ideals in the Fifties* (New York: Free Press, 1961).

20. Ibid., 207. See also Clifford Geertz, *Negara: The Theater State in Nineteenth-Century Bali* (Princeton: Princeton University Press, 1980).

21. Geertz, *Negara*, 123; see also Clifford Geertz, "Centers, Kings, and Charisma: Reflections on the Symbolics of Power," in *Local Knowledge: Further Essays in Interpretive Anthropology*, 121–46 (New York: Basic Books, 1983).

22. Leslie Dwyer and Degung Santikarma, "'When the World Turned to Chaos': 1965 and Its Aftermath in Bali, Indonesia," in Robert Gellately and Ben Kiernan, eds., *The Specter of Genocide: Mass Murder in Historical Perspective* (New York: Cambridge University Press, 2003), 290.

23. Geoffrey Robinson, *The Dark Side of Paradise: Political Violence in Bali* (Ithaca: Cornell University Press, 1995), 5, 8.

24. Geertz, *The Interpretation of Cultures*, quoted in Robinson, *The Dark Side of Paradise*, 8. In a later, partly autographical essay, however, Geertz does engage with the incidents in 1965 at some length. See Clifford Geertz, *After the Fact: Two Countries, Four Decades, One Anthropologist* (Cambridge: Harvard University Press, 1995). For a critique of the depiction of the Bali massacre presented in Geertz's essay, see Stephen P. Reyna, "Right and Might: Of Approximate Truths and Moral Judgment," *Identities* 4, nos. 3–4 (1998): 431–66.

25. Robinson, *The Dark Side of Paradise*, Green quoted on 277, everything else from 304–7 and 313.

26. George Kahin, *Nationalism and Revolution in Indonesia* (Ithaca: Cornell University Press, 1952). See also Geertz, "Ideology as a Cultural System," 225, and Clifford Geertz, "The Integrative Revolution: Primordial Sentiments and Civil Politics in the New States," in *The Interpretation of Cultures*, 255–310.

27. The first quote comes from Geertz, "Ideology as a Cultural System," 224, and the second from Geertz, *Negara*, 121.

28. Arendt quoted in Mark J. Osiel, *Mass Atrocity, Ordinary Evil, and Hannah Arendt: Criminal Consciousness in Argentina's Dirty War* (New Haven: Yale University Press, 1997), 9; Giorgio Agamben, *The State of Exception*, translated by Kevin Attell (Chicago: University of Chicago Press, 2005).

29. Tzvetan Todorov, *The Conquest of America: The Question of the Other* (New York: Harper and Row, 1984).

32. George Kennan, *Memoirs, 1925–1950* (Boston: Little, Brown, 1967).

31. May, *Homeward Bound*, 10–29.

32. Clifford Geertz, "Thick Description: Toward an Interpretive Theory of Culture," in *The Interpretation of Cultures*, 5.

33. Geertz, *Negara*, 111–12.

34. Adam Kuper, *Culture: The Anthropologists' Account* (Cambridge: Harvard University Press, 1999), 80–81.

35. Clifford Geertz, *Available Light: Anthropological Reflections on Philosophical Topics* (Princeton: Princeton University Press, 2000), 42–43.

36. Ibid., 55.

37. The "death-world" concept is from Edith Wyschogrod, *Spirit in Ashes: Hegel, Heidegger, and Man-Made Mass Death* (New Haven: Yale University Press, 1985), 20–23; see also the conclusion in the present book.

Conclusion

1. Gallup Poll number 557 (December 6, 1955), available online at http://brain.gallup.com/documents/questionnaire.aspx?STUDY=AIPO0557. See also Kenneth Osgood, *Total Cold War: Eisenhower's Secret Propaganda Battle at Home and Abroad* (Lawrence: University Press of Kansas, 2006), 1–2.

2. William H. McNeill, *The Rise of the West: A History of the Human Community* (Chicago: University of Chicago Press, 1991), 797.

3. Quoted in John Lewis Gaddis, "The Cold War, the Long Peace, and the Future," in Michael J. Hogan, ed., *The End of the Cold War: Its Meaning and Implications* (New York: Cambridge University Press, 1992), 21. See also Mary Kaldor, *New and Old Wars: Organized Violence in a Global Age* (Stanford: Stanford University Press, 2001), 29.

4. Kaldor, *New and Old Wars*, 29–30.

5. Paul Fusell, *The Great War and Modern Memory* (London: Oxford University Press, 1975).

6. Stephan Kern, *The Culture of Time and Space, 1880–1918* (Cambridge: Harvard University Press, 1983), 152–53.

7. John Golding, *Cubism: A History and an Analysis* (London: Faber and Faber, 1959), 17.

8. Kern, *The Culture of Time and Space*, 153.

9. Stein quoted in ibid., 288.

10. Edith Wyschogrod, *Spirit in Ashes: Hegel, Heidegger, and Man-Made Mass Death* (New Haven: Yale University Press, 1985).

11. Quoted in Greg Grandin, *The Last Colonial Massacre: Latin America in the Cold War* (Chicago: University of Chicago Press, 2004), 170.

12. Ibid., 3.

13. Steve J. Stern, *Remembering Pinochet's Chile*, vol. 1 (Durham: Duke University Press, 2004).

BIBLIOGRAPHY

Agamben, Giorgio. *The State of Exception*. Translated by Kevin Attell. Chicago: University of Chicago Press, 2005.

Anderson, Benedict. *Imagined Communities: Reflections on the Origin and Spread of Nationalism*. London: Verso, 1991.

——. *Language and Power: Exploring Political Cultures in Indonesia*. Ithaca: Cornell University Press, 1990.

Appadurai, Arjun. "Grassroots Globalization and the Research Imagination." In Arjun Appadurai, ed., *Globalization*, 1–21. Durham: Duke University Press, 2001.

——. *Modernity at Large: Cultural Dimensions in Globalization*. Minneapolis: University of Minnesota Press, 1996.

Appy, Christian G., ed. *Cold War Constructions: The Political Culture of United States Imperialism, 1945–1966*. Amherst: University of Massachusetts Press, 2000.

——. "Introduction: Struggling for the World." In Christian G. Appy, ed., *Cold War Constructions: The Political Culture of United States Imperialism, 1945–1966*, 1–8. Amherst: University of Massachusetts Press, 2000.

Arendt, Hannah. *Between Past and Future: Six Exercises in Political Thought*. New York: Viking, 1961.

——. *The Human Condition*. 2d ed. Chicago: University of Chicago Press, 1998 [1958].

——. *Men in Dark Times*. Orlando, Fla.: Harcourt Brace, 1968.

Barry, Kathleen, ed. *Vietnam's Women in Transition*. New York: St. Martin's, 1996.

Battaglia, Debbora. *On the Bones of the Serpent: Person, Memory, and Mortality in Sabarl Island Society*. Chicago: University of Chicago Press, 1990.

Bauman, Zygmunt. "After the Patronage State: A Model in Search of Class Interests." In Christopher G. A. Bryant and Edmund Mokrzycki, eds., *The New Great Transformation? Change and Continuity in East–Central Europe*, 14–35. New York: Routledge, 1993.

——. *Globalization: The Human Consequences*. Cambridge, U.K.: Cambridge University Press, 1998.

Behrend, Heike. "Power to Heal, Power to Kill." In Heike Behrend and Ute Luig, eds., *Spirit Possession: Modernity and Power in Africa*, 20–33. Oxford, U.K.: James Currey, 1999.

Behrend, Heike and Ute Luig, eds. *Spirit Possession: Modernity and Power in Africa*. Oxford, U.K.: James Currey, 1999.

Bell, Daniel. *The End of Ideology: On the Exhaustion of Political Ideals in the Fifties*. New York: Free Press, 1961.

Benedict, Ruth. *The Chrysanthemum and the Sword: Patterns of Japanese Culture*. Boston: Houghton Mifflin, 1946.

Berdahl, Daphne, Matti Bunzi, and Martha Lampland, eds. *Altering States: Ethnographies of Transition in Eastern Europe and the Former Soviet Union*. Ann Arbor: University of Michigan Press, 2000.

Bettleheim, Bruno. *Freud and Man's Soul*. New York: Random House, 1989.

Bhabha, Homi. "In the Spirit of Calm Violence." In Gyan Prakash, ed., *After Colonialism: Imperial Histories and Post-colonial Displacements*, 326–46. Princeton: Princeton University Press, 1995.

——. *The Location of Culture*. New York: Routledge, 1994.

Bobbio, Norberto. *Left and Right: The Significance of a Political Distinction*. Chicago: University of Chicago Press, 1996.

Boddy, Janice. *Wombs and Alien Spirits: Women, Men, and the Zār Cult in Northern Sudan*. Madison: University of Wisconsin Press, 1989.

Borneman, John. *After the Wall: East Meets West in the New Berlin*. New York: Basic Books, 1991.

——. *Belonging in Two Berlins: Kin, State, Nation*. New York: Cambridge University Press, 1992.

——. *Subversions of International Order: Studies in the Political Anthropology of Culture*. Albany: State University of New York Press, 1998.

Borstelmann, Thomas. *Apartheid's Reluctant Uncle: The United States and Southern Africa in the Early Cold War*. New York: Oxford University Press, 1993.

Bousquet, Gesèle. *Behind the Bamboo Hedge: The Impact of Homeland Politics in the Parisian Vietnamese Community*. Ann Arbor: University of Michigan Press, 1991.

Bradley, Mark P. *Imagining Vietnam and America: The Making of Postcolonial Vietnam, 1919–1950.* Chapel Hill: University of North Carolina Press, 2000.

——. "Slouching Toward Bethlehem: Culture, Diplomacy, and the Origins of the Cold War in Vietnam." In Christian G. Appy, ed., *Cold War Constructions: The Political Culture of United States Imperialism, 1945–1966,* 11–34. Amherst: University of Massachusetts Press, 2000.

Breckenridge, Carol A. and Peter van der Veer, eds. *Orientalism and the Postcolonial Predicament.* Philadelphia: University of Pennsylvania Press, 1993.

Bridger, Sue and Frances Pine, eds. *Surviving Post-socialism: Local Strategies and Regional Responses in Eastern Europe and the Former Soviet Union.* New York: Routledge, 1997.

Brinkley, Alan. "The Illusion of Unity in Cold War Culture." In Peter J. Kuznick and James Gilbert, eds., *Rethinking Cold War Culture,* 61–73. Washington, D.C.: Smithsonian Institution Press, 2001.

Bryant, Christopher G. A. and Edmund Mokrzycki, eds. *The New Great Transformation? Change and Continuity in East–Central Europe.* New York: Routledge, 1993.

——. "Theorizing the Changes in East–Central Europe." In Christopher G. A. Bryant and Edmund Mokrzycki, eds., *The New Great Transformation? Change and Continuity in East–Central Europe,* 1–14. New York: Routledge, 1993.

Buck-Morss, Susan. *Dreamworld and Catastrophe: The Passing of Mass Utopia in East and West.* Cambridge: MIT Press, 2000.

Buhle, Paul. "William Appleman Williams: Grassroots Against Empire." In Allen Hunter, ed., *Rethinking the Cold War,* 289–306. Philadelphia: Temple University Press, 1998.

Burawoy, Michael and Katherine Verdery, eds. *Uncertain Transition: Ethnographies of Change in the Postsocialist World.* Lanham, Md.: Rowman and Littlefield, 1999.

Butler, Judith. *Antigone's Claim: Kinship Between Life and Death.* New York: Columbia University Press, 2000.

Carafano, James J. *Waltzing Into the Cold War: The Struggle for Occupied Austria.* Austin: Texas A&M University Press, 2002.

Caute, David. *The Great Fear: The Anti-Communist Purge Under Truman and Eisenhower.* New York: Simon and Schuster, 1978.

Chakrabarty, Dipesh. *Provincializing Europe: Postcolonial Thought and Historical Difference.* Princeton: Princeton University Press, 2000.

Chari, Sharad and Katherine Verdery. "Thinking Between the Posts: Postcolonialism, Postsocialism, and Ethnography After the Cold War." *Comparative Studies in Society and History* 51, no. 1 (2009): 6–34.

Chatterjee, Partha. *The Nation and Its Fragments: Colonial and Post-colonial Histories.* Princeton: Princeton University Press, 1993.

Chomsky, Noam. *Imperial Ambitions.* New York: Metropolitan Books, 2005.

Clark, Ian. *The Post–Cold War Order: The Spoils of Peace*. New York: Oxford University Press, 2001.

Clifford, James. *The Predicament of Culture: Twentieth-Century Ethnography, Literature, and Art*. Cambridge: Harvard University Press, 1988.

Cooper, Frederick and Ann Laura Stoler, eds. *Tensions of Empire: Colonial Cultures in a Bourgeois World*. Berkeley and Los Angeles: University of California Press, 1997.

Crew, David F. and Jean-Sebastian Marcoux, eds. *Consuming Germany in the Cold War*. Oxford, U.K.: Berg, 2003.

Cumings, Bruce. *Korea's Place in the Sun: A Modern History*. New York: Norton, 1997.

——. *The Origins of the Korean War: Liberation and the Emergence of Separate Regimes, 1945–1947*. Princeton: Princeton University Press, 1981.

——. *The Origins of the Korean War: The Roaring of the Cataract, 1947–1950*. Princeton: Princeton University Press, 1990.

——. *Parallax Visions: Making Sense of American–East Asian Relations at the End of the Century*. Durham: Duke University Press, 1999.

——. "The Wicked Witch of the West Is Dead. Long Live the Wicked Witch of the East." In Michael J. Hogan, ed., *The End of the Cold War: Its Meanings and Implications*, 87–102. New York: Cambridge University Press, 1992.

Cuordileone, K. A. *Manhood and American Political Culture in the Cold War*. New York: Routledge, 2005.

Dean, Robert D. *Imperial Brotherhood: Gender and the Making of Cold War Foreign Policy*. Amherst: University of Massachusetts Press, 2001.

Demeuldre, Michel, ed. *Sentiments doux-amers dans les musiques du monde*. Paris: L'Harmattan, 2004.

Derrida, Jacques. *On Cosmopolitanism and Forgiveness*. New York: Routledge, 2001.

——. *Specters of Marx*. New York: Routledge, 1994.

Dirks, Nicholas B., ed. *Colonialism and Culture*. Ann Arbor: University of Michigan Press, 1992.

Doherty, Thomas. *Cold War, Cool Medium: Television, McCarthyism, and American Culture*. New York: Columbia University Press, 2003.

Douglas, Mary. *Implicit Meanings: Essays in Anthropology*. New York: Routledge, 1975.

Du Bois, W. E. B. *The Souls of Black Folk*. New York: Hackett, 1994 [1903].

Dudziak, Mary L. *Cold War Civil Rights: Race and the Image of American Democracy*. Princeton: Princeton University Press, 2000.

Duggan, Christopher. "Italy in the Cold War Years and the Legacy of Fascism." In Christopher Duggan and Christopher Wagstaff, eds., *Italy in the Cold War: Politics, Culture, and Society, 1948–58*, 1–24. Oxford, U.K.: Berg, 1995.

Duggan, Christopher and Christopher Wagstaff, eds. *Italy in the Cold War: Politics, Culture, and Society, 1948–58.* Oxford, U.K.: Berg, 1995.

Duiker, William J. *Vietnam: Revolution in Transition.* Boulder: Westview, 1995.

Dwyer, Leslie and Degung Santikarma. "'When the World Turned to Chaos': 1965 and Its Aftermath in Bali, Indonesia." In Robert Gellately and Ben Kiernan, eds., *The Specter of Genocide: Mass Murder in Historical Perspective,* 289–306. New York: Cambridge University Press, 2003.

Eckes, Alfred E., Jr., and Thomas W. Zeiler. *Globalization and the American Century.* New York: Cambridge University Press, 2003.

Eliot, T. S. *Selected Essays.* London: Faber, 1951.

Engerman, David C., Nils Gilman, Mark H. Haefele, and Michael B. Latham, eds. *Staging Growth: Modernization, Development, and the Global Cold War.* Amherst: University of Massachusetts Press, 2003.

Enloe, Cynthia. *The Morning After: Sexual Politics at the End of the Cold War.* Berkeley and Los Angeles: University of California Press, 1993.

——. "Women After Wars: Puzzles and Warnings." In Kathleen Barry, ed., *Vietnam's Women in Transition,* 299–315. New York: St. Martin's, 1996.

Fabian, Johannes. *Time and the Other: How Anthropology Makes Its Object.* New York: Columbia University Press, 1983.

Family Association of the Victims of the Jeju April Third Incident. *The Chronicle of the Family Association of the Victims of the Jeju April Third Incident* (in Korean). Jeju City, Korea: Onnuri, 2005.

Fawcett, Louise and Yezid Sayigh, eds. *The Third World Beyond the Cold War: Continuity and Change.* Oxford, U.K.: Oxford University Press, 1999.

Field, Douglas, ed. *American Cold War Culture.* Edinburgh, U.K.: Edinburgh University Press, 2005.

——. "Introduction." In Douglas Field, ed., *American Cold War Culture,* 1–13. Edinburgh, U.K.: Edinburgh University Press, 2005.

——. "Passing as a Cold War Novel: Anxiety and Assimilation in James Baldwin's *Giovanni's Room.*" in Douglas Field, ed., *American Cold War Culture,* 88–108. Edinburgh, U.K.: Edinburgh University Press, 2005.

Fitzgerald, Frances. *Fire in the Lake: The Vietnamese and the Americans in Vietnam.* Boston: Little, Brown, 1972.

Forgacs, David, ed. *The Antonio Gramsci Reader.* New York: New York University Press, 2000.

Forrester, Sibelan, Magdalena Zaborowska, and Elena Gapova. "Introduction: Mapping Postsocialist Cultural Studies." In Sibelan Forrester, Magdalena Zaborowska, and Elena Gapova, eds., *Over the Wall/After the Fall: Post-Communist Cultures Through an East–West Gaze,* 1–40. Bloomington: Indiana University Press, 2004.

——, eds. *Over the Wall/After the Fall: Post-Communist Cultures Through an East–West Gaze*. Bloomington: Indiana University Press, 2004.

Forty, Adrian and Susanne Küchler, eds. *The Art of Forgetting*. Oxford, U.K.: Berg, 1999.

Franklin, Bruce. *Vietnam and Other American Fantasies*. Amherst: University of Massachusetts Press, 2000.

Fukuyama, Francis. *The End of History and the Last Man*. New York: Penguin, 1992.

Fusell, Paul. *The Great War and Modern Memory*. London: Oxford University Press, 1975.

Gaddis, John L. "The Cold War, the Long Peace, and the Future." In Michael J. Hogan, ed., *The End of the Cold War: Its Meanings and Implications*, 21–38. New York: Cambridge University Press, 1992.

——. *The Long Peace: Inquiries Into the History of the Cold War*. New York: Oxford University Press, 1987.

——. *The United States and the End of the Cold War: Implications, Reconsiderations, Provocations*. New York: Oxford University Press, 1992.

——. *We Know Now: Rethinking Cold War History*. New York: Oxford University Press, 1998.

Gardner, Lloyd C. and Marilyn B. Young, eds. *The New American Empire*. New York: New Press, 2005.

Geertz, Clifford. *After the Fact: Two Countries, Four Decades, One Anthropologist*. Cambridge: Harvard University Press, 1995.

——. *Available Light: Anthropological Reflections on Philosophical Topics*. Princeton: Princeton University Press, 2000.

——. *The Interpretation of Cultures*. New York: Basic Books, 1973.

——. *Local Knowledge: Further Essays in Interpretive Anthropology*. New York: Basic Books, 1983.

——. *Negara: The Theater State in Nineteenth-Century Bali*. Princeton: Princeton University Press, 1980.

Gellately, Robert and Ben Kiernan, eds. *The Specter of Genocide: Mass Murder in Historical Perspective*. New York: Cambridge University Press, 2003.

Gellner, Ernest. *Anthropology and Politics: Revolutions in the Sacred Grove*. Oxford, U.K.: Blackwell, 1995.

Gerolymatos, André. *Red Acropolis, Black Terror: The Greek Civil War and the Origins of Soviet–American Rivalry, 1943–1949*. New York: Basic Books, 2004.

Gettleman, Marvin, Jane Franklin, Marilyn B. Young, and H. Bruce Franklin, eds. *Vietnam and America: A Documented History*. New York: Grove, 1995.

Giddens, Anthony. *Beyond Left and Right: The Future of Radical Politics*. Cambridge, U.K.: Polity, 1994.

——. *The Third Way: Renewal of Social Democracy*. Cambridge, U.K.: Polity, 1998.

Giddens, Anthony and Will Hutton. "In Conversation." In Will Hutton and Anthony Giddens, eds., *Global Capitalism*, 1–51. New York: New Press, 2000.

Gillis, John R., ed. *Commemorations: The Politics of National Identity*. Princeton: Princeton University Press, 1994.

Gilman, Nils. *Mandarins of the Future: Modernization in Cold War America*. Baltimore: Johns Hopkins University Press, 2004.

Gluckman, Max. *Custom and Conflict in Africa*. Oxford, U.K.: Blackwell, 1955.

Golding, John. *Cubism: A History and an Analysis*. London: Faber and Faber, 1959.

Gramsci, Antonio. "Americanism and Fordism." In David Forgacs, ed., *The Antonio Gramsci Reader*, 275–99. New York: New York University Press, 2000.

Grandin, Greg. *The Last Colonial Massacre: Latin American in the Cold War*. Chicago: University of Chicago Press, 2004.

Griffith, Robert. "The Cultural Turn in Cold War Studies." *Reviews in American History* 29, no. 1 (2001): 150–57.

Gusterson, Hugh. *Nuclear Rites: Weapons Laboratory at the End of the Cold War*. Berkeley and Los Angeles: University of California Press, 1998.

Hakim, Khalifa Abdul. *Islam and Communism*. Lahore, Pakistan: Institute of Islamic Culture, 1951.

Halliday, Fred. *The Middle East in International Politics: Power, Politics, and Ideology*. Cambridge, U.K.: Cambridge University Press, 2005.

Hann, Chris M. "Farewell to the Socialist 'Other.'" In Chris M. Hann, ed., *Postsocialism: Ideals, Ideologies, and Practices in Eurasia*, 1–11. New York: Routledge, 2002.

——. "Introduction: Political Society and Civil Anthropology." In Chris Hann and Elizabeth Dunn, eds., *Civil Society: Challenging Western Models*, 1–24. London: Routledge, 1996.

——, ed. *Postsocialism: Ideals, Ideologies, and Practices in Eurasia*. New York: Routledge, 2002.

Hann, Chris and Elizabeth Dunn, eds. *Civil Society: Challenging Western Models*. London: Routledge, 1996.

Hansen, Philip B. *Hannah Arendt: Politics, History, and Citizenship*. Cambridge, U.K.: Polity Press, 1993.

Hardt, Michael and Antonio Negri. *Empire*. Cambridge: Harvard University Press, 2000.

Haynes, John E. *Red Scare or Red Menace: American Communism and Anti-communism in the Cold War Era*. Chicago: Dee, 1996.

Hendershot, Cynthia. *Anti-communism and Popular Culture in Mid-century America*. Jefferson: McFarland, 2003.

Herman, Arthur. *Joseph McCarthy: Reexamining the Life and Legacy of America's Most Hated Senator*. New York: Free Press, 2000.

Hertz, Robert. *Death and the Right Hand*. Translated by Rodney Needham and Claudia Needham. Aberdeen, U.K.: Cohen and West, 1960 [1915].

——. "The Pre-eminence of the Right Hand: A Study in Religious Polarity." In Rodney Needham, ed., *Right and Left: Essays on Dual Symbolic Classification*, 3–31. Chicago: University of Chicago Press, 1973.

Hirshfeld, Alan. *Parallax: The Race to Measure the Cosmos*. New York: W. H. Freeman, 2001.

Hixson, Walter L. *Parting the Curtain: Propaganda, Culture, and the Cold War, 1945–1961*. New York: St. Martin's, 1997.

Hobsbawm, Eric. *Age of Extremes: The Short Twentieth Century, 1914–1991*. London: Abacus, 1995.

Hochschild, Adam. *The Unquiet Ghost: Russians Remember Stalin*. New York: Penguin, 1995.

Hogan, Michael J., ed. *The End of the Cold War: Its Meaning and Implications*. New York: Cambridge University Press, 1992.

Hoover, Edgar. *A Study of Communism*. New York: Holt, Rinehart and Winston, 1962.

Humphrey, Caroline. "Does the Category 'Postsocialist' Still Make Sense?" In Chris M. Hann, ed., *Postsocialism: Ideals, Ideologies, and Practices in Eurasia*, 12–15. New York: Routledge, 2002.

——. *The Unmaking of Soviet Life: Everyday Economies in Russia and Mongolia*. Ithaca: Cornell University Press, 2001.

Hunt, Lynn. "The Paradoxical Origins of Human Rights." In Jeffrey N. Wasserstrom, Lynn Hunt, and Marilyn B. Young, *Human Rights and Revolutions*, 3–17. New York: Rowman and Littlefield, 2000.

Hunter, Allen. "Introduction: The Limits of Vindicationist Scholarship." In Allen Hunter, ed., *Rethinking the Cold War*, 1–32. Philadelphia: Temple University Press, 1998.

——, ed. *Rethinking the Cold War*. Philadelphia: Temple University Press, 1998.

Huntington, Samuel P. *The Clash of Civilizations and the Remaking of World Order*. London: Simon and Schuster, 1997.

Hutton, Will and Anthony Giddens, eds. *Global Capitalism*. New York: New Press, 2000.

Hyun, Gil-Eon. *Our Grandfather* (in Korean). Seoul: Koryŏwŏn, 1990.

Institute of 4.3 Studies. *The April Third Incident and History* (in Korean). Vol. 3. Jeju City, Korea: Kak, 2003.

Isaac, Jeffrey C. "Hannah Arendt as Dissenting Intellectual." In Allen Hunter, ed., *Rethinking the Cold War*, 271–87. Philadelphia: Temple University Press, 1998.

Isaacs, Arnold R. *Vietnam Shadows: The War, Its Ghosts, Its Legacy*. Baltimore: Johns Hopkins University Press, 1997.

Jamieson, Neil. *Understanding Vietnam*. Berkeley and Los Angeles: University of California Press, 1993.

Johnson, Chalmers. *The Sorrows of Empire: Militarism, Secrecy, and the End of the Republic*. New York: Verso, 2004.

Kahin, George. *Nationalism and Revolution in Indonesia*. Ithaca: Cornell University Press, 1952.

Kaldor, Mary. "After the Cold War." In Mary Kaldor, ed., *Europe from Below: An East–West Dialogue*, 27–42. London: Verso, 1991.

——, ed. *Europe from Below: An East–West Dialogue*. London: Verso, 1991.

——. *Global Civil Society: An Answer to War*. Cambridge, U.K.: Polity, 2003.

——. *The Imaginary War: Interpretation of East–West Conflict in Europe*. Oxford, U.K.: Blackwell, 1990.

——. *New and Old Wars: Organized Violence in a Global Age*. Stanford: Stanford University Press, 2001.

Kaledin, Eugenia. *Daily Life in the United States, 1940–1959*. Westport, Conn.: Greenwood, 2000.

Kandiyoti, Deniz. "Post-colonialism Compared: Potentials and Limitations in the Middle East and Central Asia." *International Journal of Middle East Studies* 34, no. 2 (2002): 279–97.

Kennan, George. *Memoirs, 1925–1950*. Boston: Little, Brown, 1967.

Kern, Stephan. *The Culture of Time and Space, 1880–1918*. Cambridge: Harvard University Press, 1983.

Keys, Charles F., Laurel Kendall, and Helen Hardacre, eds. *Asian Visions of Authority: Religion of the Modern States of East and Southeast Asia*. Honolulu: University of Hawai'i Press, 1994.

Kim, Gwi-Ok. *Divided Families: Neither Anti-Communist Warriors nor Red Communists* (in Korean). Seoul: Historical Criticism Press, 2004.

Kim, Kwang-Ok. "Rituals of Resistance: The Manipulation of Shamanism in Contemporary Korea." In Charles F. Keys, Laurel Kendall, and Helen Hardacre, eds., *Asian Visions of Authority: Religion of the Modern States of East and Southeast Asia*, 195–220. Honolulu: University of Hawai'i Press, 1994.

Kim, Kye-Dong. *The Partition of Korea and the Korean War*. Seoul: Seoul National University Press, 2000.

Kim, Seong-Nae. "Chronicles of Violence, Rituals of Mourning: Cheju Shamanism in Korea." Ph.D. diss., University of Michigan, 1989.

——. "Lamentations of the Dead: Historical Imagery of Violence." *Journal of Ritual Studies* 3, no. 2 (1989): 251–86.

King, Charles. "Post-postcommumism: Transition, Comparison, and the End of 'Eastern Europe.' " *World Politics* 53 (2000): 143–72.

Kirby, Dianne, ed. *Religion and the Cold War*. New York: Palgrave, 2003.

——. "Religion and the Cold War—An Introduction." In Dianne Kirby, ed., *Religion and the Cold War*, 1–22. New York: Palgrave, 2003.

Klein, Christina. *Cold War Orientalism: Asia in the Middlebrow Imagination, 1945–1961*. Berkeley and Los Angeles: University of California Press, 2003.

——. "Family Ties and Political Obligation: The Discourse of Adoption and the Cold War Commitment to Asia." In Christian G. Appy, ed., *Cold War Constructions: The Political Culture of United States Imperialism, 1945–1966*, 35–66. Amherst: University of Massachusetts Press, 2000.

Klor de Alva, J. Jorge. "The Postcolonization of the (Latin) American Experience: A Reconsideration of 'Colonialism,' 'Post-colonialism,' and 'Mestizaje.'" In Gyan Prakash, ed., *After Colonialism: Imperial Histories and Post-colonial Displacements*, 241–77. Princeton: Princeton University Press, 1995.

Krantz, Frederik. *History from Below: Studies in Popular Protest and Popular Ideology*. New York: Blackwell, 1988.

Krugler, David F. *The Voice of America and the Domestic Propaganda Battles, 1945–1953*. Columbia: University of Missouri Press, 2000.

Kumaraswamy, P. R. "South Asia After the Cold War: Adjusting to New Realities." In Louise Fawcett and Yezid Sayigh, eds., *The Third World Beyond the Cold War: Continuity and Change*, 170–99. Oxford, U.K.: Oxford University Press, 1999.

Kuper, Adam. *Culture: The Anthropologists' Account*. Cambridge: Harvard University Press, 1999.

Kuznick, Peter J. and James Gilbert. "Introduction: U.S. Culture and the Cold War." In Peter J. Kuznick and James Gilbert, eds., *Rethinking Cold War Culture*, 1–13. Washington, D.C.: Smithsonian Institution Press, 2001.

——, eds. *Rethinking Cold War Culture*. Washington, D.C.: Smithsonian Institution Press, 2001.

Kwon, Heonik. *After the Massacre: Commemoration and Consolation in Ha My and My Lai*. Berkeley: University of California Press, 2006.

——. *Ghosts of War in Vietnam*. Cambridge, U.K.: Cambridge University Press, 2008.

——. "North Korea's Politics of Longing." *Critical Asian Studies* 42, no. 1 (2010): 2–25.

——. "The Wealth of Han." In Michel Demeuldre, ed., *Sentiments doux-amers dans les musiques du monde*, 47–55. Paris: L'Harmattan, 2004.

LaFeber, Walter. *The American Age: United States Foreign Policy at Home and Abroad Since 1750*. New York: W. W. Norton, 1989.

——. "An End to Which Cold War?" In Michael J. Hogan, ed., *The End of the Cold War: Its Meaning and Implications*, 13–19. New York: Cambridge University Press, 1992.

——. *The Origins of the Cold War, 1941–1947*. New York: John Wiley, 1971.

Laïdi, Zaki. *A World Without Meaning: A Crisis of Meaning in International Politics.* New York: Routledge, 1998.

Leach, Edmund. *Political Systems of Highland Burma: A Study of Kachin Social Structure.* London: Bell, 1964.

Lederer, William J. and Eugene Burdick. *The Ugly American.* New York: W. W. Norton, 1958.

Lee, Steven H. *Outposts of Empire: Korea, Vietnam, and the Origins of the Cold War in Asia, 1949–1954.* Liverpool, U.K.: Liverpool University Press, 1995.

Leffler, Melvyn P. *For the Soul of Mankind: The United States, the Soviet Union, and the Cold War.* New York: Hill and Wang, 2007.

——. *The Specter of Communism: The United States and the Origins of the Cold War, 1917–1953.* New York: Hill and Wang, 1994.

Leffler, Melvyn P. and David Painter, eds. *The Origins of the Cold War: An International History.* New York: Routledge, 2005.

Levering, Ralph B. and Verena Botzenhart-Viehe. "The American Perspective." In Ralph B. Levering, Vladimir O. Pechatnov, Verena Botzenhart-Viehe, and C. Earl Edmondson, eds., *Debating the Origins of the Cold War: American and Russian Perspectives,* 1–62. Lanham, Md.: Rowman and Littlefield, 2002.

Levering, Ralph B., Vladimir O. Pechatnov, Verena Botzenhart-Viehe, and C. Earl Edmondson, eds. *Debating the Origins of the Cold War: American and Russian Perspectives.* Lanham, Md.: Rowman and Littlefield, 2002.

Little, Douglas. *American Orientalism: The United States and the Middle East Since 1945.* Chapel Hill: University of North Carolina Press, 2002.

Lowe, Peter. *Origins of the Korean War.* New York: Longman, 1986.

Lowen, Rebecca S. *Creating the Cold War University: The Transformation of Stanford.* Berkeley and Los Angeles: University of California Press, 1997.

Lundestad, Geir, ed. *East, West, North, South: Major Developments in International Politics, 1945–1990.* Oslo: Norwegian University Press, 1991.

——. "The End of the Cold War, the New Role for Europe, and the Decline of the United States." In Michael J. Hogan, ed., *The End of the Cold War: Its Meaning and Implications,* 195–206. New York: Cambridge University Press, 1992.

Luong, Hy Van. "Economic Reform and the Intensification of Rituals in Two North Vietnamese Villages, 1980–90." In Bore Ljunggren, ed., *The Challenge of Reform in Indochina,* 259–91. Cambridge: Harvard Institute for International Development, 1993.

——, ed. *Postwar Vietnam: Dynamics of a Transforming Society.* New York: Rowman and Littlefield, 2003.

——. *Revolution in the Village: Tradition and Transformation in North Vietnam, 1925–1988.* Honolulu: University of Hawai'i Press, 1992.

Lutz, Catherine A., and Jane L. Collins. *Reading National Geographic*. Chicago: University of Chicago Press, 1993.

Malarney, Shaun K.. *Culture, Ritual, and Revolution in Vietnam*. Surrey: Routledge-Curzon, 2002.

——. "Return to the Past? The Dynamics of Contemporary and Ritual Transformation." In Hy Van Luong, ed., *Postwar Vietnam: Dynamics of a Transforming Society*, 225–56. New York: Rowman and Littlefield, 2003.

Mamdani, Mahmood. *Good Muslim, Bad Muslim: America, the Cold War, and the Roots of Terror*. New York: Pantheon, 2004.

Mandler, Peter. "One World, Many Cultures: Margaret Mead and the Limits to Cold War Anthropology." *History Workshop Journal* 68 (2009): 149–72.

May, Elaine T. *Homeward Bound: American Families in the Cold War Era*. New York: Basic Books, 1999.

May, Lary. "Introduction." In Lary May, ed., *Recasting America: Culture and Politics in the Age of Cold War*, 1–16. Chicago: University of Chicago Press, 1989.

——, ed. *Recasting America: Culture and Politics in the Age of Cold War*. Chicago: University of Chicago Press, 1989.

Mazower, Mark, ed. *After the War Was Over: Reconstructing the Family, Nation, and State in Greece, 1943–1960*. Princeton: Princeton University Press, 2000.

——. *Dark Continent: Europe's Twentieth Century*. New York: Penguin, 1999.

——. "Introduction." In Mark Mazower, ed., *After the War Was Over: Reconstructing the Family, Nation, and State in Greece, 1943–1960*, 1–22. Princeton: Princeton University Press, 2000.

——. "Three Forms of Political Justice: Greece, 1944–1945." In Mark Mazower, ed., *After the War Was Over: Reconstructing the Family, Nation, and State in Greece, 1943–1960*, 24–41. Princeton: Princeton University Press, 2000.

McAlister, Melani. *Epic Encounters: Culture, Media, and U.S. Interests in the Middle East Since 1945*. Berkeley and Los Angeles: University of California Press, 2001.

McConachie, Bruce. *American Theater in the Culture of the Cold War: Producing and Contesting Containment, 1947–1962*. Iowa City: University of Iowa Press, 2003.

McNeill, William H. *The Rise of the West: A History of the Human Community*. Chicago: University of Chicago Press, 1991.

Mernissi, Fatema. "Palace Fundamentalism and Liberal Democracy." In Emran Qureshi and Michael A. Sells, eds., *The New Crusades: Constructing the Muslim Enemy*, 51–67. New York: Columbia University Press, 2003.

Mosse, George. *Fallen Soldiers: Reshaping the Memory of the World Wars*. Oxford, U.K.: Oxford University Press, 1990.

Murray, Robert K. *Red Scare: A Study in National Hysteria, 1919–1920*. New York: McGraw-Hill, 1955.

Nadel, Alan. "Cold War Television and the Technology of Brainwashing." In Douglas Field, ed., *American Cold War Culture*, 146–63. Edinburgh, U.K.: Edinburgh University Press, 2005.

——. *Containment Culture: American Narratives, Postmodernism, and the Atomic Age.* Durham: Duke University Press, 1995.

Nashel, Jonathan. *Edward Lansdale's Cold War.* Amherst: University of Massachusetts Press, 2005.

Nelson, Deborah. *Pursuing Privacy in Cold War America.* New York: Columbia University Press, 2002.

Nicholson, Steve. *British Theatre and the Red Peril: The Portrayal of Communism, 1917–1945.* Exeter, U.K.: University of Exeter Press, 1999.

Obeyesekere, Gananath. *The Apotheosis of Captain Cook: European Mythmaking in the Pacific.* Princeton: Princeton University Press, 1993.

O'Hanlon, Rosalind and David Washbrook. "After Orientalism: Culture, Criticism, and Politics in the Third World." *Comparative Studies in Society and History* 34, no. 1 (1992): 141–67.

Ohnuki-Tierney, Emiko. *Culture Through Time: Anthropological Approaches.* Stanford.: Stanford University Press, 1990.

Olson, James S. and Randy Roberts. *My Lai: A Brief History with Documents.* Boston: Bedford Books, 1998.

Osgood, Kenneth. *Total Cold War: Eisenhower's Secret Propaganda Battle at Home and Abroad.* Lawrence: University Press of Kansas, 2006.

Osgood, Robert E. *America and the World: From the Truman Doctrine to Vietnam.* Baltimore: Johns Hopkins University Press, 1970.

Osiel, Mark J. *Mass Atrocity, Ordinary Evil, and Hannah Arendt: Criminal Consciousness in Argentina's Dirty War.* New Haven: Yale University Press, 1997.

Pechatnov, Vladimir O. and C. Earl Edmondson. "The Russian Perspective." In Ralph B. Levering, Vladimir O. Pechatnov, Verena Botzenhart-Viehe, and C. Earl Edmondson, eds., *Debating the Origin of the Cold War: American and Russian Perspectives*, 85–151. Lanham, Md.: Rowman and Littlefield, 2001.

Pelley, Patricia. *Post-colonial Vietnam: New Histories of the National Past.* Durham: Duke University Press, 2002.

Perica, Vjekoslav. *Balkan Idols: Religion and Nationalism in Yugoslav States.* New York: Oxford University Press, 2002.

Pierpaoli, Paul G., Jr. *Truman and Korea: The Political Culture of the Early Cold War.* Columbia: University of Missouri Press, 1999.

Pieterse, Jan Naderveen and Bhikhu Parekh, eds., *The Decolonization of Imagination: Culture, Knowledge, and Power.* London: Zed, 1995.

———. "Shifting Imaginaries: Decolonization, Internal Decolonization, Post-colony."
In Jan Naderveen Pieterse and Bhikhu Parekh, eds., *The Decolonization of Imagination: Culture, Knowledge, and Power*, 1–19. London: Zed, 1995.

Pine, Frances and Sue Bridger. "Introduction: Transitions to Post-socialism and Cultures of Survival." In Sue Bridger and Frances Pine, eds., *Surviving Post-socialism: Local Strategies and Regional Responses in Eastern Europe and the Former Soviet Union*, 1–15. New York: Routledge, 1997.

Pollock, Sheldon, Homi K. Bhabha, Carol A. Breckenridge, and Dipesh Chakrabarty. "Cosmopolitanisms." *Public Culture* 12, no. 3 (2000): 577–89.

Porter, Dennis. "Orientalism and Its Problems." In Patrick Williams and Laura Chrisman, eds., *Colonial Discourse and Post-colonial Theory: A Reader*, 150–61. Hemel Hempstead, U.K.: Harvester Wheatsheaf, 1993.

Powell, Colin. *A Soldier's Way: An Autobiography*. London: Hutchinson, 1995.

Prakash, Gyan, ed. *After Colonialism: Imperial Histories and Post-colonial Displacements*. Princeton: Princeton University Press, 1995.

Qureshi, Emran, and Michael A. Sells. "Introduction: Constructing the Muslim Enemy." In Emran Qureshi and Michael A. Sells, eds., *The New Crusades: Constructing the Muslim Enemy*, 1–47. New York: Columbia University Press, 2003.

———, eds. *The New Crusades: Constructing the Muslim Enemy*. New York: Columbia University Press, 2003.

Reyna, Stephen P. "Right and Might: Of Approximate Truths and Moral Judgment." *Identities* 4, nos. 3–4 (1998): 431–66.

Robin, Ron. *The Making of the Cold War Enemy: Culture and Politics in the Military–Intellectual Complex*. Princeton: Princeton University Press, 2001.

Robinson, Geoffrey. *The Dark Side of Paradise: Political Violence in Bali*. Ithaca: Cornell University Press, 1995.

Roeder, Philip G. "The Revolution of 1989: Postcommunism and the Social Sciences." *Slavic Review* 58, no. 4 (1989): 743–55.

Rogin, Michael. *Ronald Reagan, the Movie, and Other Episodes in Political Demonology*. Berkeley and Los Angeles: University of California Press, 1987.

Rose, Kenneth D. *One Nation Underground: A History of the Fallout Shelter*. New York: New York University Press, 2001.

Rowlands, Michael. "Remembering to Forget: Sublimation as Sacrifice in War Memorials." In Adrian Forty and Susanne Küchler, eds., *The Art of Forgetting*, 129–46. Oxford, U.K.: Berg, 1999.

Ryan, David. "Mapping Containment: The Cultural Construction of the Cold War." In Douglas Field, ed., *American Cold War Culture*, 50–68. Edinburgh, U.K.: Edinburgh University Press, 2005.

Ryang, Sonia. *North Koreans in Japan: Language, Ideology, and Identity*. Boulder: Westview, 1997.

Said, Edward W. "The Clash of Definitions." In Emran Qureshi and Michael A. Sells, eds., *The New Crusades: Constructing the New Muslim Enemy*, 68–87. New York: Columbia University Press, 2003.

———. *Orientalism: Western Conceptions of the Orient*. New York: Penguin, 1991 [1978].

San Juan, E., Jr. *Beyond Postcolonial Theory*. New York: St. Martin's, 1998.

Schaub, Thomas H., ed. *American Fiction in the Cold War*. Madison: University of Wisconsin Press, 1991.

Schimmelfennig, Frank. *The EU, NATO, and the Integration of Europe: Rules and Rhetoric*. New York: Cambridge University Press, 2003.

Schlesinger, Arthur, Jr. *The Vital Center*. Cambridge: Da Capo, 1988 [1949].

Scott, James C. *The Moral Economy of the Peasant: Rebellion and Subsistence in Southeast Asia*. New Haven: Yale University Press, 1976.

Shannon, Christopher. *A World Made Safe for Differences: Cold War Intellectuals and the Politics of Identity*. New York: Rowman and Littlefield, 2001.

Shultz, George P. *Turmoil and Triumph*. New York: Macmillan, 1993.

Slezkine, Yuri. "The USSR as a Communal Apartment, or How a Socialist State Promoted Ethnic Particularism." *Slavic Review* 53, no. 2 (1994): 414–52.

Sontag, Susan. *Against Interpretation*. New York: Farrar, Straus and Giroux, 1986.

Stern, Lewis M. *The Vietnamese Communist Party's Agenda for Reform: A Study of the Eighth National Party Congress*. Jefferson: McFarland, 1998.

Stern, Robert. *Hegel and the Phenomenology of Spirit*. New York: Routledge, 2002.

Stern, Steve J. *Remembering Pinochet's Chile*. Vol. 1. Durham: Duke University Press, 2004.

Stocking, George W., Jr. *Race, Culture, and Evolution: Essays in the History of Anthropology*. Chicago: University of Chicago Press, 1982.

Stoler, Ann. "Mixed-Bloods and the Cultural Politics of European Identity in Colonial Southeast Asia." In Jan Naderveen Pieterse and Bhikhu Parekh, eds., *The Decolonization of Imagination: Culture, Knowledge, and Power*, 128–48. London: Zed, 1995.

———. "Sexual Affronts and Racial Frontiers: European Identities and the Cultural Politics of Exclusion in Colonial Southeast Asia." In Frederick Cooper and Ann Laura Stoler, eds., *Tensions of Empire: Colonial Cultures in a Bourgeois World*, 198–237. Berkeley and Los Angeles: University of California Press, 1997.

Strathern, Marilyn. *Reproducing the Future: Essays on Anthropology, Kinship, and the New Reproductive Technologies*. New York: Routledge, 1992.

Suny, Ronald. *The Revenge of the Past: Nationalism, Revolution, and the Collapse of the Soviet Union*. Stanford: Stanford University Press, 1993.

Tai, Hue-Tam Ho, ed. *The Country of Memory: Remaking the Past in Late Socialist Vietnam*. Berkeley and Los Angeles: University of California Press, 2001.

———. "Introduction: Situating Memory." In Hue-Tam Ho Tai, ed., *The Country of Memory: Remaking the Past in Late Socialist Vietnam*, 1–19. Berkeley and Los Angeles: University of California Press, 2001.

———. *Radicalism and the Origins of Vietnamese Revolution*. Cambridge: Harvard University Press, 1992.

Tan, Viet. *Viec ho* (The Work of Family Ancestor Worship). Hanoi: Nha Xuat Ban Van Hoa Dan Toc, 2000.

Taussig, Michael. *Law in a Lawless Land: Diary of a Limpieza*. New York: New Press, 2003.

Taylor, Philip. *Goddess on the Rise: Pilgrimage and Popular Religion in Vietnam*. Honolulu: University of Hawai'i Press, 2004.

Thomas, Nicholas. *Colonialism's Culture: Anthropology, Travel, and Government*. Cambridge: Polity Press, 1994.

Thompson, E. P. *Beyond the Cold War*. London: Merlin Press, 1982.

———. *Customs in Common*. New York: New Press, 1993.

———. "Ends and Histories." In Mary Kaldor, ed., *Europe from Below: An East–West Dialogue*, 7–25. London: Verso, 1991.

———. *The Making of the English Working Class*. London: Gollancz, 1963.

Todorov, Tzvetan. *The Conquest of America: The Question of the Other*. New York: Harper and Row, 1984.

Trullinger, James W. *Village at War: An Account of Conflict in Vietnam*. Stanford: Stanford University Press, 1994.

Tuttle, William M., Jr. "America's Children in an Era of War, Hot and Cold: The Holocaust, the Bomb, and Child Bearing in the 1940s." In Peter J. Kuznick and James Gilbert, eds., *Rethinking Cold War Culture*, 14–34. Washington, D.C.: Smithsonian Institution Press, 2001.

Van Boeschoten, Riki. "The Impossible Return: Coping with Separation and the Reconstruction of Memory in the Wake of the Civil War." In Mark Mazower, ed., *After the War Was Over: Reconstructing the Family, Nation, and State in Greece, 1943–1960*, 122–41. Princeton: Princeton University Press, 2000.

Verdery, Katherine. "Transnationalism, Nationalism, Citizenship, and Property: Eastern Europe Since 1989." *American Ethnologist* 25, no. 2 (1998): 291–306.

———. *What Was Socialism, and What Comes Next?* Princeton: Princeton University Press, 1996.

———. "Whither Postsocialism?" In Chris M. Hann, ed., *Postsocialism: Ideals, Ideologies, and Practices in Eurasia*, 15–28. New York: Routledge, 2002.

Vermaak, Christopher J. *Red Trap: Communism and Violence in South Africa*. Johannesburg: A. P. B. Publishers, 1966.

Wade, Peter. *Race, Nature, and Culture*. London: Pluto, 2002.

Wagner, Roy. *The Invention of Culture*. Chicago: University of Chicago Press, 1981.

Wagnleitner, Reinhold. "The Irony of American Culture Abroad: Austria and the Cold War." In Lary May, ed., *Recasting America: Culture and Politics in the Age of Cold War*, 285–300. Chicago: University of Chicago Press, 1989.

Wall, Wendy L. "America's 'Best Propagandists': Italian Americans and the 1948 'Letters to Italy' Campaign." In Christian G. Appy, ed., *Cold War Constructions: The Political Culture of United States Imperialism, 1945–1966*, 89–109. Amherst: University of Massachusetts Press, 2000.

Wasserstrom, Jeffrey N., Lynn Hunt, and Marilyn B. Young, eds. *Human Rights and Revolutions*. New York: Rowman and Littlefield, 2000.

Wendt, Alexander. *Social Theory of International Politics*. New York: Cambridge University Press, 1999.

Werbner, Richard, ed. *Memory and the Postcolony*. London: Zed, 1998.

Westad, Odd Arne. *Decisive Encounters: The Chinese Civil War, 1946–1950*. Stanford: Stanford University Press, 2003.

——. *The Global Cold War: Third World Interventions and the Making of Our Times*. New York: Cambridge University Press, 2005.

Whitfield, Stephen J. *The Culture of the Cold War*. Baltimore: Johns Hopkins University Press, 1991.

Williams, Patrick. "Kim and Orientalism." In Patrick Williams and Laura Chrisman, eds., *Colonial Discourse and Post-colonial Theory: A Reader*, 480–97. Hemel Hempstead, U.K.: Harvester Wheatsheaf, 1993.

Williams, Patrick and Laura Chrisman, eds. *Colonial Discourse and Post-colonial Theory: A Reader*. Hemel Hempstead, U.K.: Harvester Wheatsheaf, 1993.

Williams, William A. *Empire as a Way of Life*. New York: Oxford University Press, 1980.

Winter, Jay and Jean-Louis Robert. *Capital Cities at War: Paris, London, Berlin, 1914–1919*. New York: Cambridge University Press, 1997.

Winter, Jay and Emmanuel Sivan, eds. *War and Remembrance in the Twentieth Century*. New York: Cambridge University Press, 1999.

Wittgenstein, Ludwig. *Culture and Value*. Oxford, U.K.: Blackwell, 1980.

Wolf, Eric R. *Europe and the People Without History*. Berkeley and Los Angeles: University of California Press, 1982.

——. *Peasant Wars of the Twentieth Century*. New York: Harper and Row, 1969.

Woods, Jeff. *Black Struggle, Red Scare: Segregation and Anti-communism in the South, 1948–1968*. Baton Rouge: Louisiana State University Press, 2004.

Wyschogrod, Edith. *Spirit in Ashes: Hegel, Heidegger, and Man-Made Mass Death*. New Haven: Yale University Press, 1985.

Yeğenoğlu, Meyda. *Colonial Fantasies: Towards a Feminist Reading of Orientalism*. New York: Cambridge University Press, 1998.

Young, John W. *Cold War Europe, 1945–1991: A Political History.* 2d ed. London: Edward Arnold, 1996.

Young, Marilyn B. "Epilogue: The Vietnam War in American Memory." In Marvin Gettleman, Jane Franklin, Marilyn B. Young, and H. Bruce Franklin, eds., *Vietnam and America: A Documented History*, 515–22. New York: Grove, 1995.

——. "Preface." In Jeffrey N. Wasserstrom, Lynn Hunt, and Marilyn B. Young, eds., *Human Rights and Revolutions*, vii–xii. New York: Rowman and Littlefield, 2000.

——. *The Vietnam Wars, 1945–1990.* New York: HarperPerennial, 1991.

Yun, Taik-Lim. *Red Village: A History* (in Korean). Seoul: Historical Criticism Press, 2003.

Žižek, Slavoj. "The Spectre of Ideology." In Slavoj Žižek, ed., *Mapping Ideology*, 1–33. London: Verso, 1994.

Žižek, Slavoj, ed. *Mapping Ideology.* London: Verso, 1994.

INDEX